ACKNOWLEDGMENTS

Many thanks are owed to the people who proved instrumental in this book's development. The members of our publishing team, Robert Franek, Pia Aliperti, Stephen Koch, and Scott Harris; Tyler Corvin, Sharon Forward, Deanna Hughes, Lorna Kenyon, Andrea O'Brien, Courtney Thompson, Dr. Richard Weismab and Jennifer Welch, who kindly set aside time to detail the particulars of their institution's admissions process; and, of course, the amazing students who took time out of their anatomy labs and study hours to offer examples of their writing for the benefit of future generations of medical school applicants—thank you all.

D0348739

CONTENTS

Introduction 1

    Why Did We Produce This Book? 3

    How Can This Book Help You? 4

    Why'd They Do It? 5

    Where'd They Get In? 5

    The Parts of This Book 9

    Editor's Note 11

**Chapter 1: Following Directions: A Brief Overview
of the Medical School Application Process** 13

    A View to Admissions 15

    The Premedical Timeline 17

    The Notorious GPA 20

    MCAT on a Hot Tin Roof 21

    Invest in Extracurricular Activities 23

    Letters of Recommendation 24

    How to Apply 26

    Round #2: Secondary Applications 29

    The Art of the Interview 30

**Chapter 2: Getting Personal: Primary
and Supplemental Essays** 33

    The Personal Statement 35

    An Angle on Secondary Applications 36

**Chapter 3: Having Heart: What Really
Makes an Essay Tick** 39

    Guidance, If Needed 41

    The Secrets to Your Success 41

    Get to Know Yourself Better 41

    Three Approaches 43

    Road Map to Greatness 44

    The Benefits of Peer Pressure 47

    Dos and Don'ts 48

**Chapter 4: They're, Their, and There:
Grammar and Writing Tips** 49

    Good Grammar = Good Form 51

    Most Common Grammar Mistakes 51

Grammar Chart..58

Using Punctuation Correctly...60

Writing Clearly 63

    Eliminating Wordiness..63

    Eliminating Fragments and Run-Ons.........................67

    Limiting Your Use of Passive Voice...........................67

    Using Non-Sexist Language......................................69

    Avoid Clichés Like the Plague...................................70

Style Chart..72

Navigating the Minefield 73

Excuses, Excuses..75

Ready, Set, Write!..76

Chapter 5: Making Ends Meet: Financial Aid Overview........ 77

Making Friends with Money 79

What Is Financial Aid?..79

Financial Assistance: Your Basic Options.........................80

Don't Go It Alone 81

How Much? 82

A Little Help from the Family..82

More on Loans and Scholarships 83

Evaluating Your Financial Aid Package.............................87

Financial Aid Pitfalls 87

Smart Money 88

Chapter 6: Being a Doctor: Things You Should Know 89

The Meaning of an MD 91

Patient Care..93

Compensation..94

Prestige...95

Trends in Medicine 95

A Very Big Adventure...106

Chapter 7: Q&A with Admissions Officers........................... 107

Chapter 8: Real Personal Statements
and Secondary Essays 129

Chapter 9: Where They Got In... 251

Introduction

WHY DID WE PRODUCE THIS BOOK?

Too many freaked-out premeds with outstanding academic records, enviable MCAT scores, and impressive experiences outside the classroom encounter frustration with their medical school personal statement. Given the task of boiling down their desire to be a doctor to a single page of prose, many don't even know where to start. This book is designed to show that there are many different ways to approach the personal statement and that, if a student reflects on what's most important in his or her life, he or she will indeed have something to write about. Our evidence is enclosed herewith: actual personal statements that got living, breathing premeds into medical school.

The personal statements in this book display a range of creativity and sophistication with the written word. Some are so good they may intimidate you; others may hardly impress you. We think you'll find, as we have, that the most memorable ones illuminate their writers and edify their cause. They're believable and perhaps relatable—but above all else, they're sincere.

Of course, personal statements don't stand alone; they have a place within the larger admissions context. In this book, we give you the whole picture: the college GPA; graduate school GPA, if applicable; extracurriculars; hometown; race; and Medical College Admissions Test (i.e., MCAT) scores of the student who wrote each personal statement we feature. Some students were also generous enough to provide essays they wrote for secondary applications. Finally, we include a list of admissions decisions for every single applicant whose personal statement you'll read. We hope to provide you with an understanding of the relative selectivity of the medical schools that the students in this book applied to and the admissions context within which the personal statement functions. Sure, you can find the average MCAT scores and GPAs of last year's freshman class in most college guides, but what you'll find here are the complete profiles of individual applicants who are currently enrolled in, or have recently graduated from, U.S. medical schools.

HOW CAN THIS BOOK HELP YOU?

The early chapters of this book are primarily a guide to medical school admissions and the writing that med school applications entail, with some extra information that you may find helpful as you decide whether to pursue a career in medicine. These chapters will fill in any gaps in your knowledge and make you a well-informed premed.

The personal statements, secondary essays, applicants, and admissions results in this book are presented without commentary. Among the personal statements and secondary essays, not every sentence is eloquent, nor every comma perfectly placed. However, they all passed the ultimate test for medical school application soundness: Their authors gained acceptance into at least one of the medical schools to which they applied. Ideally, these personal statements and secondary essays will inspire you, supply you with paradigms for narrative and organizational structures, teach you ways to express yourself that you hadn't yet considered, and help you write exactly what you wish to communicate.

This book should also help prepare you to encounter both success and failure in the admissions process. You're going to be a bit perplexed when UCSF accepts, Penn waitlists, and Mt. Sinai rejects a student in the book. As you'll see, even wunderkinds—we've profiled plenty of them—get denied admission to top-flight schools. In fact, very few of the students you will encounter in this book got into every medical school to which they applied. So what should this mean to you? It means that disappointment is a part of life, even when you worked your buns off toward a particular goal. But even if you do get a rejection letter, there's no reason to feel completely bereft: a few fat envelopes are probably wending their way to you.

WHY'D THEY DO IT?

Why would current medical school students and recent grads allow us to publish their personal statements, test scores, grades, and biographical information? They realize the value their stories have for prospective medical school students. After all, gaining admission to medical school is no small feat. Many said they were honored to have been chosen for publication and to have been given the chance to help the next generation of medical school students.

WHERE'D THEY GET IN?

Students with personal statements published in this book received offers of admission from the following U.S. medical schools:

Albany Medical College

Baylor College of Medicine

Boston University, School of Medicine

Brown University, Brown Medical School

Case Western Reserve University, School of Medicine

Cleveland Clinic Lerner College of Medicine

Columbia University, College of Physicians and Surgeons

Cornell University, Joan & Sanford I. Weill Medical Center

Creighton University, School of Medicine

Dartmouth Medical School

Drexel University, College of Medicine

Duke University, School of Medicine

Eastern Virginia Medical School

Edward Via Virginia College of Osteopathic Medicine

Emory University, School of Medicine

Florida State University, College of Medicine

George Washington University, School of Medicine and Health Sciences

Georgetown University, School of Medicine

Harvard Medical School

Howard University, College of Medicine

Johns Hopkins University, School of Medicine

Loma Linda University, School of Medicine

Louisiana State University, School of Medicine

Loyola University of Chicago, Stritch School of Medicine

Mayo Clinic College of Medicine, Mayo Medical School

Medical College of Georgia, School of Medicine

Medical College of Wisconsin

Medical University of South Carolina

Meharry Medical College, School of Medicine

Michigan State University, College of Osteopathic Medicine

Morehouse Medical School

Mount Sinai School of Medicine

New York University, Mount Sinai School of Medicine

New York University, NYU School of Medicine

Northwestern University, Feinberg School of Medicine

Ohio State University, College of Medicine and Public Health

Oregon Health & Science University, School of Medicine

Pennsylvania State University, College of Medicine

Philadelphia College of Osteopathic Medicine

Rush University, Rush Medical College

Saint Louis University, School of Medicine

Southern Illinois University, School of Medicine

Stanford University, School of Medicine

State University of New York—Downstate Medical Center

State University of New York—Stony Brook University, School of Medicine

State University of New York—University at Buffalo, School of Medicine and
	Biomedical Sciences

State University of New York—Upstate Medical University, College of Medicine

Temple University, School of Medicine

Thomas Jefferson University, Jefferson Medical College

Tufts University, School of Medicine

Tulane University, School of Medicine

UMDNJ, New Jersey Medical School

UMDNJ, Robert Wood Johnson Medical School

University of Alabama—Birmingham, School of Medicine

University of California—Irvine, College of Medicine

University of California—Los Angeles, David Geffen School of Medicine

University of California—San Diego, School of Medicine

University of California—San Francisco, School of Medicine

University of Chicago, Pritzker School of Medicine

University of Florida, College of Medicine

University of Illinois at Chicago, UIC College of Medicine

University of Iowa, Roy J. and Lucille A. Carver College of Medicine

University of Kentucky, College of Medicine

University of Maryland, School of Medicine

University of Massachusetts, Medical School

University of Miami, Miller School of Medicine

University of Miami, Miller School of Medicine at Florida Atlantic University

University of Michigan, Medical School

University of Minnesota—Duluth, Medical School

University of Minnesota—Twin Cities, Medical School

University of North Carolina at Chapel Hill, School of Medicine

University of North Dakota, School of Medicine and Health Services

University of Pennsylvania, School of Medicine

University of Pittsburgh, School of Medicine

University of Rochester, School of Medicine and Dentistry

University of South Alabama, College of Medicine

University of South Dakota, School of Medicine

University of South Florida, College of Medicine

University of Southern California, Keck School of Medicine

University of Tennessee—Memphis, College of Medicine

University of Toledo, Health Science Campus

University of Virginia, School of Medicine

University of Wisconsin—Madison, School of Medicine and Public Health

Vanderbilt University, School of Medicine

Virginia College of Osteopathic Medicine

Virginia Commonwealth University, School of Medicine

Wake Forest University, School of Medicine

Washington University in St. Louis, School of Medicine

West Virginia University, School of Medicine

Western University of Health Sciences, College of Osteopathic Medicine of the Pacific

Yale University, School of Medicine

Yeshiva University, Albert Einstein School of Medicine

After considering the information for applicants who were accepted to a given medical school, you'll start to get an idea of what you will need—in terms of academic competitiveness, personal statement quality, extracurricular experiences, etc.—to gain admission to it. Even if you do not plan to apply to the same schools as the students included in this book, the quality of the students' personal statements and the overall strength of their applications can be used to measure your own writing and credentials.

THE PARTS OF THIS BOOK

CHAPTER 1

Following Directions: A Brief Overview of the Medical School Application Process

Before we get down to the business of your personal statement and secondary essays, we place them both in the context of your application; we also place your application in the larger context of the medical school admissions process.

CHAPTERS 2–4

Getting Personal: Primary and Supplemental Essays
Having Heart: What Really Makes an Essay Tick
They're, Their, and There: Grammar and Writing Tips

These three chapters address how to write a great personal statement and first-rate secondary essays for admission to medical school. There's no magic recipe, of course; nevertheless, if you follow our advice about what to put in and what to leave out, we're very confident that you'll end up with memorable pieces of writing that will differentiate you from the applicant pool at large and make you a more competitive candidate. We'll also give you a refresher course on GUMS (that's grammar, usage, mechanics, spelling) to prevent a few misplaced modifiers from casting a pall over your application.

CHAPTER 5

Making Ends Meet: Financial Aid Overview

Your basic financial aid options are laid out here. We present good strategies to adopt and common pitfalls to avoid.

CHAPTER 6

Being a Doctor: Things You Should Know

Is medicine the right career for you? This chapter presents a discussion of modern medical practice and current trends in medicine.

Chapter 7

Q&A with Admissions Officers

This part of the book consists of interviews with eight medical school admissions professionals—five from allopathic schools and three from an osteopathic school. Read about what they do and don't like to see in applications, how their admissions office works, and just how much the personal statement and secondary essays are worth at their school. We think you'll find their opinions intriguing; they also lend a human perspective to the sometimes harrowing medical school admissions process.

Chapter 8

Real Personal Statements and Secondary Essays

This part of this book contains 64 actual, unexpurgated personal statements written and submitted by real medical school applicants to a variety of schools. Each student profile is broken down into manageable chunks. The name of the student[1] and a photograph (if he or she provided one) come first. We then offer a short paragraph summarizing the major accomplishments and activities the student highlighted on his or her applications. Next, we provide statistical information, which appeared on the student's apps and a list of schools to which the student applied. Below that you will see the *unedited* personal statement that the student wrote for his or her American Medical College Application Service (AMCAS) primary application.[2] For any non-AMCAS schools to which the applicant applied, he or she would have had to prepare an additional application or applications, which may not have included the personal statement shown.[3] It is not uncommon, however, for premeds to use their AMCAS personal statement for a non-AMCAS primary application if the prompt is general enough.

---

1 Some students wished to have their profiles listed anonymously. Their profiles can be found at the end of the chapter.

2 A list of medical schools participating in AMCAS for the 2015 entering class can be found at Aamc.org/students/applying/amcas/participating-schools/. Please note that the schools participating in AMCAS changes somewhat annually—schools on this list may not have been participating when a given applicant applied to medical school.

3 All osteopathic schools participate in the American Association of Colleges of Osteopathic Medicine (AACOM)'s Application Service (AACOMAS), discussed in chapter one of this book. Some allopathic schools also do not participate in the AMCAS, though the number of schools in that category has steadily decreased over the last decade. *Medical School Admissions Requirements*, a book annually published by the American Association of Medical Colleges (AAMC), provides contact information for non-AMCAS schools.

Students profiled in this book also shared one or more essays written as part of a secondary application. Secondary essays are always written for a specific school, in response to prompts that are more explicit than those found on primary apps. Though chances are you won't encounter the exact essay prompts that these students received, these real-life examples can help to demystify this part of the application. The particulars of primary and secondary applications are discussed in more detail in chapters one and two of this book.

In this section, we did not group the applicants into any categories or organize them by school; you will find them in alphabetical order by first name. The location of the page listing each applicant's admissions decision(s) can be found at the end of his or her profile. While you read, you may want to consult the medical school profiles on our website, PrincetonReview.com. In each school profile, you will find information about students who applied in the most recent academic year, including the average MCAT score and average college GPA of the entering class, as well as the school's acceptance rate. We also provide admissions requirements and suggestions for each school, as well as a description of its admissions process.

CHAPTER 9

Where They Got In

This is an index of the admissions decisions each student received. Below the name of the student is the name of the medical school he or she decided to attend. Try putting yourself in the position of the admissions officer; you may be surprised by some admissions results! This index is also alphabetized by the student's first name.

EDITOR'S NOTE

Though it goes without saying, *don't* plagiarize the personal statements and essays in this book. Your response must be in your own words. We encourage you to note themes, structures, and words that you like, but draw the line at copying paragraphs, sentences, or even phrases. There's a chance you'll get caught, and then you wouldn't get into medical school at all. Penalties notwithstanding, plagiarism is simply wrong, so don't do it.

Chapter 1

Following Directions:
A Brief Overview of the
Medical School
Application Process

A View to Admissions

If you want to be a doctor—whether you aspire to do reconstructive surgery, administer anesthesia, or treat cataracts—your first steps are clear: Fulfill your premed requirements and go to medical school.

You probably already know that medical school admissions are a challenging enterprise. Those who've succeeded, however, are often quick to point out that it is a small price to pay for the rewards reaped. You also have some help in the form of this book. In this chapter, we'll guide you through each step of the medical school admissions process, describing the hurdles you'll have to leap and the potential pitfalls. There are seven key components to the process; all are worth separate and special consideration, as admissions committees will carefully assess your performance on each one. They are as follows:

1. GPA and academic performance in college

2. MCAT score(s)

3. Extracurricular preparation

4. Letters of recommendation

5. Primary application (AMCAS or other)

6. Secondary application

7. Interview

Medical schools share a general application process, but individual schools can vary significantly in how they evaluate candidates. Here are some across-the-board commonalities. Every admissions committee does an initial evaluation by way of some type of admissions index. This system assigns a set of points or category ranking to each applicant based mainly on his or her GPA, MCAT scores, and other objectively quantifiable elements from the primary application. For example, a certain number of points might be assigned to a candidate who has to work more than 20 hours a week to pay his or her way through college. This index is most commonly used in the first round to eliminate low-performing students from further consideration. It may also be consulted in later rounds for decisions between close candidates, but this is less common.

If a student's application achieves the initial minimum index, the admissions committee then reviews his or her subjective criteria—the extracurricular preparation, letters of recommendation, and essays submitted with the primary and secondary applications.

Most top schools also consider subjective aspects of a student's academic record in this phase, such as the type and difficulty of courses taken, GPA trends, special academic projects undertaken, and the reputation of the major or school attended. Students who pass this more subjective evaluation are then offered interview spaces. After the interview, the interviewers' impressions are prepared for the student's file and final admissions decisions are made, either on a case-by-case basis or with groups of applications being ranked by committee vote.

Gaining admission to medical school is never an easy task, but in some years it can be significantly more competitive. In the "easiest" years, two out of three students who apply are accepted; in other years, it's one out of two; in the most difficult years, it's one out of three. Of course, many more potential medical school students are lost during the undergraduate years than during this stage. Though attrition rates vary by school, fulfilling premedical requirements is one of the most difficult things to do as an undergraduate—those who do so successfully should congratulate themselves!

Depending on who you are and what your preparation has been, you may find the challenges of medical school admission relatively easy, or you may find them unexpectedly difficult. One often-cited motto for minimizing procrastination is **Plan and do first those things that scare you.** If any aspect of the admissions process gives you anxiety just by thinking about it, you need to plan ahead and start working toward a solution now, rather than later. If you are anxious about maintaining your undergraduate GPA, find courses, majors, and universities that will allow you to highlight your abilities. Seek help from your school's tutoring center. If letters of recommendation scare you, go to your professors' office hours and get to know them. Become a research assistant. If it is the MCAT that concerns you, start taking sample tests. If it is the interview, you can conduct mock interviews at your career services center and take humanities courses that will improve your verbal communication skills.

Pre-Game Huddle

You may often feel pressure to be the perfect premed, but don't get caught up in competitiveness. You should minimize self-doubt and focus on your own goals. There is no set path to achievement, so embrace your individuality and be kind to yourself and others along the way—how you get there is just as important as actually getting there. Remember: You aren't alone in your endeavors. Take comfort in your friends and be on the lookout for any useful tools and tips you can pick up along the way. Learn what you can from those who have gone through this process before you and the books—such as this one—written about their experiences. If you reach out to well-chosen classmates, mentors, and friends, you can build an effective support team, whose members can motivate and encourage you along the way.

The Premedical Timeline

The traditional medical student is one who prepares for and applies to medical school during college, entering a program directly upon graduation from his or her undergraduate institution. Although there is no prescribed order in which students should complete the academic requirements for medical school (which are primarily entry-level courses), most premeds do so during the first few years of college. That said, **you can arrange your premed courses in any way that accommodates your schedule. If you feel that your academic record will suffer if you follow the standard timetable, don't adhere to it!** Think creatively and find your own path.

The requirements are the same for students who are considering allopathic or osteopathic medicine. The following is an outline of a typical premedical curriculum for a traditional, full-time undergraduate student:

Freshman Year
Academic:
- One year of general chemistry
- One year of calculus
- One year of biology
- One semester of English
- Introductory major requirements (optional)

Extracurricular:
- Explore all the various specialties of medical practice.
- Begin a healthcare-related volunteer job or internship.
- Research academic societies, premed clubs, and other student organizations and consider joining one.

Other:
- Visit your school's premed advisor, review course requirements, and create a premedical game plan.
- Continue investigating medicine. Is it right for you? Develop personal and academic goals. Write them down.
- Build relationships with professors who can later serve as mentors, offer you the opportunity to participate in research, or write recommendations on your behalf.

Sophomore Year

Academic:
- One year of organic chemistry
- Other introductory major requirements

Extracurricular:
- If you had a positive experience your freshman year, continue with the same extracurricular activity; if you didn't enjoy it or were not sufficiently challenged, begin a new one immediately.

Other:
- Toward the end of the year, begin researching medical school programs.
- Continue seeking relationships with professors and begin a list of those who might write your recommendations.

Junior Year

Academic:
- One year of calculus-based physics
- Upper division major course work

Applications:
- Begin drafting your personal statement in early spring.
- Request applications from non-AMCAS medical schools in April.
- Collect letters of recommendation to send in September of your senior year.

MCAT:
- Take the MCAT no later than mid-May to receive your scores in June.

Summer Before Senior Year

Applications:
- Complete primary medical school applications. You may start this process as soon as April and, ideally, you should complete it by June or July. As the vast majority of medical schools review applications as they come in and assign interview spots on a rolling basis, your chances of scoring an interview are significantly higher if you apply early. If you want to be considered seriously for a position, you'll want to submit all application

material no later than September. Your chances of acceptance go down
steadily after the J's and rapidly after September.

- Research financial aid options.

MCAT:

- Premeds who did not take the MCAT earlier or want to retake the exam
  should take the MCAT as early in the summer as possible.

SENIOR YEAR
Academic:

- Finish remaining premed requirements.
- Finish remaining major/university requirements.
- Take upper-division or graduate-level courses in medically related subjects such as physiology, histology, pharmacology, and anatomy, if you
  have time. This will allow you some breathing room during the first two
  years of medical school.

Applications:

- Do more comprehensive research about the medical schools to which
  you applied.
- Complete secondary applications and send in letters of recommendation
  between September and January.
- Submit FAFSA.
- Prepare for interviews and wait for invitations to interview. Interviews
  typically take place in the fall, winter, and, at some schools, early spring.
- Interview and wait for letters!

Bear in mind that this list represents only the minimum requirements for admission to most
medical school programs. Some medical schools ask applicants to take additional courses as
prerequisites to their programs. If you have your heart set on a certain medical school program,
you should do research about its prerequisites.

THE NOTORIOUS GPA

Your undergraduate academic performance will be the most important factor in your admissions decisions. In 2013, the average GPA for medical school applicants was 3.54; the average GPA for students who successfully matriculated was 3.69.[4]

Since your GPA is an average of all your grades, you don't need to perform at a B-plus/A-minus (3.33/3.67) level in all your classes, though that would be ideal. If your average science subject (biology, chemistry, physics, and math) GPA—what AMCAS calls BCPM—is around 3.35, you can still be accepted to medical school. Chances are, however, that you will need the GPA of your other course work to compensate. In fact, committees expect you to perform measurably better in those courses as most non-science GPAs tend to be higher, on average, then science GPAs for most medical school applicants.

While medical schools do evaluate the rigor of science courses, they first look for students with high grade point averages (3.5 or above). Therefore, unless you are extremely talented in science, it is better to take all the prerequisite courses in college. Even if you took AP Biology and were able to pass out of the introductory course, you should take first-year bio with all the other premeds and receive a high mark.

Most medical schools will evaluate an applicant's GPA in the context of his or her entire academic history. Medical schools look favorably on students who overcome adversity to achieve as well as students who come from disadvantaged or minority backgrounds. A demanding work schedule of more than twenty hours per week during college may also receive special consideration. Also of importance, particularly for top-tier medical schools, is the quality of the college or university attended. Some allowance may be made for lower grades at a top public, Ivy League, technical university. **Admissions officers, however, are most impressed by sustained periods of high GPA.** Think of your premedical curriculum as a marathon, not a series of sprints followed by walking. Shoot for consistent, strong performance in all your academic work.

4   Association of American Medical Colleges, "MCAT Scores and GPAs for Applicants and Matriculants, 2002–2013," https://www.aamc.org/download/321494/data/2013factstable17.pdf (accessed September 10, 2014).

MCAT on a Hot Tin Roof

The MCAT is a standardized exam written and administered by the AAMC and designed to test the general critical thinking abilities and introductory science knowledge of medical school applicants. Since there is a wide range of difficulty in curricula at U.S. colleges, the MCAT helps medical schools to contextualize or "normalize" an applicant's GPA, evaluating his or her basic knowledge and critical reasoning abilities on a standard measure. (But don't be fooled. If medical school admissions committees want to see what you know, all they have do to is look at your transcripts. What they really want to see, though, is how you *think*. Especially, how you think under pressure. And that's what your MCAT score will tell them.) The MCAT is also designed to serve as a barometer for how a student will perform in medical school, though it is not always very successful in that endeavor.

Virtually all U.S. and Canadian allopathic and osteopathic medical schools require the MCAT. You should, if possible, sit for the test in the spring of your junior year. Most medical schools have rolling admission policies, so earlier test dates, as long as you've finished your prerequisite course work, are better. Of course, not all applicants' academic schedules realistically allow them to take the April test.

The test attempts to be culturally neutral, indifferent to a student's real-world background, skills, and environmental influences. In that sense, the MCAT has major limits as a tool for evaluating an applicant's unique abilities. Fortunately, most students can do well on it, regardless of background, with a program of advanced preparation. It is far more a test of your preparation technique and test-taking skills than it is of your innate learning.

But what is it? The MCAT is a seven-and-a-half hour, computer-based test, designed to determine your ability to rapidly apply basic sciences knowledge and critical analysis skills. It's important to note that this test is not adaptive. Adaptive tests base your next question on whether or not you've answered the current question correctly, but the MCAT is *fixed-form*. Questions are in a pre-determined order and do not change based on your answers. The test is mostly passage based, meaning that students must read and then answer a set of conceptual questions that follow each passage. Still, about ¼ of the questions in the sciences sections are freestanding questions, which means these questions are independent of any passage information. The test is divided into four scored sections: Chemical and Physical Foundations of Biological Systems, Critical Analysis and Reasoning Skills, Biological and Biochemical Foundations of Living Systems, and Psychological, Social, and Biological Foundations of Behavior. By the time you have finished your prerequisites, you have already learned everything you need to know for the MCAT. Unfortunately, **success in premed course work does not translate directly into success on the MCAT**. It is not so much a test of your basic science knowledge as it is a test of your ability to interpret and apply that knowledge to different situations. Premedical students are generally exposed to the information tested on the MCAT over the course of several years and, especially after doing some review, are reasonably comfortable with the concepts and research principles being tested. It's the *application of this knowledge* to new and unfamiliar situations that is challenging. Therefore, it is imperative to design an effective method of preparation early on.

As you're reading a book published by The Princeton Review, you're correct in assuming that we're a little biased as to how we think you should study for the MCAT. The short answer here is that, for most people, taking a course to prepare for the MCAT is worth both the time and the money. MCAT scores are heavily weighted on your medical school application—at some schools, they are weighed as heavily as undergraduate GPA. As this book dedicated to the essay attests, final acceptance into medical school depends on a wide variety of factors. Still, a high GPA and good MCAT scores can make it a little easier to get your foot in the door. A class forces you to study in a reasonable way, cover the material efficiently, and get plenty of practice. It also gives you the resources to shore up any gaps in your academic preparation. The MCAT is a tedious and wretched business; it's nice to have a class full of fellow sufferers who can make you feel less alone in your pain. Simply put, an investment in studying for the MCAT is an investment in your future, and the more you invest, the better you'll likely do.

You can register for the MCAT online at the AAMC website (www.aamc.org).

INVEST IN EXTRACURRICULAR ACTIVITIES

Extracurriculars are a key component of one's medical school application. Most schools carefully review students' postsecondary nonacademic experiences to learn more about personality and interests. Qualities that cannot be measured by GPA and MCAT scores—such as humanity, maturity, and leadership—are often measured by one's prolonged involvement in an extracurricular activity.

You're probably saying, "Wait, where do I find the time for that?" Thankfully, **extracurricular activities are not necessarily time-consuming. On average, the time commitment is four hours a week.** This means that no matter how busy you are, you shouldn't have too much trouble fitting an extracurricular activity into your schedule.

Look at it this way: Most medical students have a strong academic record, and schools need additional ways to distinguish among candidates. The extracurricular activities you participate in can show schools that you not only have the intelligence but the personality and character necessary to make a great physician. They are great indicators of the personal qualities and work ethic that would make you both happy and productive in medicine. Participating in four years' worth of extracurricular activities (four hours of extracurriculars a week, for four years) is best as sustained long-term commitment to an activity showcases that other quality admissions officers are on the prowl for: follow-through. For instance, you might continue with an extracurricular you were involved in in high school, particularly if the activity was medically related.

It is important to emphasize, however, that you should not approach extracurricular activities as something you must do in order to satisfy an admissions committee. Students who are passionate about medicine often find volunteer and internship opportunities to be rewarding, life-enhancing, and interesting experiences. In addition, sustained commitment to a well-chosen extracurricular activity can demonstrate qualities that medical schools find desirable, such as leadership ability, altruism, and maturity. On top of that, extracurricular activities often provide excellent material for personal statements and secondary essays. They are also generally discussed in your interview, so you should be able to talk about why you chose a given activity and what you have taken from it.

If you have questions about how much a certain extracurricular program, such as a summer internship, might be valued on your application, consult your premed advisor.

LETTERS OF RECOMMENDATION

In most cases, medical schools request of applicants either a minimum of three recommendations or a premedical committee letter. The latter can be a letter written by the undergraduate premedical committee specifically recommending you, or it can be a letter that summarizes your achievements and suitability for medicine and lists your class rank and comments various faculty members have made about you.

If you are a student who is still in school and you have access to pre-health advising, your letters will probably be handled by that office, and at least one of your letters will probably be from the pre-health advisor. If your school does not have a premedical committee or you are a returning adult, you may have to take care of all the requests and letters yourself.

Letters of recommendation for medical school work in the same way other such letters do—**you will have much better luck if you approach your potential recommender courteously and with a copy of your resume, transcript, and personal statement.** Make an appointment to speak with each potential recommender and explain why you are applying to each school on your list and make your case. The key is to start early and be conscientious about following up with your letter writers throughout the process.

As a rule of thumb, a strong application file typically will contain at least two letters from a professor in the sciences and one letter from a professor outside the sciences. Unless specifically instructed not to send additional letters (some schools request that you send no more than three), more competitive applicants commonly send as many as six recommendations. Sending more letters than the minimum allows you to include those from additional academic sources, clinical mentors, supervisors in extracurricular activities, and research sources, and it allows you to course-correct for a recommendation letter that was unexpectedly lukewarm. Even if you have been out of school for a while, you should try to get at least one letter from a former professor. During your undergrad years (or your post-bacc program), you should build relationships with faculty members so they can write something meaningful about you. Don't ask for a letter from someone famous unless they know you pretty well. Name-dropping is not considered to be particularly attractive in a prospective medical student.

Although many returning adults feel awkward approaching professors they might not have spoken with in several years, most are pleasantly surprised to discover that, for the most part, professors do tend to remember their students, and most are happy to write letters of recommendation.

As with all aspects of your application, it is good to submit a well-rounded set of recommendations, including letters from people who can attest to your personal qualities, as well as your academic abilities. Aside from the obligatory faculty recommendations, you may wish to submit additional recommendations from supervisors you had at research, volunteer, or professional positions, who can discuss your nonacademic strengths, such as compassion, dedication to service, and professionalism. Both current and former students should also consider asking for letters from doctors with whom they have worked or volunteered. Those applying to an osteopathic school must submit a letter of recommendation from a doctor of osteopathy (DO). Again, unless a medical school specifically limits the number of recommendations you can send, you can send up to double the number they request. More than that, however, would be overkill. While you should definitely consider nonacademic supervisors as a source of recommendations, do not send letters from family, friends, or graduate students.

How to Apply

There are 158 accredited allopathic medical schools that confer the MD degree—137 in the United States, 4 in Puerto Rico, and 17 in Canada—and 30 accredited osteopathic medical schools that confer the DO degree. The main difference between allopathic and osteopathic programs is philosophical—the latter usually have a greater focus on preventative medicine, holistic healing, and patient care skills. They also incorporate training in "manipulation," a traditional form of healing that is intended to promote musculoskeletal health. An advantage to osteopathic schools is that admissions standards are generally less stringent than they are for allopathic schools, which can be very enticing to older applicants or students who lack a perfect academic record, but nonetheless have a strong desire to be a doctor. However, those interested in entering a specialized allopathic medical field or engaging in clinical medical research will find that attending an osteopathic school severely limits certain choices. The moral herein: Do your homework before applying.

Whether applying to allopathic schools, osteopathic schools, or both, it is a good idea to **apply broadly—the typical premed applies to ten to fifteen schools. In competitive states, such as California, the average is often as high as 25.** Make sure to include "safety" schools where you will most likely be accepted—perhaps as many as six, if you are applying to twenty-four schools. In addition to admissions competitiveness, there are many factors to consider when evaluating medical school programs, including location, reputation, affiliated teaching hospitals, pre-clinical and clinical curriculum, teaching methodology, and student life.

Most allopathic medical schools use the AMCAS application, a standardized form handled by the AAMC. The medical schools in Ontario, Canada, use the Ontario Medical School Application Services application (www.ouac.on.ca/omsas/index.html) and the medical schools at the University of Texas use their own central application service (www.utsystem.edu/tmdsas). For some schools, you will need to request a specific application.

In the spring of 2001, the AAMC switched to an entirely Web-based AMCAS application. This online application is available directly from www.aamc.org and costs $160 for the first school you apply to and $36 for each additional school. If you have significant financial hardship, you can apply directly to AMCAS for a fee waiver—through the Fee Assistance Program—on their website.

When you begin the AMCAS application, you will be prompted fill in your undergraduate course work and grades, your work experience and extracurricular activities, and the personal comments section, where you'll have exactly one typewritten, single-spaced page to explain your life and convince admissions officers that you should be one of the chosen few. Needless to say, this part of the application takes time and patience—we will address it in more detail in the following chapters.

You will also need to prepare transcript requests for every postsecondary school you ever attended, even if you only took one class there or the credits transferred elsewhere. You can download official transcript request forms as part of the online AMCAS application. Undergraduate colleges will send your transcripts to AMCAS, who will use them to verify the information on your application. AMCAS begins accepting transcripts on roughly around March 15 each year and completed applications on June 1. It will take about six weeks for AAMC to process everything, a procedure that includes a "Verification" of your coursework. You can contact AAMC to check the status of your application (you can reach them on the Web at www.aamc.org or by phone at 202-828-0400).

When you are choosing which schools to apply to, make sure that you check in-state residency requirements. Although many allopathic schools are private, there are quite a few public schools that receive free money every year from out-of-state applicants they are prohibited from accepting into their programs. It doesn't matter how qualified you are; if you aren't a state resident, you can't get in.

Osteopathic schools use their own internal system, AACOMAS, which in many respects works exactly the same way as AMCAS: You can download a paper application from their website, fill one out online at www.aacom.org, or call 301-968-4100. The application costs $195 for the first school and $35 for additional schools, and there is also a fee waiver available for applicants who qualify. Like the AMCAS application, the AACOMAS application takes some time to fill out, so make sure you get started early. It also includes a personal statement, but it's even shorter than the AMCAS's—you only have about half a page to explain why you want to be an osteopathic physician. You will also need to get a recommendation from a DO, a fact that takes some applicants by surprise. If you are serious about osteopathic school, search for a mentor DO as early as possible. One of the nice things about AACOMAS is that all osteopathic schools use it—you don't have to worry about tracking down additional applications. Because osteopathic schools are private institutions, they don't have state residency requirements (although some may have tuition breaks for residents of particular states). If you are interested in studying osteopathic medicine, investigate all of the colleges and choose based on your interest in the program and living conditions in the area.

Another rule of thumb, regardless of the schools you apply to, is to apply as early as you can in the process. In general, premedical students begin the application process in the spring semester of their junior year, or approximately a year and a half before they want to enter medical school. The vast majority of medical schools engage in some type of rolling admissions, which means that they read and evaluate applications as the folders arrive. However, they will not begin evaluating an applicant until all of his or her admissions materials (e.g., application, transcripts, MCAT scores) have been received. In practical terms, this means that if you take the MCAT in the spring and get your applications in by late June, you will have a distinct advantage over someone taking the test in the summer, who may not have their application materials submitted until early September. Each year, students are accepted with summer test scores and applications that arrived late in the process. Unfortunately, there are also large numbers of students who are not accepted but would have had a decent chance had they applied earlier. Basically, you should try for every possible advantage. Turning in your application early can certainly help to give you an edge. Also, procrastinators take note: AMCAS is serious about its deadlines. If an application or transcript is late, you'll get it back.

ROUND #2: SECONDARY APPLICATIONS

If you take the MCAT in the spring, you will get a short breather after submitting your primary applications. Traditionally, premeds take advantage of this time with a well-deserved vacation. But keep the phone handy during this leisurely interlude; only a few weeks after you submit your primaries, medical schools will start mailing secondary applications.

Most schools send secondary applications indiscriminately, meaning that every living, breathing candidate who submitted a primary application will get a secondary. The main reason schools send out secondary applications without reviewing the primary application first is that they charge fees, ranging from $35 to $120 per school, for the privilege of filling one out. And while there are a few student-friendly schools that will review GPA and MCAT scores before sending a secondary application, in most cases you will receive a secondary application even if you have no chance of acceptance. If you find that the cost of sending back secondaries becomes prohibitive, you should call the schools and request fee waivers, especially if you were already eligible for a waiver from AMCAS.

Needless to say, spending countless hours filling out secondaries for schools that would decline to interview applicants based on their primary applications is a source of irritation for many. Keep this in mind and don't have false hopes that a secondary application means any more than it does. The types of questions you'll find on secondary applications are discussed in the following chapter, *Getting Personal: Primary and Supplemental Essays*.

THE ART OF THE INTERVIEW

To many admissions committees, the interviewer's opinions matter even more than recommendations, partly because recommendations often come from unknown sources. Again, if you consider the expense and hassle involved in setting up a personal interview for every possible admit, you have an idea of how much medical schools value the process. The interview is a chance to get a real sense of the candidate as a person, and the school's opportunity to hear a medical professional's first-hand evaluation of an applicant.

For highly desirable applicants, the interview will not be a deal-breaker unless something dramatically bad happens. For top-tier candidates, the interview is primarily an opportunity for the medical school to confirm credentials and verify that the actual person roughly matches the impressive application. Even if they don't dazzle their interviewers, top applicants are still very likely to be accepted.

For students who have high potential but are not at the top of the stack, in other words, for the average applicant, the interview is an important opportunity to make a positive, distinctive impression on the admissions committee. Therefore, it is important to spend some time preparing for the interview by reviewing sample questions and rehearsing answers. You might also spend some time reading the newspaper or science magazines, as your interviewer may ask you about current issues in medicine. Even if you are naturally charming and charismatic, resist the temptation to wing it in the interview.

Regardless of which category you fall into, simply by being invited for an interview, you officially join the ranks of "desirable" applicants. Remember: It would be too costly and time-consuming for medical schools to interview all possible candidates; therefore, it is only the most promising who are invited. That said, **about 50 percent of interviewed candidates are not offered admission—you have to use every advantage you can.** The earlier you interview, the sooner the admissions committee can begin evaluating you for a position. Whenever possible, you should take the earliest interview date you are offered. As a rule, don't put off or delay interviews unnecessarily.

Nonetheless, you will want to control travel costs by scheduling interviews for schools that are in similar geographic regions within the timeframe of a single trip. Schools understand students' desire to minimize costs and will often accommodate changes. If you receive an interview request from one school and have applied to another school in the same area, you may consider calling the second school and asking politely if they are planning to interview you. Explain that you have another interview at a school in the area and were wondering if you should also be planning to visit their campus. In that case, schools are often happy to let you know whether they will be able to interview you in the same timeframe.

Interviewees often have the option of staying with a current medical student the night before the interview. If you are comfortable with new people and short on cash, this option is a good way to save some money and get to know more about the school. Be sure to ask your host for his or her honest opinion of the strengths and weaknesses of the school. A friendly host may also be able to offer a couple last-minute interview tips. If, however, you would feel stressed or are unwilling to sleep on someone else's sofa, look for accommodations on or near campus. The key is to be prepared, even if it costs a few extra bucks. Your future self will thank you.

Chapter 2

Getting Personal: Primary and Supplemental Essays

THE PERSONAL STATEMENT

The AMCAS and AACOMAS applications both feature a personal comments section, also referred to as "the personal statement" or "the essay." It is the first and best opportunity you have to speak directly to admissions officers. Don't underestimate its power to make a strong, positive impression on an admissions committee. Whether you're a budding wordsmith or have daily nightmares about the written page, it presents an opportunity to give your application a voice—your voice. Medical schools are looking for passionate, humane, and interesting individuals who can add diversity of thought and distinct experiences to the incoming class. The essay is your chance to convince the committee that you are more than the sum of your academic record, and that you deserve a shot at an interview.

Neither AMCAS nor AACOMAS will provide you with a specific prompt for your personal comments. They will, however, provide topics to consider. These topics typically concern your motivation for a medical career and the experiences, situations, and ideas that have influenced your life and academic career and are not mentioned elsewhere in your application. Considering this, most personal statements tend to utilize one or more of the following basic themes:

- A life-changing personal experience with medicine, as a patient or as a person close to a patient, which led to an interest in a career as a doctor.
- A relationship with a mentor, or another inspiring individual.
- The decision to pursue a medically related career.
- An experience that challenged or changed your perspective about medicine.
- A challenging personal experience and its effects on your life.
- An insight into the nature of medical practice or the future of medical technology, and your perceived relation to this insight.

No one theme is inherently better than another—there are excellent personal statements written using commonplace themes and poor ones written using extraordinary themes. The best, however, tend to focus on a single theme supported by a few well-chosen, illustrative examples.

When brainstorming ideas for your personal statement, consider events that have strongly influenced or affected you. You've probably had a number of experiences that have affirmed or challenged your sense of purpose, or led you to reconsider a long-held opinion. Think about how these moments have shaped you. Make a list of them and begin to look for a connection between them. What have you learned in the past few years? How have you and your perspectives changed? What part of medicine was not like you expected it to be? What has been the most difficult thing for you to accept? What has been the most enlightening?

Whichever topic you choose will require thorough care and consideration. For example, you may decide to write about a complex, tragic experience that challenged your faith in medicine, such as the death of a loved one. When writing this, you could simply retell the story, explaining what happened, how you felt about medicine before the event, and how you felt after. A better approach, perhaps, would be to consider the deeper issues related to this experience. This approach might explore how the health care system functions on the individual level, what preventive care was missing from your loved one's experience, or it might define the lack of technology or science that could have provided a solution to your loved one's problem. You could discuss the physical aspects of the health care setting, describing the hospital room, ambulances, other patients, and the nursing staff. You might also discuss the positive aspects of the experience, such as the influence of a trusted doctor or nurse. In addition, you could explain how this experience affected other parts of your life, what you did and didn't do as a result of it, and how it might impact you as a medical student or a doctor.

The main point is: **Whatever you say, it shouldn't be simple.** Medicine is a complex, interdisciplinary, and wholly human profession. Though you should have a clear subject and theme—they might even be "well-worn"—take the time to write something truly heartfelt and original. The goal isn't to rewrite history but to suggest that, if given the chance, you could change it for the better.

An Angle on Secondary Applications

Unlike primary applications, secondary applications ask specific questions about your goals, experiences, and personal views on a wide range of topics. This is not a time to get lazy, so don't rely on copying and pasting boilerplate responses from a previous draft of your personal statement. **Your secondaries will be read to see how they complement what you have already said in your primary application.** You may have an opportunity to highlight achievements or experiences that received less attention in your primary application. You should not, however, force subject matter that does not pertain to the question or questions asked. At the most basic level, your secondary is another test to see whether you can adequately understand and follow instructions—this time, the school's specific directions.

As you write your secondaries, you can refer briefly to themes in your personal statement, but you should focus more on new material. If, for example, you wrote in your personal statement about a primary care experience, you may want to point out some research experience in your secondary application, showing that you are an even broader applicant than your initial application suggested—just make sure not to bring in new material that in any way casts doubt on your original statements.

If given enough room on certain questions, you may want to follow the thesis, body, and conclusion structure that you would use for a longer essay. Don't, however, try to squeeze in extra words by using a font more than a point smaller than your AMCAS application. The admissions committee will notice and you'll come across as a rule bender, which isn't the most ideal image to portray.

POTENTIAL QUESTIONS

Secondary questions run the gamut from personal to political to pointless. If you want to see what to expect, you can contact your premed advisor as they often keep a file with the previous year's secondary applications. Here are a few questions from recent apps:

- "Write a short autobiography of your life. You should include childhood and elementary school experiences, all the way to college."
- "Compare and contrast managed care and traditional fee-for-service medical care."
- "Describe a challenge or obstacle you have overcome, and what you learned from the experience."
- "Describe an instance where you helped someone in need."
- "Describe your greatest accomplishment."

STRATEGIZE AND PRIORITIZE

As you begin to receive secondary applications, there are several different approaches you can take. Some students focus first on the schools that they would most like to attend. Other students realize that their last secondaries will be better written than their first. Thus they hold off sending secondaries to the more competitive schools until they've sent out a few to the less competitive ones. Still other students reply first to schools whose secondaries ask questions to which they can easily give solid answers. This allows them to work their way up to the more difficult applications. Finally, a few students practice writing secondary essays even before they get their first ones, so that they're ready to respond to their top choices first. In many cases, schools reveal what type of student they're looking for in the type of secondary questions they ask. Therefore, the stronger the answers you have for their questions, the more likely it is that you have the characteristics they're looking for in an applicant.

Ultimately, only you know which approach will work best for you, so trust your instincts. If you want to make sure that you are not wasting time and money by filling out secondary applications for particular schools, research their admissions requirements before you write them checks.

Chapter 3

Having Heart: What Really Makes an Essay Tick

GUIDANCE, IF NEEDED

Writing a personal statement is a unique experience. In fact, it is something of a genre of its own. Even if you're an English major and have written 101 papers on the writings of famous authors, you might find yourself tongue-tied when attempting to pen the story of your life thus far. A good way to get an idea of how to approach your personal statement is to read other students' attempts. Later in this book, we reproduce 65 personal statements and 11 secondary essays written by real medical school applicants. Your premed advisor also may have some examples of exemplary personal statements on file. For an even wider perspective, you might consider reading law or business school applications to see what students in other disciplines have written about themselves (our own *Law School Essays that Made a Difference* and *Business School Essays that Made a Difference* are good resources for this task).

THE SECRETS TO YOUR SUCCESS

The keys to success when approaching your personal statement are compression and clarity. As it's extremely difficult to write about anything important in a page or less, assume that you'll be spending a lot of quality time with your computer. To get started, you can try a couple of different approaches to get your fingers moving.

GET TO KNOW YOURSELF BETTER

The subject matter of your medical school admissions essay is: You (and why you want to go to medical school). You probably know yourself pretty well, but it can be helpful to come up with answers to the following questions before you get started writing:

- Who has been the biggest influence on your life and your decision to apply to medical school?
- If you were exiled to a deserted island and only allowed to take three books with you, which would they be? Have any of these works influenced you and your desire to be a doctor? What do your choices reveal about you?
- What work experience or extracurricular activity is most meaningful for you? What have you learned from participating in this activity?
- What has been the most disappointing/challenging experience of your life? How has this experience shaped your medical school readiness and who you are today?

- What character trait separates you from the crowd? How did you develop this character trait?
- Where do you see yourself in ten years, fifteen years, twenty years? How will medical school help you actualize this vision? What will be your definition of success when looking back on your life at your retirement?

Your responses to these questions may provide a gateway to talk about your desire for a medical school education. At the very least, they will force you into a state of self-reflection that is always conducive to writing (especially when writing about oneself).

CLUSTERING

Another approach is to get a large blank piece of paper and write down a few words to describe what has led you to apply to medical school. You can also jot down some interesting, sad, or memorable experiences and try to link them to your interest in medicine. You don't have to write these items in any particular order, just scatter your thoughts across the page. After you have several topics to work with, see if you can spot any patterns. Some of the topics will probably be interrelated. Next, generate longer descriptions of the words you wrote. For example, try to explain what you meant by "intellectual challenge." Was there a particular class you took? A paper you wrote? After you have some ideas on paper, try to pull them together based on the patterns of relationships you see between the topics. When writing your personal statement, **it is often more effective to let the reader draw conclusions than to spell things out.** Relate how you felt while treating a patient and let the reader see that you are compassionate. Don't write, "That experience demonstrates my compassion." The key is to show, not tell—imply, never spell out.

FREE WRITING

This is particularly helpful if you find that you're having trouble figuring out where to start. All you have to do is sit down and force yourself to write about anything that comes to mind. Don't worry about punctuation or grammar—just write for several pages. After ten or fifteen minutes (some people find it helpful to set a timer), take a break and look back at what you wrote. Underline everything you like or find interesting, even if it's just a word or phrase. Most of the time, you'll be surprised to discover the beginnings of an idea. Make sure to keep a notepad with you and by your bed so you can jot down ideas as they arrive.

TALK, TALK, TALK

If you have serious writer's block, you can talk into a tape recorder or bribe a friend to write as you speak. If you go the latter route, have your friend write down what he or she thinks is interesting or important as you explain why you want to go to medical school. You shouldn't expect to generate your essay in this way, but you will be able to produce some material from which you can start writing.

THREE APPROACHES

There are many different ways to structure the personal essay, but here are three basic approaches that can be used alone or in combination:

"MY HISTORY IN SCHOOL"

This essay focuses on college experiences. It works well for people whose grades are fairly high, and who want to emphasize their growth during college. If you go this route, you should write about your development, specialties, and strengths. **The best essays of this genre usually have specific examples—it helps to have a specific class, professor, paper, or experience that crystallizes your experiences and ties into your goals.** One of the benefits of this essay is a built-in chronology and organizational structure.

"MY LIFE HISTORY"

In this essay, focus on a few events or main ideas that illustrate the qualities you can bring to medicine. If your whole life clearly leads up to being a physician—even if it didn't seem that way at the time—this can be a good choice. One of the pitfalls of this genre is that it can free you to ramble and lose clarity. As you give a brief overview of your life, you should concentrate your paragraphs around individual ideas.

"THE STORY"

This is often the most effective genre if it's done correctly. It has the potential to be the most fun for admissions officers to read; it's also the most likely to be coherent and cohesive. Focus on one or two stories that illustrate your key points. You don't have to go overboard with adjectives or turns of phrase to write an effective narrative. Just pick a couple of moments that clearly define why you want to be in medicine.

ROAD MAP TO GREATNESS

Great personal statements are, well, personal. They're also on topic—i.e., medically oriented. And all your application essays should be well organized, thoughtful, clear, honest, and unique. It's a tall order, but essays that feature all these qualities can make your application truly memorable. As you write your essays, keep the below points in mind. Where does your essay shine and where can it be improved?

PERSONAL

The best personal statements are those that tell a real story from your real life. Adding an original, intimate component will make your statement stand out among the thousands seen by admissions officers every year. Though you may feel like you have the same experiences as every other premed, that is never the case. Everyone takes their own path. Take time to think back on your life and review your experiences; you'll likely come up with many small (or large) ways in which you are an original person.

MEDICALLY ORIENTED

A good personal statement clearly explains why an applicant is interested in a medical career. In fact, the central theme of the essay should demonstrate the applicant's interest in or commitment to medicine. If you choose to write about an experience that is not directly related to health care, you'll need to explain immediately how that experience contributed to your desire to go to medical school or how it'll specifically inform your experience as a medical student.

WELL ORGANIZED

Choose one central theme and stick to it. Make sure your essay has a thesis statement or overriding purpose. Good organization comes from a thorough outline, so before you begin writing, organize your essay into clear paragraphs, with a beginning, middle, and end. Your essay should flow from beginning to end and move logically sentence by sentence. Organization makes your points understandable and is essential in a great personal statement.

THOUGHTFUL

Take the time to develop a theme for your essay. Pick out some memorable experiences that relate to the theme and explore each one. Why did that experience affect you? How does it pertain to medicine and the type of physician you want to become? As you can see, *why* and how [italic] are the best starters to questions that will force you to dig deep and find meaning under the surface of an experience

CLEAR

Don't try to outshine other essays by using fancy words and terminology, and never underestimate the power of a short declarative statement. If you use a flowery or over-wrought writing style, you may muddle your main point. Though you should certainly try to vary sentence structure and word choice throughout the essay, resist the temptation to pull out your thesaurus and replace adjectives with bigger, more impressive variations. Simpler and shorter sentences are often the clearest way to convey your message; after all, it worked for Hemingway.

HONEST

Admissions committees are quick to distinguish between essays that describe a real personal experience and those that describe an exaggerated or contrived event. In addition, your interviewers will occasionally follow up on the things you said in your personal state-ment, asking you further questions about the experiences you described. It doesn't pay to be dishonest. What's more, there's no reason to be. If you feel like something you have to say is inadequate or uninteresting, consider why that is the case rather than masking it with a synthetic emotion. For example, if you worked in the oncology ward of a hospital for two years but found yourself generally uninspired by the job, don't pretend that the experience was life-changing or moving just because you think that's what an admissions committee wants to hear. Instead, consider what your reaction to the situation says about you or medicine. What could have been improved? Why weren't you able to make an emotional connection with the patients? How did the shortcomings of that experience inform your view of medicine? The answers to your questions may not always be the "right" ones; however, if you take the time to reflect and carefully consider your experience, you will ultimately find a satisfying, original, and thoughtful response.

UNIQUE

Admissions essays have a tendency to sound the same. Knowing this, some applicants try to make their essay stand out by telling jokes, writing in the third person, inserting heady intellectual quotations or commentary, or telling a story from a very unusual perspective (e.g., a patient or a child). While you do want your statement to be unique, you don't need to resort to such gimmicks. Remember, a good story shines through every time—a classic tale of con-tent over style. Make your essay special by telling a personal story in a personal way. Why is your essay about you and not about any other medical school applicant? What qualities are special about you or the circumstances you are describing? The details will set you apart: a well-chosen verb, a crisp image, or a clear crystallization of an idea is more engaging to read than writing that is vague or abstract. For example, you may feel tempted to write about what a "powerful" experience it was to volunteer at the children's hospital, but the admissions committee will feel more connected to you if you can show them the value of that experience. Bring your own voice, perspective, and experiences to the story to give it a truly unique and memorable flavor.

Finally, you can make your essay unique by occasionally using powerful, original language, as long as it is not overdone. You might start with a great opening line that catches the reader's attention, expressing an original sentiment or thought.

THE BENEFITS OF PEER PRESSURE

Writing is an ongoing process of drafts and revisions. If you've been taking mandatory writing-based humanities courses, you know how long it can take to craft a perfect paper. (And, to be brutally frank, the paper never will be perfect. "Perfect" is a subjective evaluation about and by you. How could something like that ever be perfect?) To improve your essay's quality, seek out a small circle of reviewers to help in the revision process.

The first person to recruit should be someone with an *admissions background*, such as your premed advisor, who can tell you whether the essay is addressed appropriately to your medical school audience. The second reader should be someone who *knows you very well* and can analyze the content of the essay based on what they know about you and your passions. The third reader should be someone with an *English or composition background* who can identify whether your statement is appropriately organized, grammatically correct, and tells a compelling story. If you think you're particularly weak in your insights about medicine, in your personal introspection abilities, or in your composition abilities, you might think about recruiting more than one of a particular reader type.

When looking for readers, start by asking people who are in your immediate circle. In particular, you may have trouble finding a composition reader. If you don't know anyone who's a great writer and willing to spend an hour carefully critiquing your essay, you'll need to specifically recruit someone for the job. Humanities TAs and paid writing tutors, who will review your essay for grammar, syntax, organization, and content, are good bets.

QUESTIONS FOR YOUR ADMISSIONS READER:
- Does my personal statement compliment my application?
- Is my interest in medicine and medical school evident?
- Are there any other aspects of my premedical experience that I should address?

QUESTIONS FOR YOUR PERSONAL READER:
- Have I forgotten to include any important aspects of my background or personality?
- Does this essay reflect me as a person?
- Do I represent myself well?

QUESTIONS FOR YOUR COMPOSITION READER:
- Is my essay well structured?
- Is there a central theme?

- Are my ideas expressed well?
- Do I use proper vocabulary?

With hard work and good editing, you will eventually recognize your personal statement as a well-crafted testament to your desire to attend medical school. When this time comes, leave it alone—further tinkering will only reduce its impact and originality.

DOS AND DON'TS

- **Do** focus on a single theme or thesis. Elaborate on your theme through details, opinions, and experiences.
- **Do** outline your theme and main points before you start writing. Aim for an organized, direct statement.
- **Do** tell a personal story, rather than make generalizations.
- **Do** write about something medically oriented.
- **Do** start your essay with a solid, attention-grabbing sentence.
- **Do** end your essay with a strong conclusion.
- **Do** spend time on your personal statement—it isn't a "throw away" part of the application.
- **Do** proofread carefully.
- **Do** spell check and spell check again.
- **Do** have three different reviewers, but not many more than that.

- **Don't** list all your awards and achievements, or try to include everything you have ever done on a single page.
- **Don't** be overly philosophical or abstract (a common mistake).
- **Don't** be self-aggrandizing or try too hard to impress the admissions committee; tell a real story and let the details speak for themselves.
- **Don't** use clichés or resort to attention-getting gimmicks to stand out. Use real, honest detail to make your personal statement unique.
- **Don't** lie or exaggerate.
- **Don't** use too much detail. Aim to be succinct and direct.
- **Don't** be too controversial. Avoid topics that may raise eyebrows.
- **Don't** make negative statements unless you can show how they lead to a positive counter-argument.
- **Don't** use the word "I" too often. If you state an opinion, the reader will assume it's yours. Tell a story and let the details speak for themselves.

Chapter 4

They're, Their, and There: Grammar and Writing Tips

GOOD GRAMMAR = GOOD FORM

You should strive to make your writing 100 percent grammatically accurate. Think of each essay you write as a building. If it doesn't have structural integrity, medical school admissions officers will tear through it with a wrecking ball.

Let's face it: You can write the most rip-roaring yarn this side of Clive Cussler, but without grammatical accuracy, it'll fall apart. **Though a thoughtful essay that offers true insight will undoubtedly stand out, it will not receive serious consideration if it's riddled with poor grammar and misspelled words.** It's critical that you avoid grammatical errors. We can't stress this enough. Misplaced modifiers, fragments, or spelling that belongs in a text message not only distract from your ideas but also cast doubt on your abilities, not to mention your intelligence.

Most Common Grammar Mistakes

Chances are you know the difference between a subject and a verb. So we won't spend time here reviewing the basic components of English sentence construction (however, if you feel like you could use a refresher, check out our book, *Grammar Smart*.) Instead we will focus on problems of usage.

Below is a brief overview to the seven most common usage errors among English speakers. These are errors we all make (some more than others) and knowing what they are will help you snuff them out in your own writing.

Mistake #1: Misplaced Modifier

A modifier is a descriptive word or phrase inserted into a sentence to add dimension to the thing it modifies. For example:

Because he could talk, Mr. Ed was a unique horse.

Because he could talk is the modifying phrase in the sentence. It describes a characteristic of Mr. Ed. Generally speaking, a modifying phrase should be right next to the thing it modifies. If it's not, the meaning of the sentence may change. For example:

Every time he goes to the bathroom outside, John praises his new puppy for being so good.

Who's going to the bathroom outside? In this sentence, it's John! There are laws against that! The descriptive phrase *every time he goes to the bathroom outside* needs to be near *puppy* for the sentence to say what it means.

When you are writing sentences that begin with a descriptive phrase followed by a comma, make sure that the thing that comes after the comma is the person or thing being modified.

MISTAKE #2: PRONOUN AGREEMENT

As you know, a pronoun is a little word that is inserted to represent a noun (*he, she, it, they, etc.*). Pronouns must agree with their nouns: The pronoun that replaces a singular noun must also be singular, and the pronoun that replaces a plural noun must be plural.

During your proofreading, be sure your pronouns agree with the nouns they represent. The most common mistake is to follow a singular noun with a plural pronoun (or vice versa), as in the following:

If a writer misuses words, they will not do well on the MCAT.

The problem with this sentence is that the noun ("writer") is singular, but the pronoun ("they") is plural. The sentence would be correctly written as follows:

If a writer misuses words, he or she will not do well on the MCAT.

Or

If writers misuse words, they will not do well on the MCAT.

This may seem obvious but it is also the most commonly violated rule in ordinary speech. How often have you heard people say, *The class must hand in their assignment before leaving. Class* is singular. But *their* is plural. Class isn't the only tricky noun that sounds singular but is actually plural. Following is a list of "tricky" nouns—technically called collective nouns. They are nouns that typically describe a group of people, but are considered singular and therefore need a singular pronoun:

Family
Jury
Group
Team
Audience
Congregation
United States

If different pronouns are used to refer to the same subject or one pronoun is used to replace another, the pronouns must also agree. The following pronouns are singular:

Either
Neither
None
Each
Anyone
No one
Everyone

If you are using a pronoun later in a sentence, double-check to make sure it agrees with the noun/pronoun it is replacing.

Mistake #3: Subject-Verb Agreement

The rule regarding subject-verb agreement is simple: singular with singular, plural with plural. If you are given a singular subject (*he, she, it*), then your verb must also be singular (*is, has, was*).

Sometimes you may not know if a subject is plural or singular, making it tough to determine whether its verb should be plural or singular. (Just go back to our list of collective nouns that sound plural but are really singular.)

Subjects joined by *and* are plural:

Bill and Pat *were* going to the show.

However, nouns joined by *or* can be singular or plural—if the last noun given is singular, then it takes a singular verb; if the last noun given is plural, it takes a plural verb.

Bill or Pat *was* going to get tickets to the show.

When in doubt about whether your subjects and verbs agree, trim the fat! Cross out all the prepositions, commas, adverbs, and adjectives separating your subject from its verb. Stripping the sentence down to its component parts will allow you to quickly see whether your subjects and verbs are in order.

Mistake #4: Verb Tense

As you know, verbs come in different tenses—for example, *is* is present tense, while *was* is past tense. The other tense you need to know about is "past perfect."

Past perfect refers to some action that happened in the past and was completed (perfected) before another event in the past. For example:

I had already begun to volunteer at the hospital when I discovered my passion for medicine.

You'll use the past perfect a lot when you describe your accomplishments to admissions officers. For the most part, verb tense should not change within a sentence (e.g., switching from past to present).

Mistake #5: Parallel Construction

Remember this from your SATs? Just as parallel lines line up with one another, parallelism means that the different parts of a sentence line up in the same way. For example:

Jose told the career counselor his plan: he will be taking the MCAT, attend medical school, and become a pediatrician.

In this sentence, Jose is going to *be taking, attend*, and, *become*. The first verb, *be taking* is not written I the same form as the other verbs in the series. In other words, it is not parallel. To make this sentence parallel, it should read:

Jose told the career counselor his plan: he will take the MCAT, attend medical school, and become a pediatrician.

It is common to make errors of parallelism when writing sentences that list actions or items. Be careful.

MISTAKE #6: COMPARISONS

When comparing two things, make sure that you are comparing what can be compared. Sound like double talk? Look at the following sentence:

Larry goes shopping at Foodtown because the prices are better than Shoprite.

Sound okay? Well, sorry—it's wrong. As written, this sentence says that the prices at Foodtown are better than Shoprite—the entire store. What Larry means is that the prices at Foodtown are better than the *prices* at Shoprite. You can only compare like things (prices to prices, not prices to stores).

The English language uses different comparison words when comparing two things than when comparing more than two things. Check out these examples:

more (for two things) vs. **most** (for more than two)
Ex.: Given Alex and David as possible dates, Alex is the *more* appealing of the two.
In fact, of all the guys I know, Alex is the *most* attractive.

less (for two things) vs. **least** (for more than two)
Ex.: I am *less* likely to be chosen than you are.
I am the *least* likely person to be chosen from the department.

better (for two things) vs. **best** (for more than two)
Ex.: Taking a cab is *better* than hitchhiking.
My organic chemistry professor is the *best* professor I have ever had.

between (for two things) vs. **among** (for more than two)
Ex.: Just *between* you and me, I never liked her anyway.
Among all the people here, no one likes her.

Keep track of what's being compared in a sentence so you don't fall into this grammatical black hole.

Mistake #7: Diction

Diction means choice of words. There are tons of frequently confused words in the English language and can be broken down into words that sound the same but mean different things (*there, they're, their*), words and phrases that are made up (*irregardless*) and words that are incorrectly used as synonyms (*fewer, less*).

Words that sound the same but mean different things are homonyms. Some examples are:

there, they're, their: *There* is used to indicate a location in time or space. *They're* is a contraction of "they are." *Their* is a possessive pronoun.

it's/its: *It's* is a contraction of "it is." *Its* is a possessive pronoun.

effect/affect: *Effect* is the result of something. *Affect* is to influence or change something.

conscience/conscious: *Conscience* is Freudian, and is a sense of right or wrong. *Conscious* is to be awake.

principle/principal: *Principle* is a value. *Principal* is the person in charge at a school.

eminent/imminent: *Eminent* describes a person who is highly regarded. *Imminent* means impending.

Imaginary words that don't exist but tend to be used in writing include:

Alot: Despite widespread use, *alot* is not a word. *A lot* is the correct form.

Irregardless: *Irregardless* is not in anybody's dictionary—it's not a real word. *Regardless* is the word that you want.

Sometimes people don't know when to use a word. How often have you seen this sign?

Express checkout: Ten items or less.

Unfortunately, supermarkets across America are making a blatant grammatical error when they post this sign. When items can be counted, you must use the word fewer. When something cannot be counted, you would use the word less. For example:

If you eat fewer French fries, you can use less ketchup.

Here are some other words people make the mistake of using interchangeably:

number/amount: Use *number* when referring to something that can be counted. Use *amount* when it cannot.

aggravate/irritate: *Aggravate* and *irritate* are not synonymous. To *aggravate* is to make worse. To *irritate*, is to annoy.

disinterested/uninterested: *Disinterest* means impartiality; absence of strong feelings about something, good or bad. *Uninterest*, on the other hand, indicates boredom.

Diction errors require someone to cast a keen, fresh eye on your essay because they trick your ear and require focused attention to catch.

Here's a handy chart to help you remember the most common grammar usage errors:

GRAMMAR CHART

Grammatical Category	What's the Rule?	Bad Grammar	Good Grammar
Misplaced Modifier	A modifier is word or phrase that describes something and should go right next to the thing it modifies.	1. Eaten in Mediterranean countries for centuries, **northern Europeans** viewed the tomato with suspicion. 2. A **former greenskeeper** now about to become the Masters champion, **tears** welled up in my eyes as I hit my last miraculous shot.	1. Eaten in Mediterranean countries for centuries, the tomato was viewed with suspicion by Northern Europeans. 2. I **was a former greenskeeper** who was now about to become the Masters champion; **tears** welled up in my eyes as I hit my last miraculous shot.
Pronoun Agreement	A pronoun must refer unambiguously to a noun, and it must agree in number with that noun.	1. Although **brokers** are not permitted to know executive access **codes**, **they** are widely known. 2. The **golden retriever** is one of the smartest breeds of dogs, but **they** often **have** trouble writing **personal statements** for law school admission. 3. Unfortunately, both **candidates** for whom I worked sabotaged their own **campaigns** by accepting a **contribution** from illegal **sources**.	1. Although **brokers** are not permitted to know executive access **codes, the codes** are widely known. 2. The **golden retriever** is one of the smartest breeds of dogs, but often **it has** trouble writing **a personal statement** for law school admission. 3. Unfortunately, both **candidates** for whom I worked sabotaged their own **campaigns** by accepting **contributions** from illegal **sources**.

Grammatical Category	What's the Rule?	Bad Grammar	Good Grammar
Verb Tense	Always make sure your sentences' tenses match the time frame being discussed.	1. After he finished working on his law school essays he **would go** to the party.	1. After he finished working on his law school essays he **went** to the party.
Parallel Construction	Two or more ideas in a single sentence that are parallel need to be similar in grammatical form.	1. The two main goals of the Eisenhower presidency were a **reduction** of taxes and to **increase** military strength.	1. The two main goals of the Eisenhower presidency were **to reduce** taxes and **to increase** military strength.
		2. **To provide a child** with the skills necessary for survival in modern life is **like guaranteeing their** success.	2. **Providing children** with the skills necessary for survival in modern life is **like guaranteeing their** success.
Comparisons	You can only compare like things.	1. The **rules** of written English are **more stringent** than spoken **English.**	1. The rules of written English are **more stringent than those of** spoken **English.**
		2. The **considerations** that led many colleges to impose admissions quotas in the last few decades *are similar to the quotas* imposed in the recent past by large businesses.	2. The **considerations** that led many colleges to impose admissions quotas in the last few decades **are similar to those** that led large businesses to impose quotas in the recent past.
Diction	There are many words that sound the same but mean different things.	1. Studying had a very positive **affect** on my score.	1. Studying had a very positive **effect** on my score.
		2. My high SAT score has positively **effected** the outcome of my college applications.	2. My high SAT score has positively **affected** the outcome of my college applications.

Using Punctuation Correctly

Now that we've got that covered, it's time to talk about punctuation. As a member of the LOL generation you might be great at turning punctuation into nonverbal clues, but colons and parentheses have other uses besides standing in as smiley faces at the end of your texts.

A formal essay is not like the notes you take in econometrics. "W/" is not an acceptable substitute for *with*, and neither is "b/c" for *because*. Symbols are also not acceptable substitutes for words (@ for *at*, & for *and*, etc.). (In fact, try to avoid the use of "etc."; it is not entirely acceptable in formal writing. Use "and so forth" or "among others" instead.) And please don't indulge in any "cute" spelling ("nite" for *night*, "tho" for *though*). This kind of writing conveys a message that you don't care about your essay. Show the admissions officers how serious you are by eliminating these shortcuts.

The overall effectiveness of your medical school application essay is greatly dependent on your ability to use punctuation wisely. Here's what you need to know:

Apostrophes (')

Use apostrophes in contractions or to show possession. Where you place the apostrophe depends on whether the word is singular or plural (the exception being plural words that don't end with s.) Are you trying to make a word plural? Don't use an apostrophe.

- "Writer's block is only a failure of the ego." *Norman Mailer*
- Karen was proud of her friends' test scores since she knew they had been studying for months.

Commas (,)

Very few people understand every rule for proper comma use in the English language.

This lack of understanding leads to two disturbing phenomena: essays without commas and essays with commas everywhere. Here is a quick summary of proper comma use:

Use Commas to Set Off Introductory Elements.
- Breezing through my application essay, I wondered if everyone were as well prepared as I.
- Incidentally, I got a 35 on the MCAT.
- Before you jump to any conclusions, I was only taking a mote out of her eye.

Use Commas to Separate Items in a Series.

- She made hot chocolate, cinnamon toast, scrambled eggs with cheese, and coffee cake.

[Note: There's always great debate as to whether the final serial comma (before the *and*) is necessary. In this case, the comma must be added; otherwise, there will be a question about the contents of the scrambled eggs. In cases where no such ambiguity exists, the extra comma seems superfluous. Use your best judgment. When in doubt, separate all the items in a series with commas.]

Use a Comma to Separate Independent Clauses.

(Use a comma when the independent clauses are joined by the proper conjunction: for, and, nor, but, yet, so.)

- Lindsay ate a big breakfast, but her tummy was still rumbling on test day.

Use Commas Around a Phrase or Clause that Could Be Removed Logically from the Sentence.

- The Essay section, the first section of the SAT, always makes my palms sweat.
- Xavier, the student whose test was interrupted by marching band practice, would have liked to have had ear plugs.

Use a Comma to Separate Coordinate (Equally Important) Adjectives. *Do Not* Use a Comma to Separate Noncoordinate Adjectives.

- It was a dark, stormy night.
- It was a messy triple bypass.

***Do Not* Use a Comma to Separate a Subject and a Verb.**

- Incorrect: My new MCAT study group, meets at the local café.
- Correct: My new MCAT study group meets at the local café.

***Do Not* Use a Comma to Separate Compound Subjects or Predicates.**

(A compound subject means two "do-ers"; a compound predicate means two actions done.)

- Incorrect: My best friend Xavier, and his brother Lou always tell me the truth about my practice essays.
- Correct: My best friend Xavier and his brother Lou always tell me the truth about my practice essays.
- Incorrect: Because of the strange tickling in the back of my throat, I stayed in bed, and gave myself a break from studying.

- Correct: Because of the strange tickling in the back of my throat, I stayed in bed and gave myself a break from studying.

Colons (:)

Use a colon to introduce an explanation or a list.

- "I think you judge Truman too charitably when you call him a child: He is more like a sweetly vicious old lady." *Tennessee Williams*
- "When I am dead, I hope it may be said: 'His sins were scarlet, but his books were read.'" *Hilaire Belloc*
- "Everything goes by the board to get the book written: honor, pride, decency..." *William Faulkner*

Semicolons (;)

Use a semicolon to join related independent clauses in a single sentence (a clause is independent if it can logically stand alone).

- "An artist is born kneeling; he fights to stand." *Hortense Calisher*
- "Why had I become a writer in the first place? Because I wasn't fit for society; I didn't fit into the system." *Brian Aldiss*

Dashes (—)

Use a dash for an abrupt shift. Use a pair of dashes (one on either side) to frame a parenthetical statement that interrupts the sentence. Dashes are more informal than colons.

- "Like a lot of what happens in novels, inspiration is a sort of spontaneous combustion—the oily rags of the head and heart." *Stanley Elkin*
- "Writers should be read—but neither seen nor heard." *Daphne du Maurier*
- "Of all the cants which are canted in this canting world—though the cant of hypocrites may be the worst—the cant of criticism is the most tormenting." *Laurence Sterne*

Exclamation Points (!)

Use exclamation points sparingly. Try to express excitement, surprise, or rage in the words you choose. A good rule of thumb is *one* exclamation point per essay, at the most.

- "You don't know what it is to stay a whole day with your head in your hands trying to squeeze your unfortunate brain so as to find a word. Ah! I certainly know the agonies of style." *Gustave Flaubert*

Question Marks (?)

Use a question mark after a direct question. Don't forget to use a question mark after rhetorical questions (ones that you make in the course of argument that you answer yourself).

- "Why shouldn't we quarrel about a word? What is the good of words if they aren't important enough to quarrel over? Why do we choose one word over another if there isn't any difference between them?" *G. K. Chesterton*

Quotation Marks (" ")

Use quotation marks to indicate a writer's exact words. Use quotation marks for titles of songs, chapters, essays, articles, or stories—a piece that is part of a larger whole. Periods and commas always go inside the quotation mark. Exclamation points and question marks go inside the quotation mark when they belong to the quotation and not to the larger sentence. Colons, semicolons, and dashes go outside the quotation mark.

- "That's not writing, that's typing." *Truman Capote* on *Jack Kerouac*

WRITING CLEARLY

Now that you've gotten a refresher in the building blocks of good writing, it's time to talk about the other half of the equation: style. If grammar and punctuation represent the mechanics of your writing, style represents the choices you make in sentence structure, diction, and figures of thought that reveal your personality to admissions officers. We can't recommend highly enough that you read *The Elements of Style*, by William Strunk Jr., E. B. White, and Roger Angell. This little book is a great investment. Even if you've successfully completed a course or two in composition without it, it will prove invaluable and become your new best friend—and hopefully also your muse.

ELIMINATING WORDINESS

Remember: Good writing is writing that's easily understood. You want to communicate, not conceal your point behind clichéd language and wordiness. Don't ramble, repeat, or talk vaguely. Make your prose clear and direct. **If an admissions officer has to struggle to figure out what you're trying to say, there's a good chance he or she might not bother reading further.** Abide by word limits and avoid the pitfall of overwriting. Here are some suggestions that will help clarify your writing by eliminating wordiness:

Address One Idea at a Time

Don't try to put too much information into one sentence. If you're ever uncertain whether a sentence needs three commas and two semicolons or two colons and a dash, just make it into two separate sentences. Two simple sentences are better than one long convoluted one. Which of the following examples seems clearer to you?

Example #1:

Many people, politicians for instance, act like they are thinking of the people they represent by the comments made in their speeches, while at the same time they are filling their pockets at the expense of the taxpayers.

Example #2:

Many people appear to be thinking of others, but are actually thinking of themselves. For example, many politicians claim to be thinking of their constituents, but are in fact filling their pockets at the taxpayers' expense.

Use Fewer Words to Express an Idea

In a 500-word essay, you don't have time to mess around. In an attempt to sound important, many of us "pad" our writing. Always consider whether there's a shorter way to express your thoughts. We are all guilty of some of the following types of clutter:

Cluttered	Clear
due to the fact that	because
with the possible exception of	except
until such time as	until
for the purpose of	for
referred to as	called
at the present time	now
at all times	always

Test Yourself: Eliminating Wordiness Exercise

Another way in which unnecessary words may sneak into your writing is through the use of redundant phrases. Pare each phrase listed below down to a single word:

cooperate together _____

resulting effect _____

large in size _____

absolutely unprecedented _____

disappear from sight _____

new innovation _____

repeat again _____

totally unique_____

necessary essentials _____

Use Fewer Qualifiers

A qualifier is a little phrase we use to cover ourselves. Instead of plainly stating that "Former President Reagan sold arms in exchange for hostages," we feel more comfortable stating "*It's quite possible* that former President Reagan *practically* sold arms in *a kind* of exchange for people who were *basically* hostages." Over-qualifying weakens your writing by making you sound wishy-washy or unsure. Prune out these words and expressions wherever possible:

kind of	basically
a bit	practically
sort of	essentially
pretty much	in a way
rather	quite

Another type of qualifier is the *personal qualifier*, where instead of stating the truth, I state the truth "in my opinion." Face it: Everything you state (except perhaps for scientific or historical facts) is your opinion. Personal qualifiers like the following can often be pruned:

to me

in my opinion

in my experience

I think

it is my belief

it is my contention

the way I see it

Use Fewer Adverbs

If you choose the right verb or adjective to begin with, an adverb is often unnecessary.

Use an adverb only if it does useful work in the sentence. It's fine to say "the politician's campaign ran smoothly up to the primaries," because the adverb "smoothly" tells us something important about the running of the campaign. The adverb could be eliminated, however, if the verb were more specific: "The politician's campaign sailed up to the primaries." The combination of the strong verb *and* the adverb, as in "the politician's campaign sailed smoothly up to the primaries," is unnecessary because the adverb does no work. Here are other examples of unnecessary adverbs:

very unique

instantly startled

dejectedly slumped

effortlessly easy

absolutely perfect

totally flabbergasted

completely undeniable

Similarly, precise adjectives can help you remove pesky clutter like the adverb *not* ("not clear" becomes "unclear" or "not moving" becomes "still"). Deletions like these add up when, as in the case of the AMCAS application, you only have 5,300 characters at your disposal.

ELIMINATING FRAGMENTS AND RUN-ONS

Sentences with too few words are just as annoying to admissions officers as those with too many.

A fragment is an unfinished sentence. It may lack a subject or verb, or it may be a dependent clause. Use this test for sentence fragments: Can the fragment logically stand alone, without the previous or following sentences?

- Fragment: My pencil broke during the last five minutes of the test. Pieces rolling beneath my chair.
- Correct Sentence: My pencil broke during the last five minute of the test, and the pieces rolled beneath my chair.

A run-on is an instance where two sentences run together when they should be separate. Sometimes the author forgets the necessary conjunction or the proper punctuation. Sometimes the two sentences are simply too long to fit together well.

- Run-on: Regardless of the weather, I will go spear fishing in Bali the water is as clear as glass.
- Correct Sentences: Regardless of the weather, I will go spear fishing in Bali where the water is as clear as glass.

Make sure your sentences don't contain these fatal errors.

LIMITING YOUR USE OF PASSIVE VOICE

Consistently writing in the active voice and limiting your use of the passive voice can make your writing more forceful, authoritative, and interesting. Look at the sentences below. They convey essentially the same basic idea, but they have very different effects on the reader.

- The Tobacco Industry deliberately withheld data about the dangers of second-hand smoke.
- Data about the dangers of second-hand smoke were deliberately withheld [by the Tobacco Industry].

The first sentence is in the active voice; the second, in the passive voice. The active voice has a clear subject-verb relationship which illustrates that the subject is doing the action. A sentence is in the passive voice when the subject of the sentence, instead of acting, is acted upon. By distancing the subject from the verb, the passive voice makes it appear that the action is being done to the subject. The passive voice uses a form of be (is, am, are, was, were, been) plus the main verb in past participle form. The "do-er" of a passive voice sentence is either absent or relegated to the end of the sentence in a "by" phrase.

Test Yourself: Eliminating the Passive Voice Exercise

Put each of the following sentences into the active voice:

1. The Constitution was created by the Founders to protect individual rights against the abuse of federal power.

_____

_____

_____

_____

2. Information about the Vietnam War was withheld by the government.

_____

_____

_____

_____

3. The right to privacy was called upon by the Supreme Court to form the foundation of the Roe v. Wade decision.

_____

_____

_____

_____

Using Nonsexist Language

Pronoun agreement problems often arise because the writer is trying to avoid a sexist use of language. Because there is no gender-neutral singular pronoun in English, many people use *they* incorrectly. But there are other, more grammatically precise ways of getting around this problem.

One common, albeit quite awkward, solution is to use *he/she* or *his/her* in place of *they* or *their*. For example, instead of writing, "If someone doesn't pay income tax, then they will go to jail," you can write, "If someone doesn't pay income tax, then he or she will go to jail." A more graceful (and shorter) alternative to *he/she* is to use the plural form of both noun and pronoun: "If people don't pay income tax, they will go to jail." Using nonsexist language also means finding alternatives for the word *man* when you are referring to humans in general. Instead of *mankind* you can write *humankind* or *humanity*; instead of *mailman*, you can use *mail carrier*; rather than stating that something is *man-made* you can call it *manufactured* or *artificial*.

There are a number of good reasons for you to use nonsexist language. For one thing, it is coming to be the accepted usage; that is, it is the language educated people use to communicate their ideas. Many publications now make it their editorial policy to use only non-gendered language. In addition, nonsexist language is often more accurate. Some of the people who deliver mail, for example, are female, so you are not describing the real state of affairs by referring to all of the people who deliver your mail as *men* (since it is no longer universally accepted that *man* refers to all humans). Finally, there is a good chance that at least one of your readers will be female, and that she—or, indeed, many male readers—will consider your use of the generic "he" to be a sign that you either are not aware of current academic conventions or do not think that they matter. It is best not to give your readers that impression.

Use of non-sexist language can feel awkward at first. Practice until it comes to seem natural; you may soon find that it is the old way of doing things that seems strange.

Avoid Clichés Like the Plague

Clichés are comfortable. When we're stuck for the next word, a cliché will suddenly strike us, and we'll feel lucky. We write something like "this tried and true method" or "he was one of the best and brightest." A cliché may let the writer off the hook, but the reader will be turned off. The reason a cliché is a cliché is because it is overused. Try something original instead of the following overused clichés:

"I've Always Wanted to Be a Doctor."

A great personal statement should clearly illustrate the applicant's commitment to and interest in medicine. Even so, avoid throwaway lines and generic statements that could be repeated by any other premed. Many students who choose to study medicine truly feel the decision is the result of a long-term life calling, but making such statements will not distinguish you from the crowd. Instead, focus on illustrating how you have demonstrated that commitment to medicine academically and through your activities.

"I Want to Become a Doctor to Help People."

Let's be clear: If you really want to spend your life saving lives, then by all means write about it. Just keep in mind that many other people will go this route as well. Although some of these people really do want to save lives, way down in the cockles of their hearts, most just say it because they want to look good and are motivated by less altruistic desires to attend medical school.

Here's the rub: Many essays about saving lives and healing will appear bogus and insincere. Even if you're heartfelt, your essay may get tossed into the same pile as all the insincere ones. Admissions officers will take your professed altruistic ambitions (and those of the hundreds of other applicants with identical personal statements) with a sizeable grain of salt. The key is to demonstrate your commitment to public service through examples of the work you have done. If you can in good conscience say that you're committed to a career in the public interest, you must show the committee something tangible on your application and in your essay that will allow them to see your statements as more than hollow assertions.

Speak from experience, not from desire. This is exactly where those details we've already discussed come into play. If you can't show that you're already a veteran in the good fight, then don't claim to be. While medical schools value altruism and philanthropy, there are many other worthy reasons to study medicine, such as the intellectual challenge, a love of science and research, and the ability to participate in one of the most dynamic professional fields while making a positive contribution to society. Be forthright. Nothing is as impressive to the reader of a personal statement as the truth.

Style Category	What's the Rule?	Bad Style	Good Style
Wordiness	Sentences should not contain any unnecessary words.	1. The medical school is accepting applications **at this point in time.** 2. She carries a book bag that is made out of leather **and textured**.	1. The medical school is accepting applications **now.** 2. She carries a **textured, leather** book bag.
Fragments	Sentence should contain a subject and a verb and express a complete idea.	1. And I went to the library.	1. I went to class and I went to the library.
Run-ons	Sentences that consist of two independent clauses should be joined by the proper conjunction.	1. The test has a lot of difficult information **in it, you should** start studying right away.	1. The test has a lot of difficult information **in it, and you should** start studying right away.
Passive/Active Voice	Choose the active voice, in which the subject performs the action.	1. **The ball was hit by the bat.** 2. **My time and money were wasted** trying to keep www.justdillpickles.com afloat single-handedly.	1. **The bat hit the bat.** 2. **I wasted time and money** trying to keep www.justdillpickles.com afloat single-handedly.
Nonsexist Language	Sentences should not contain any gender bias.	1. A professor should correct **his** students' papers according to the preset guidelines. 2. From the beginning of time, **mankind** used language in one way or another. 3. Are there any **upperclassmen** who would like to help students in their Lit classes?	1. Professors should correct **their** students' papers according to the preset guidelines. 2. From the beginning of time, **humans** used language in one way or another. 3. Are there any **seniors** who would like to help students in their Lit classes?

NAVIGATING THE MINEFIELD

Besides grammatical concerns, premeds should keep in mind the following points while writing their admissions essays:

Don't Repeat Information from Other Parts of Your Application

That is, don't repeat information from other parts of your application unless you can spin it to elucidate previously unmentioned facets of your personality and perspectives. The admissions staff already has your transcripts, MCAT score, and list of academic and extracurricular achievements. The personal statement is your only opportunity to present all other aspects of yourself in a meaningful way. Even if you don't mind wasting your own time, admissions officers will mind if you waste theirs.

In General, Avoid Generalities

Admissions officers have to read an unbelievable number of boring essays. You'll find it harder to be boring if you write about particulars. It's the details that stick in a reader's mind. As Ludwig Mies van der Rohe wrote, "God is in the details."

Don't Go On at Length About Your Goals

Face it: You have only an imprecise idea of what medical school will be like. Everyone's goals change through the years. Your goals are especially likely to change because medical school will change you. So leave the seventy-five-year plan out of your personal statement.

Maintain the Proper Tone

Your essay should be memorable without being outrageous and easy to read without being too formal or sloppy. When in doubt, err on the formal side.

Don't Try to Be Funny, Unless What You Have to Say is Actually Funny

An applicant who can make an admissions officer laugh never gets lost in the shuffle. No one will be able to bear tossing your application into the "reject" pile if you garner a genuine chuckle. But beware! Only a select few are able to pull off humor in this context.

Stay Away from Anything Even Remotely Off-Color

Avoid profanity. It's not a good idea to be irreverent in admissions essays. Also, there are some things admissions officers don't need (or want) to know about you, so keep those things to yourself.

Circumvent Political Issues if Possible

Admissions officers don't care about your political perspectives as long as your viewpoints are thoughtful. They don't care what your beliefs are as long as you are committed to the preservation of human life. The problem is that if you write about a political issue, you may come across as the type of person who is intolerant or unwilling to consider other viewpoints. In medical school (and certainly in your career as a medical practitioner), you'll occasionally be challenged to defend a position with which you disagree—and you don't want to seem like someone who is so impassioned that you are incapable of arguing both sides of an issue. If you opt to write about politics, be very careful.

Consider Your Audience if You Want to Write About Religion

As a general rule, don't make religion the focal point of your essay unless you're applying to a medical school with a religious affiliation. Don't misunderstand us—religion is not taboo. It's totally fine to mention religion in any personal statement; just make sure to put it within the context of the whole, dynamic person you are.

Put the Fraternity Bakesale Behind You

The same goes for the juggling club juggle-a-thon and the like. It's definitely worth noting on your resume if you were the president of your sorority or of any such institutionally affiliated organization. That said, achievements in a Greek organization or any club or student group are not the kind of life-changing events that have made you the person you fundamentally are today. Make sure what you write about has had an actual impact on your life (and better yet, on the lives of others).

No Gimmicks, No Gambles

Avoid tricky stuff. You want to differentiate yourself but not because you are some kind of daredevil. Don't rhyme. Don't write a satire or mocked-up front-page newspaper article. Gimmicky personal statements mostly appear contrived and, as a result, they fall flat, taking you down with them.

EXCUSES, EXCUSES...

Admissions officers have seen every excuse in the book for bad grades and lousy test scores. Rather than make excuses, you want to come across as resolute and capable of doing better.

"My MCAT Score isn't Great, But I'm Not a Good Test Taker."

Don't dwell on a low MCAT score in your personal statement. If there were extenuating circumstances, you can briefly mention them or you can include a separate note in your application. If there were no such circumstances, it's best to avoid mention of your score.

There's a reason for the test being taken before entrance to medical school—it's a primer, the first of many tests that you will take as a medical student. If you don't take tests well and the MCAT confirms it, don't make excuses for it; instead, resolve to do better.

Consider also that a low MCAT score speaks for itself—all too eloquently. It doesn't need you to speak for it too. The MCAT may be a flawed test, but don't argue the unfairness of the test to admissions officers who use it as a primary factor in their admissions decisions. We feel for you, but you'd be barking up the wrong tree there.

"My College Grades Weren't That High, But. . ."

This issue is a little more complicated than the low MCAT score. If your grades fall below average acceptance criteria to most medical programs, or if there are certain anomalous periods of low achievement on your transcript, it's probably best to offer some form of explanation—especially if you have a good reason for lower performance, such as illness, pregnancy, or a demanding work schedule. Medical school admissions committees will be more than willing to listen to your interpretation of your college performance, but only within limits. Keep in mind that medical schools require official transcripts for a reason. Members of the admissions committee will be aware of your academic credentials even before they read your essay.

If your grades are unimpressive, the best strategy is to offer the admissions committee something else by which to judge your abilities. Many admissions committees say that they are willing to consider students whose grades or MCAT scores fall slightly below the average acceptance criteria, particularly if they've demonstrated extraordinary altruism or service to the community. Again, the best argument for looking past your college grades is evidence of achievement in another area, whether it is your MCAT score, extracurricular activities, overcoming economic hardship as an undergraduate, or career accomplishments.

READY, SET, WRITE!

Hopefully what you've read here will help guide you through the process of writing a great personal essay and stand-out secondaries. Though there's no magic recipe, we're confident that if you follow our advice about what to put in and what to leave out, you'll end up with a memorable personal statement that will differentiate you from the larger applicant pool and make you a more competitive candidate. Take our word for it and give it your best shot.

Chapter 5

Making Ends Meet: Financial Aid Overview

MAKING FRIENDS WITH MONEY

Few people enjoy the process of thinking about and researching financial aid. As no one requires them to do it, most manage their school finances poorly. With a little effort, you can avoid the mistake of putting this issue off until the last minute and avoid taking out big loans to pay for medical school. Though you may not want to put in any time on financial issues, think about it this way: **If someone were willing to pay you $10,000 for a week or two of your time, you probably wouldn't hesitate to take the job.** But with financial aid planning, you could save far more than $10,000 if you take just a few days to research and consider your options.

For specialized tasks that you don't enjoy, get help. Ask a parent who's good at managing the family funds or see a financial planner. Every medical school has a financial aid officer who's usually happy to give advice over the phone, even to prospective students. Most current medical students don't talk to financial aid officers nearly as much as they should, perhaps because they are afraid of dealing with money issues or thinking about displeasing topics such as debt. You'll quickly overcome your fears simply by taking proactive steps, talking to the helpful experts at your medical college (or prospective medical college), and making a plan.

WHAT IS FINANCIAL AID?

Financial aid is money given or loaned to students to help cover the gap between their and their families' resources and the amount needed to pay for an education. Some schools and independent foundations offer scholarships, grants, and fellowships to students based on their academic performance or other factors. In most cases, however, medical students receive financial aid awards based on their demonstrated financial need.

Given the large price tag of a medical education, almost everyone is eligible for at least some financial assistance. To apply for financial aid, you will need to file an application for medical school admission and a standardized need analysis form. Generally, med schools require you to submit the Free Application for Federal Student Assistance (FAFSA) as well as their own financial aid forms. The FAFSA is available via the Web at www.fafsa.ed.gov.

FINANCIAL ASSISTANCE: YOUR BASIC OPTIONS

Medical school isn't cheap, and the majority of medical students need some form of financial assistance to help cover schooling costs. Students usually fund their education through one or more of the following:

LOANS

Taking out student loans is the most common form of covering medical educational expenses. Medical students may participate in subsidized federal loan programs (Stafford loans), as well as proprietary loan programs through private schools, associations, and financial institutions. As we'll discuss shortly, each has different terms and conditions, and you will save thousands by finding one that's best suited to your needs.

SCHOLARSHIPS AND GRANTS

Qualified students can receive "free money" in the form of scholarships or grants from the school they're attending. The amount can vary significantly from school to school. In addition, some private sources of scholarship money are available for medical students, though these resources are limited and harder to locate. Check to make sure that any third-party grants or scholarships will offset your loans and not your school-based grants. If they offset your school-based grants, third-party awards will not lower your overall costs; they'll just save your school some money.

Though scholarships and grants are generally awarded to students who display both financial need and academic prowess, federal service programs, such as the National Health Service Corps, can cover the entire cost of a medical education in exchange for several years of service in the military or in underserved communities. Other federal programs you might explore are the Armed Forces Health Professions Scholarship and the National Medical Fellowships. These programs can be particularly excellent choices for students with primary care practice interests. Be sure to investigate them thoroughly to understand the options they provide.

SAVINGS

Though it's unlikely that you'll have extra money after your undergraduate years, those lucky few who were thinking ahead may have some savings to help cover the cost of med school. **If you're an undergrad, ask your financial advisor if there are any savings programs they would recommend.**

Teaching Assistant/Research Assistant Fellowships

Some institutions will cover a significant portion of a student's tuition in exchange for his or her services as a graduate research assistant or as a TA to undergraduate classes. Availability of this type of opportunity varies by institution and is usually limited to a small subset of students.

Don't Go It Alone

Finding viable financial aid options is near impossible without help. To get more information on the variety of available loans, scholarships, and grants, you will need to dedicate some time and resources to researching these topics. Here are some of the best places to start looking.

Financial Aid Brochures

Request a financial aid brochure from at least three prestigious, private medical schools. Most will send one to you at little or no cost. Expensive colleges typically do the best job finding and explaining financial aid options to help struggling students and parents offset their high annual tuition. Review these brochures to acquaint yourself with the wide range of financing tools available to you.

Internet

The Internet is one of the cheapest and most efficient ways to get information about scholarships and loan programs. In fact, it is usually more effective than private aid search services, which differ greatly in quality. A number of independent websites can help you locate free money and financing options. Official financial aid sites provide useful information, eligibility requirements, and forms.

Books and Publications

There are several good books published on the topic of financial aid and scholarships. The Princeton Review's *Paying for College Without Going Broke* is among the best and most comprehensive guides on the market.

Private Consultants

Financial aid options are so vast and confusing that it can be difficult to navigate the terrain alone. Consider seeking the help of a professional, such as a certified financial planner (CFP) or certified public accountant (CPA), who can help you create a viable, long-term financial strategy. Many CFPs, as well as the more expensive CPAs, can also handle your annual tax returns for a low fee.

How Much?

By any standard, medical school is extremely pricey. Tuition and fees generally represent the most sizable expense, especially for students attending private institutions. Even students at public schools may discover that the cost of their education is far from reasonable, given living expenses, equipment, transportation, and incidental costs. How much can you expect financial aid to cover? When determining your eligibility for financial aid, schools factor in the following:

- Tuition and fees
- Room and board
- Supplies, including lab equipment
- Medical and licensing exams
- Transportation to and from school or hospital

They do NOT generally include:

- Family expenses for married students or student-parents
- Relocation expenses
- Debt or other financial obligations

When you consider these factors, you can actually begin to determine what you will have to pay to attend medical school.

A Little Help from the Family

In most cases, your expected family contribution (EFC) is calculated using the federal methodology, which takes into consideration the income and assets of both the student and parents, then subtracts taxes, standard living expenses, and asset protection allowances (in the case of the parents, this depends on the age of the oldest parent). If more than one family member is attending college, the parent contribution is divided into equal portions for each student. The basic formula for determining financial need is:

Costs of Attendance − Expected Family Contribution = Financial Need

This formula, however, can be more complicated in reality. **Many students are surprised to hear that their parents' income is factored into their financial aid package, especially**

if the student has already graduated from college and has been living independently for several years. All U.S. Department of Health and Human Services programs, as well as most institutional loans, grants, and scholarships, consider students dependent by default, regardless of their age or whether they actually receive financial support from their family. U.S. Department of Education (ED) programs, however, consider students independent; parental contributions are not factored into ED calculations.

Your financial aid package will fluctuate every year, based on changes in your and your family's life and finances. If, for example, one of your siblings graduates from college, you may be eligible for less financial aid the following year.

MORE ON LOANS AND SCHOLARSHIPS

LOANS

Most students take out loans to pay for medical school. The average debt shouldered by 2013 graduates was $169,901.[5] Since doctors are, on average, the highest paid professionals in the United States, most schools assume that students will be able to deal with the consequences of a significant amount of debt. You should be aware, however, that student loans vary widely with regard to interest rates, terms, repayment plans, and deferment options.

Federal Loans:

Loans offered through the federal government are generally attractive to students because they offer lower interest rates than commercial student loans. Medical students who demonstrate financial need are eligible for Federal Perkins Loans and most medical students are eligible for the William D. Ford Federal Direct Loan Program (Unsubsidized) and the Direct PLUS Loan Program, for which financial need is not required. These programs differ with regard to interest rate, repayment method, borrowing limits, deferment options, fees, application procedures, and eligibility requirements.

State Loans:

If you plan to attend medical school in the state in which you are a resident, you may be eligible for need-based state loans. State loans have lower interest rates than commercial loans and are generally available to minority or disadvantaged students. Some states also have service programs that grant full tuition in exchange for service in disadvantaged communities after graduation.

5   Includes premed borrowing. American Medical Association, "Medical Student Debt Advocacy," Medical Student Section (MSS), http://www.ama-assn.org/ama/pub/about-ama/our-people/member-groups-sections/medical-student-section/advocacy-policy.page? (accessed September 11, 2014) .

Institutional Loans:

Many schools offer their own loan programs for medical students. However, the amount of money available, interest rates, and repayment methods vary greatly by institution. While some schools have a great deal of money to offer students, others have none. **If you're offered a loan through your medical school, you'll need to carefully evaluate whether that loan is better than something you could find through a federal, state, or private source.**

Private Loans:

Students can also get loans from banks or private lending institutions. The federal government does not subsidize these loans. Many private loans are not very good options, as they have high interest rates and strict repayment plans. But terms and conditions vary, and a private loan may be very helpful in a pinch.

In addition to loans from traditional lending institutions, some private foundations, corporations, charities, and associations make charitable loans to medical students. These loans may have lower interest rates or other benefits over traditional private loans. Charitable loans are usually designed to assist a certain segment of the population, such as students with disabilities. To find the best option or to locate a good private source for which you qualify may take some research.

SCHOLARSHIPS

Though they're considerably harder to come by, some students are eligible to receive scholarships, which are awarded to cover tuition costs. Scholarships are administered, like loans, through federal funds, state funds, private institutions, and associations. Usually, scholarships are either merit- or need-based, and aimed at helping students of a particular demographic.

Federal Scholarships:

The U.S. Department of Education and the U.S. Department of Health and Human Services have some limited funds available for medical students. Usually the awards are need-based, but they also consider other factors. Scholarships for Disadvantaged Students (SDS) are awarded through the U.S. Department of Health and Human Services. These scholarships are reserved for students from disadvantaged backgrounds, who are extremely financially needy. You can obtain more information about these from your school's financial aid office.

Institutional Scholarships:

Most medical schools have some proprietary funds, which they award to qualified students based on merit or a combination of merit and need. Through these scholarships, students receive what amounts to a discount on their tuition. These funds often come from an endowment and involve specific criteria, such as a student's ethnic background or research interests.

Obligatory Scholarship/Service Options:

A number of federal scholarships are available to students who are willing to serve in organizations such as the Army, Navy, or National Health Service Corps upon graduation. The service "repayment" process usually begins after residency and is usually directly proportional to the number of years of support. Most programs cover up to $25,000 of tuition cost annually, as well as a monthly stipend for living expenses. On top of that, the subsequent service experience can be in a very desirable training environment. Students should be prepared, however, for a seven- to ten-year-long service commitment after leaving the classroom. For those who require more independence, these programs may not be ideal; for those with an interest in community service, however, they are an option to carefully consider. Some examples of obligatory scholarship/service programs are described below.

- *National Health Service Corps*

  If you're interested in primary care medicine, you have the option of participating in the National Health Service Corps (NHSC), a scholarship program that covers a medical student's tuition, expenses, and offers a monthly stipend. In return, students are obligated to work in Health Professional Shortage Areas, such as rural communities, assigned by the NHSC. Again, the number of years a recipient is required to serve is directly proportional to the number of years he or she received support, with a maximum of four years. These scholarships are very competitive. For more information, visit their website at http://nhsc.hrsa.gov.

- *Armed Forces Health Professions Scholarships*

  The Army, Navy, and Air Force operate scholarship programs for students training in professional health fields. Students in the program receive full coverage of their tuition and fees, reimbursement for books and supplies, a monthly stipend, and a $20,000 sign-on bonus. In return, scholarship recipients commit to one year of active duty service for each year of support they received. The minimum number of years served is three. These scholarships are very competitive as well, but can be tremendously rewarding. Dr. Stephen Nelson, a pediatrician and MCAT tutor for The Princeton Review, describes his experience: "I funded my medical school through the Health Professions Scholarship Program. I am now completing my pediatric residency while on active duty in the Air Force and will be spending next year as a Flight Surgeon (deploying with a fighter wing, doing operational medicine, flying in the jets), and then will start my pediatric neurology fellowship. I owe the Air Force four years of service after residency for my medical school training, and will incur an additional three years of commitment for my fellowship (since my fellowship is three years). Do not think that military scholarships will prevent you from doing the residency that you want, because the military trains physicians in all specialties. Furthermore, because you do your residency on active duty, you make about $15,000 per year more than your civilian colleagues. As a fellow, you may receive about $45,000 per year more than your civilian counterparts. Also, you gain many unique experiences that they will never have, such as: going on medical missions to other countries, military transports of patients to other hospitals/states/countries, medical care in field environments, and many other unique benefits. During medical school you hold the rank of Second Lieutenant (Ensign in the Navy) and after graduation are commissioned to the rank of Captain (Lieutenant in the Navy). I highly encourage anyone who has an interest in serving his or her country to explore this option."

- *Army National Guard*

  Medical students have a couple of funding options through the Army National Guard like the Medical/Dental Student Stipend program, which offers a monthly stipend of around $2,000 for students unconditionally accepted into the educational program for which they seek funding. In return, participants commit to one year of active duty service for each six months of support they received. Other incentive programs like the Specialized Training Assistant Program and the Health Professional Loan Repayment Program are worth looking into as well. Visit their website at http://www.nationalguard.com/ for more details.

Evaluating Your Financial Aid Package

After you receive an offer of admission from a school, you will be offered a financial aid package to help cover your estimated need—as determined by the FAFSA—through a combination of loans, scholarships, grants, and/or employment. If you have other options, **don't automatically accept everything in the aid package (or any of it, for that matter).** Don't automatically accept the school either, even if it's your first choice. Before you start packing, you need to think about how you'll pay for your education. Is the offer sufficient to accept? How will you cover the difference? When you're finished with medical school, what will your debt be? What is the interest rate and repayment schedule? If you have more than one offer, you should compare the two options carefully. If one school makes you a great offer but you have your heart set on another, use the difference between the two packages as bargaining leverage. Students in the enviable position of having multiple acceptances can save thousands to tens of thousands of dollars by negotiating better financial aid packages.

Financial Aid Pitfalls

While today's financial aid programs make it possible for almost everyone to pay for higher education, there are some common pitfalls that can inhibit your ability to participate in loan programs—especially low-interest and subsidized loans. Watch out for the following problems:

Missing Deadlines

Like all aspects of your application, the earlier you submit your financial aid materials, the better. Financial aid deadlines are strongly enforced. Keep careful records and be sure to send everything on time.

Poor Credit History

As long as you have good credit, you can borrow money to pay for your education. However, if your credit is bad when you start medical school, you may be ineligible for loans, even high-interest loans. If you have a bad credit rating, get started on credit repair now. In this case, you may need to seek professional assistance. There are a number of credit rating repair services, but beware: some are scams. Get a referral to a reputable agency from a certified financial planner. Even if you don't have bad credit, you should check your credit rating before applying for financial aid. Sometimes even a few late payments on your car or credit card will show up in your credit history.

Defaulting on Undergraduate Loans

If you've not met your undergraduate loan payments, you'll have a hard time qualifying for medical school loans, especially federal loans. **Before you apply for aid, try to clear up any problems with your undergraduate student loans.** Again, you may want to seek professional assistance from a financial planner. If you have undergraduate loans and are still in school, talk to financial aid officers about deferment options.

Smart Money

Hopefully this chapter will help you to better understand and successfully navigate the murky world of medical school finances. By cultivating good financial habits now, you can not only secure funding for your degree, but also get an early start on providing for your family, buying a home, caring for your aging parents, and, eventually, saving for your own retirement. Think of today as the first day of the rest of your financially secure life.

Chapter 6

Being a Doctor: Things You Should Know

THE MEANING OF AN MD

Before you apply to medical school, you should carefully consider the following questions:

Do you want to spend your life helping others?

Doctors heal people, save lives, and help others—often through direct, face-to-face interactions. According to a recent survey of medical school students, "helping others" is the primary motivation for pursuing an MD/DO. If this is your motivation, you're in good company. However, there are other altruistic careers out there and they all involve less schooling and less debt than medical school. **The desire to help others should be one, but not the only, reason for becoming a doctor.**

Do you enjoy working hard?

Medicine is an incredibly challenging field. This was the case a hundred years ago when doctors worked to fight yellow fever, polio, and influenza, and it is the case today as health professionals try to prevent and treat heart disease, cancer, and AIDS while dealing with the constraints of managed care. So consider medicine only if you know you want tremendous challenge in your professional life. As you read this chapter, think about whether the challenges involved in practicing medicine are the ones that appeal to you. For example, a physician who is 20 years out of medical school is still expected to be familiar with the latest medical developments. A commitment to lifelong learning is one of the challenges of practicing medicine.

It should also be noted that doctors don't just work hard; they work long hours—most put in about 60 hours a week.

Are you interested in science and health issues?

If you enjoyed some aspects of your science courses—few people enjoy all aspects of premedical course work—and you find yourself drawn to health issues, there's a good chance that you will enjoy studying and practicing medicine. Although medicine has changed significantly over the years, its roots remain in basic science.

Do you like working with different people?

With the exception of a few fields, medicine involves working with people, many of whom may be very different from you. If science interests you but working with people does not, you may wish to consider an advanced degree other than an MD/DO; chances are it will involve less debt. You might also look into an MD/DO that allows you to do only research.

The above should give you an idea of what it has been and is currently like to be a doctor. But what will it take to be a doctor in the world of tomorrow? Although it will depend a great deal your on specialty, geographic region, and employment situation, the main criteria will be whether or not you feel compelled to be a doctor—is practicing medicine your calling? Consider the following:

Compassion—a critical part of healing

Advocacy—for your patients and for those without health care

Leadership—in improving health care at the team, hospital, and policy level

Lifelong learning—there will always be more to know

Interpersonal skills—communication with patients and among providers is key

Negotiation—to work around bureaucratic constraints

Grasp—of increasing amounts of medical knowledge and of a health care system in flux

If you feel the C.A.L.L.I.N.G. acronym describe qualities and desires that you have, congratulations!—you should have what it takes to become a successful and adaptable doctor. The more you know about what to expect, the more prepared you can be for it when it arrives.

PATIENT CARE

Most doctors spend their time seeing patients and generally work in one of three situations: solo, as part of a group practice, or as an employee of a hospital or organization. The most common reason people go to the doctor is for some sort of check-up or test. Other common reasons for doctor visits are respiratory, gastrointestinal, and psychological complaints. **An important responsibility of the primary care physician is to identify potentially serious issues during routine examinations.** On the other side of the spectrum, doctors with highly specialized training—e.g., oncologists, cardiologists, and surgeons—are charged with saving and improving the lives of those affected by serious medical issues. In 2011, the most recent year for which data was available, the following were the ten most common causes of mortality in the United States[6]:

1. Heart diseases
2. Malignant neoplasms (cancer)
3. Chronic lower respiratory diseases
    (e.g, emphysema, asthma, bronchitis)
4. Cerebrovascular diseases (stroke)
5. Accidents
6. Alzheimer's disease
7. Diabetes mellitus (diabetes type 2)
8. Influenza and pneumonia
9. Nephritis, nephrotic syndrome, and nephrosis (kidney disease)
10. Self-harm

Note that all of the above except Alzheimer's are preventable. As such, it is important for the modern physician to be well-versed in preventative medicine.

6   Centers for Disease Control and Prevention, "10 Leading Causes of Death by Age Group, United States—2007, Injury Prevention & Control: Data & Statistics, http://www.cdc.gov/injury/wisqars/LeadingCauses.html (accessed September 11, 2014).

COMPENSATION

A survey of physicians in various medical specialties yielded the following results[7]:

Specialty	Average Annual Salary (in USD)
Anesthesiology	277,900
Cardiology	433,408
Cardiovascular Surgery	558,719
Colorectal Surgery	291,000
Dermatology	308,000
Emergency Medicine	216,000
Endocrinology	221,900
Family Practice	177,330
Gastroenterology	492,000
General Surgery	291,000
Hematology-Oncology	444,000
Internal Medicine	176,000
Nephrology	269,000
Neurology	263,800
Neurosurgery	541,000
Obstetrics/Gynecology	261,000
Ophthalmology	314,000
Oral and Maxofacial Surgery	515,000
Orthopedic Surgery	459,000
Otorhinolaryngology (ENT)	311,000
Pediatrics	175,000
Plastic Surgery	412,000
Psychiatry	201,000
Pulmonary Medicine	288,000
Radiology	354,000
Rheumatology	229,000
Urology	358,000
Vascular Surgery	329,000

7   Medical Resource Group, "Physician Salary Survey Results," Medical Education Guide, www.studentdoc.com/salaries.html (accessed September 11, 2014).

The figures listed above don't account for residents, who are notoriously overworked and underpaid. Currently, a number of organizations, including the American Medical Association (AMA) and American Medical Students Association (AMSA), are pressing for more legislation to protect residents from extreme working conditions. In fact, the Accreditation Council for Graduate Medical Education (AGME), set new standards back in July 2011 that limit the working hours of residents to 80 hours per week. Why are residents required to work so hard? In part, it's because hospitals depend on residents as a cheap source of labor, since they are paid much less than other physicians and somewhat less than nurses and other health professionals.

You should be aware of the ongoing debate surrounding federal funding of Graduate Medical Education (a.k.a. residencies), which could affect your ability to match with a residency program after you've completed (and paid) for medical school. With an aging patient population plus an influx of newly insured individuals entering the health care system under the Affordable Care Act (more about that later), the AAMC expects a national shortage of 45,000 primary care physicians and 46,000 specialists by 2020. Medical schools are increasing their enrollment numbers, but a 10-year old cap on the number of Medicare-supported residents in teaching hospitals could mean that there will be more graduates then there are training positions. Keep your eye on legislation proposals to increase Medicare-supported residency slots and train more doctors. It behooves you to research this issue carefully.

PRESTIGE

Almost universally, being a doctor carries prestige. Doctors are thought by the general public to be smart, well educated, hardworking, caring, and dedicated. **Even in this era of managed care and malpractice lawsuits, doctors are well respected.** You should consider the degree to which having a prestigious career is important to you. Other health professions, although perhaps less glamorous, also involve healing and helping others.

TRENDS IN MEDICINE

Several trends of the past few decades are likely to continue well into the twenty-first century. These trends have implications for you, the aspiring doctor. They will impact the nature of your work, the structure of the organization in which you work, your salary, the relationship you have with patients, and, above all, the quality of the health care you deliver.

In the sections to come, we'll consider the following trends (with a disclaimer that predicting the future is difficult) affecting medicine in the twenty-first century:
- Development of new technology
- Increased health care costs
- Evolution of health care delivery and payment systems

- Greater reliance on primary and preventive care
- More guidelines for patient care
- Better gender and ethnic diversity among physicians
- An aging patient population
- The emergence of new ethical issues
- Changes in academic medicine and medical education

Note that the above list is by no means complete. Many of the trends listed are inter-related and they are not necessarily presented in order of importance.

New Technology

Health care has improved during the past few decades largely due to technological advancement and there are more exciting developments on the horizon. The term technology is often used broadly. In the health care arena, it means the development of new drugs, procedures, techniques, and means of communication that, if used correctly, have the potential to improve diagnosis, care, and patient outcomes.

Medications and Procedures:

The increase in life expectancy over the past few decades is partially due to improvements in medications and procedures. For example, the death rate due to heart disease is declining because of better drugs (hypertension, heart, and cholesterol medications) and surgical techniques.

Laboratory Techniques:

Often, improvements in laboratory tools or techniques lead to important discoveries. For example, better tools allowed the human genome to be mapped.

The Internet:

The Internet can allow a patient to arrive at the doctor's office well-informed about his or her illness. On the other hand, the Internet houses a great deal of misinformation. The physician who is Web-savvy can guide patients to informative websites and Web-based support groups. The Internet is invaluable for research.

Telemedicine:

Telemedicine is defined by the American Telemedicine Association as "the use of medical information exchanged from one site to another via electronic communications to improve patients' health status."[8] The sharing of radiographic images and patient information

8   American Telemedical Association, About Telemedicine, www.americantelemed.org/i4a/pages/index.cfm?pageID=333 (accessed July 9, 2012).

via computer between physicians is an important current application. In the future, we may see telemedicine bringing the expertise of specialists to rural or other remote areas.

Other Computer Applications:

Computerized database systems are used for billing and patient records. Some physicians take advantage of software programs made for hand-held devices. These can be used for note-taking, reference, or even patient management. Not surprisingly, it is often the younger doctors (and medical students) who are the most comfortable with computer technology. An understanding of relevant computer applications can give you an advantage when it comes to working with older, more experienced doctors; in addition to learning from them, you will have something to contribute.

HEALTH CARE COSTS

The United States spends more money per capita on health care than any other country in the world. Some believe that the U.S. offers the best medical care in the world, thereby justifying the cost. Others assert that, according to indicators such as life expectancy and infant mortality, the U.S. lags behind other industrialized countries. Regardless, the amount annually spent on health care in this country is rising. In 2012, 17.2 percent of the U.S. Gross Domestic Product (GDP) was spent on health care. That percentage is expected to reach 19.3 by 2023.[9] There are many theories as to what is causing this escalation—hospital consolidation, inefficient spending for inpatient care and hospital bureaucracy, the cost of prescription medication, the prevalence of expensive technology, and a lack of incentive programs are all commonly invoked reasons. Two are discussed below.

Technology:

As discussed earlier, technological advances usually serve to improve health care and health outcomes. Technology, however, is often cited as a major cause of rising health care costs. When new tools are developed and advertised, hospitals and physicians may feel pressure to purchase and use them, sometimes even if the benefit of the new device is questionable. Someone ultimately pays for such purchases, and thus we see rising health care costs. It is important to remember, however, that technological advances can also serve to reduce costs. By preventing illnesses and reducing the spread of disease, new vaccines (anti influenza, for example) lower the costs of treatment for society overall. New surgical instruments and the development of medications in pill form facilitate the use of outpatient procedures instead of expensive hospital stays.

9   U.S. Department of Health and Human Services, "National Health Expenditure Data," NHE Fact Sheet, www.cms.gov/Research-Statistics-Data-and-Systems/Statistics-Trends-and-Reports/NationalHealthExpendData/NHE-Fact-Sheet.html (accessed September 11, 2014).

Incentives:

Patients are generally far removed from the cost of their care, and therefore have little incentive to keep costs down. Employers and the government—not patients themselves—foot most of the bill for health care, creating a system of "third-party payers." Some believe that since patients don't pay much for their own health care, they overuse it, thereby driving government and employer health care expenditures up.

As a physician, you'll undoubtedly feel pressure to keep health care costs down. In many practice settings, insurers scrutinize doctors on the basis of the cost of the tests and treatments they prescribe. For example, primary care doctors are sometimes encouraged to limit referrals to specialists. All doctors may be monitored for "overuse" of expensive tests and equipment. Physicians face difficult decisions as they attempt to provide excellent care at a lower cost: if a patient has a slim chance of benefiting from an expensive treatment, should that treatment be employed? The physician must balance the cost of treating with the risk of not treating.

HEALTH CARE DELIVERY SYSTEMS

One of the most important trends of the past few decades has been the replacement of simple fee-for-service plans by the growth of the managed care industry.

Fee-for-Service:

Before managed care, health care was delivered on a "fee-for-service" basis. Under a fee-for-service system, doctors and hospitals perform a service—a check-up, an operation, etc.—and charge a fee for the service. Typically, the patient's health insurance company pays this fee. The patient pays the health insurance company monthly premiums or, if the patient has health benefits from his or her employer, the employer pays the monthly premiums. The insurance company calculates monthly premiums based on how much it pays out to hospitals and doctors each year for all people enrolled in the insurance plan.

Managed Care:

Managed care was introduced as a response to rising health care costs, and has succeeded in slowing the rate at which health care costs are rising. Thus, the trend toward managed care will probably continue. Although managed care is often thought to be synonymous with Health Maintenance Organizations (HMOs), an HMO is, in fact, just one of many systems for managing care.

Managed care usually involves set monthly premiums that are lower than those in fee-for-service plans, and this makes those paying the premiums (usually employers) happy. How do managed care organizations keep their premiums down? It's simple—by keeping their financial outlays down. Under managed care, expenditures are typically controlled through several mechanisms:

- Participants in a managed care plan agree to use doctors and hospitals that are part of the plan, and these providers are either paid yearly salaries or charge reduced fees for services rendered.
- Primary care physicians serve as "gatekeepers" in limiting the use of expensive medical specialists. (Many patients find that nurses and other health care professionals are responsible for a large amount of their care, and that they usually have less access to physicians.)
- Guidelines and regulations are implemented that attempt to limit the use of expensive tests and equipment in unnecessary situations.
- Inpatient care is reduced and there is greater emphasis on outpatient services (care that does not involve an overnight hospital stay).

Managed care has generated discontent among some patients and providers. Patients are often frustrated by red tape, the inability to choose one's doctor, short visits, long waits, obstacles to seeing specialists, and limitations on coverage. Many doctors object to managed care because the cost-cutting mechanisms can compromise patient care; their salaries and autonomy are also reduced in these arrangements.

There can be some advantages, however, to working for a managed care organization. For one, doctors are often salaried, which means that they earn a specified amount each year and their income does not depend on finding clients. Doctors also tend to work fewer hours a week, which is probably good for both doctors and patients. For better or for worse, being a doctor in the twenty-first century is likely to involve practicing in a managed care environment of some form.

The Affordable Care Act:

You should be familiar with the Obama administration's health care reform law, enacted in March 2010. As future doctors, the consequences of this law will affect the way you practice medicine as well as how your patients will access health care services. The short version is that the law expands access to health care coverage, controls health care costs, and includes provisions aimed to improve the health care delivery system. Among other things, ACA requires all individuals to have insurance, with an on-line insurance marketplace to help them comparison shop; expands Medicare to cover more people, with financial assistance for those who cannot afford coverage; and ensures coverage of those with pre-existing conditions. While opinions are mixed about the overall success of ACA, the bottom line is that it will one day be your obligation to educate and assist your patients in navigating their health care needs. The US. Department of Health and Human Service's overview is a good place to start familiarizing yourself with the facts (www.healthcare.gov).

Uninsured:

A discussion of health care delivery would be incomplete without mention of the uninsured. Approximately 15.4 percent of people in the United States have no health insurance[10]. The U.S. is unique among industrialized nations in that respect, and it's not exactly something to be proud of. Individuals without health insurance tend to seek medical care—typically through an emergency room—only after a health problem has become really serious. This is obviously bad for the patient, who, with early treatment, might have avoided serious complications. It's also costly to society, because prevention and early treatment are less expensive than late intervention. Most people—physicians and nonphysicians alike—believe that everyone should have access to health care. However, there is less agreement on how universal access should be achieved and funded. Doctors must speak out to ensure that this issue is addressed as soon, and as equitably, as possible.

GREATER EMPHASIS ON PRIMARY AND PREVENTIVE CARE

Most observers predict that as managed care grows, primary care physicians will continue to play a very important role, and the demand for primary care doctors will remain relatively high. In addition, **it has become increasingly clear that investing in preventative care is more cost-effective than treating advanced illness.** Therefore, there has been a growing emphasis on encouraging preventative treatment.

Gatekeepers:

Before the days of managed care, if a person discovered an odd-looking spot on his skin, he could go directly to a dermatologist and be reimbursed by his insurance company for the visit. An important tenet of managed care has been the requirement that enrollees see a primary care physician prior to visiting a specialist. Family practice, pediatrics, internal medicine, geriatrics, and ob/gyn are typically considered primary care fields. The primary care physician serves as a "gatekeeper," presumably reducing unnecessary visits to expensive specialists.

Without the training of a specialist, however, the primary care physician may not be equipped to judge the seriousness of some conditions. Missing a pre-cancerous skin lesion,

---

10 United States Census Bureau, "Income, Poverty, and Health Insurance Coverage: 2012," http://www.census.gov/hhes/www/hlthins/data/incpovhlth/2012/tables.html (accessed September 11, 2014).

for example, may cause hardship for the patient later on. On the other hand, if a primary care doctor refers all patients with skin lesions to the dermatologist, the system has failed because each patient required two doctor visits rather than one.

Integrated Approach:

A benefit of this emphasis on primary care is that, in theory, patients develop a long-term relationship with their primary care doctor, who is better able to understand the social, economic, and community-related issues associated with their health. The primary care doctor presumably has an understanding of all physiologic systems. This comprehensive knowledge facilitates diagnosis or at least allows the physician to make the initial decision about what steps will lead to diagnosis. Primary care physicians are well-positioned to address behavioral changes, such as exercise programs, that aid in the prevention of disease.

Prevention:

Several of the major causes of morbidity (illness) and mortality (death) in the U.S. are preventable. Emphysema, for example, is often the result of heavy smoking. The most common type of diabetes is linked with obesity. We have learned that the spread of HIV can be reduced through educational programs and behavioral interventions. The high death rate in this country due to violent crime is often attributed to the prevalence of handguns, a situation that could be addressed through legislation. Advances in genetics could potentially revolutionize preventative medicine by allowing physicians to identify people who are going to get sick before they show any symptoms of disease.

Prevention is preferable to treatment for the obvious reason that, with prevention, illness is reduced or eliminated altogether. Whether prevention efforts are cost-effective depends upon the disease, its prevalence, and the technology employed. For example, checking blood pressure regularly is crucial in detecting hypertension, treatment of which can potentially reduce the risk of heart disease, stroke, and kidney failure and reduce the high costs associated with treating these outcomes. It's sensible and cost effective to offer and encourage regular blood pressure checks for people above a certain age.

GUIDELINES FOR PATIENT CARE

The doctor-patient relationship, the belief that each patient must be considered individually, and the principle that doctors should be allowed to use their best judgment when providing care are all fundamental to medicine. Do these ideals conflict with the recent trend of using guidelines in clinical medicine?

Evidenced-Based Medicine or Cookbook Medicine?

Doctors vary tremendously in their approach to medicine and disease treatment. This is why, in serious illness, a second opinion is usually recommended. In recent years, there has been increased use of Evidenced-Based Medicine (EBM) in clinical practice. EBM employs scientific evidence for the purpose of standardizing and improving patient care. Quantitative indicators such as rate of reduction of disease are typically used to evaluate procedures and treatments. The goal of EBM is to establish guidelines for clinical decision-making based on the results of studies, particularly randomized clinical trials, which are generally considered the most accurate type of study.

Some doctors worry that the trend toward EBM de-emphasizes physician judgment, results in strict guidelines for treatment, and amounts to "cookbook medicine." In fact, this hasn't been the case. EBM, with its population-based approach, actually complements the one-on-one tradition of medicine by allowing doctors to defend their decisions with data. However, there are many diseases and clinical situations for which the literature fails to provide clear evidence. In some cases, the risks and benefits of a particular therapy vary depending on the study examined.

Cost Consciousness

Occasionally, guidelines that dictate clinical care are based on cost-cutting objectives rather than on sound medical evidence. Such "guidelines" may compromise patient care. Going back to our mammogram example, an HMO might encourage physicians to recommend mammograms to all women over 50, when research suggests that mammograms are highly beneficial for women in their 40s as well. It is the physician's ethical responsibility to give his patient honest and up-to-date medical advice (in this case, to recommend mammograms after age 40). At the same time, the physician may want to support the cost-cutting goals of his employer. This is the type of conflict that doctors face in the current era of cost-consciousness. There are no easy answers, but familiarity with medical evidence and the rules of the organization should allow you to make informed and responsible decisions.

DIVERSITY AMONG PHYSICIANS

Increased diversity among physicians is a positive trend and may result in better patient care for the following:

Women:

Approximately 47 percent of matriculated medical students are women.[11] There are outstanding female physicians in every imaginable medical field. Women are especially

---

11 American Medical Association, "Table 7: Applicants, First-time Applicants, Acceptees, and Matriculants to U.S. Medical Schools by Sex, 2002-2013," FACTS, https://www.aamc.org/download/321470/data/2013factstable7.pdf (accessed September 11, 2014).

well represented in pediatrics and ob/gyn, but less well represented in surgical subspecialties. Several theories and generalizations have been put forth to help explain why women are more attracted to some fields than others—people tend to be interested in fields that have personal relevance; once there is a critical mass of women within a field, it becomes a more welcoming environment for other women; and women tend to avoid fields with the very longest residencies.

Female doctors are having an important influence on the medical field. In general, female physicians tend to spend more time with patients than their male counterparts and tend to emphasize the psychological and emotional issues related to illness. Furthermore, female physicians have begun to promote a reduction of the hours that physicians work, leaving more time for family and personal life.

Minorities:

The medical profession is slowly becoming more ethnically diverse, as increased numbers of nonwhite medical school graduates enter the workforce. This increase in diversity reflects the changing demographics of the U.S. population, the availability of better and more widely available educational opportunities, and active minority recruitment on the part of medical schools that recognize that it is extremely important to have a physician population that represents the population it serves. If this trend continues, we will someday have a physician workforce that is representative of the population at large.

AGING POPULATION

In 2010, the median age in the US was 37.2 years, up from 35.3 in 2000.[12] As the population continues to age, the demand for medical care will increase—older Americans, on average, require more doctor visits per year. This contributes to rising health care costs. Because Medicare covers almost all individuals over 65, government expenditures on health care are expected to rise steadily. The paperwork involved in treating a patient with Medicare is also notoriously time-consuming.

An older population will cause growth within certain fields, such as geriatrics, internal medicine, orthopedics, and cardiovascular medicine. The incidence of chronic disease, meaning disease that is long-lasting and often incurable, will increase. In situations such as these, physicians will often be called upon to provide palliative care that addresses symptoms rather than the underlying disease. Physician-researchers will be encouraged to find treatments for conditions that afflict the elderly, such as Alzheimer's disease.

---

12 United States Census Bureau, "2010 Census Shows Nation's Population is Aging," http://www. census.gov/newsroom/releases/archives/2010_census/cb11-cn147.html (accessed September 11, 2014).

This increase in the patient population has contributed to the current physician shortage. The U.S. government actively encourages students to consider medicine.

ETHICAL ISSUES

Physicians have always dealt with important ethical issues related to life and death. As a physician in the twenty-first century, some of your ethical dilemmas are likely to involve the conflict between saving money and saving lives. Consider the following scenario:

You're a pediatrician, seeing a patient you've never seen before. The patient is a very ill six-year-old girl without health insurance. Do you treat her, knowing you'll hear about it later? Or do you send her to the free clinic across town, even though it will entail a long bus ride for the sick girl?

With an older patient population, ethical issues about end-of-life care will become increasingly relevant. For example:

Your patient is 80 years old and suffers from terminal lung cancer, which has spread to his brain. There are no cures for him at this stage, so your care has been focused on keeping him comfortable. He can't breathe on his own, is incoherent, and has been more or less motionless in the hospital for one week. His daughter doesn't want you to remove life support. What do you do?

The rule of doctor-patient confidentiality can be another source of ethical dilemmas. Consider this situation:

You've been treating a young man in the hospital for a lung infection. During his hospital stay, he was tested for HIV and the test results were positive. He's unwilling to discuss the matter, doesn't want medications that will help his HIV symptoms, and appears to be in denial. Do you have a responsibility to alert the man's wife?

There is an increasing emphasis on the ethical and emotional issues of doctoring in medical school curriculums, and some top programs require course work in patient treatment and medical ethics. Unfortunately, some medical schools barely address ethics, leaving you on your own to learn about and think through important ethical issues. A mentor, someone whose opinion you respect, can serve as a resource for sorting out ethical questions. If you feel strongly about a particular issue, you should consider getting involved by writing, attending conferences, or engaging in dialogue about it.

CHANGES IN ACADEMIC MEDICINE AND MEDICAL EDUCATION

Most medical schools are directly affiliated with teaching hospitals. Three advantages to this arrangement are:

- Medical students have an opportunity for hands-on learning.
- Patients are treated by expert physicians and benefit from the latest technology.
- The academic environment coupled with clinical facilities provides an ideal setting for research that ultimately pushes medicine forward and improves care.

Academic medical centers throughout the country are having a tough time financially, leading some experts to question their future viability. Although medical school tuition seems incredibly high, it does not cover the complete cost of a medical education; academic medical centers have historically depended on income from clinical activities to subsidize medical education costs, research activities, and the management of a teaching hospital. As discussed earlier, the shift toward outpatient medicine has resulted in reduced earnings for hospitals. For academic medical centers, this means less revenue to cover their high costs. As more and more academic medical centers face financial crisis, there will be pressure to either cut costs or raise revenue significantly. We might see academic medical centers restrict their patients to those who can pay higher fees, or we may see an increase in government funding or medical school tuition.

In response to the changes in medicine and health care described above, most medical schools are attempting to revise their programs of study. Some of the revisions we see are:

- Less time spent in lecture. Educators recognize that in this age of technology and information, there are simply too many facts to learn. Rather than inundate students with massive amounts of information, some medical schools hope to teach students general concepts that will prepare them for a lifetime of learning.
- More clinical problem-solving during the first two years. With all that we now know and all the treatment options available today, physicians must be thinkers and problem-solvers. In fact, several top-tier medical school programs have converted to entirely problem-based programs of study, greatly reducing class time and creating more opportunities for group and independent work.

- Greater emphasis on health economics, health care management, public health, and patient care. Doctors should understand the interdisciplinary nature of health care and the forces that affect medicine. Furthermore, doctors in almost every specialty are required to interact with the public with sensitivity and candor—traits that don't come naturally to every person and were previously disregarded in medical programs.
- Better training in outpatient medicine, with the use of outpatient clinics and doctors' offices for clinical rotations of outpatient facilities.

With at least 11 years of post-high school training required, becoming a physician takes longer in the U.S. than anywhere else in the world. This is costly to society. Some people predict that, as a result of financial pressures, the amount of schooling required to become a doctor will be reduced. For the time being, however, you have a long—but exciting—road ahead of you.

A Very Big Adventure

Expect a period of massive and fantastic change in medicine over the next 15 years. If you apply yourself, deal effectively with the tasks at hand, and focus on patients and solutions by following your best knowledge and instincts, there's no reason why you won't be able to contribute to this new and adventurous era in medicine.

Chapter 7

Q&A with
Admissions Officers

We asked admissions officers at five allopathic schools and at three osteopathic schools about medical school applications, personal statements, and secondary essays. They told us what they like and don't like to read, the number of applications they read each year, and just how much the personal statement and secondary essays count. The following professionals dedicated their time to answering our questions:

- Andrea O'Brien, Associate Director of Residential Admissions, Kirksville College of Osteopathic Medicine, A.T. Still University

- Deanna Hughes, Associate Director of Residential Admissions, School of Osteopathic Medicine in Arizona, A.T. Still University

- Sharon Forward, Director of Admissions and Student Affairs, Dalhousie University Medical School

- Tyler Corvin, Director of Admissions, Virginia Campus at Edward Via College of Osteopathic Medicine–Virginia & Carolinas

- Lorna Kenyon, Director of Admissions and Student Records at The Ohio State University College of Medicine

- Jennifer Welch, Director of Admissions at State University of New York Upstate Medical University

- Courtney Thompson, Program Assistant, Admissions, College of Medicine, University of Manitoba

- Dr. Richard Weismab, Associate Dean for Admissions, Miller School of Medicine, University of Miami

For ease of reading, we introduce each officer's response to the questions we asked with the name of the institution he or she serves.

SUBJECT MATTER & WRITING

Which themes continually appear in personal statements?

ATSU—Kirksville College: Compassion. Adversities faced. Motivation for medicine.

ATSU—SOMA: The desire to be a physician. Personal tragedy or triumph in overcoming an obstacle. Working with underserved populations.

Dalhousie University: Events that led them to want to be a doctor. Life events that have affected the applicant, i.e. death.

VCOM: Reasons for pursuing a degree in (osteopathic) medicine, including: life events and experiences, steps taken to present a competitive medical school application, and explanations for deficiencies in the application.

Ohio State: We see expanded discussions of applicants' involvement in the medical field, from their first interest in medicine to shadowing experiences to specific examples of patients who have had an impact on their lives. We also see detailed outlines of research, community service, and volunteer experiences.

SUNY Upstate: The story of the loss or illness of a loved one, and how this experience has influenced the applicant's decision to become a doctor.

University of Manitoba: Personal Statements are only used for Aboriginal Pool.

University of Miami: Reason and motivation for a career in medicine.

If your school requires essays as part of its secondary application, what are common topics that students address?

ATSU—Kirksville College: Characteristics of applicant that make him/her a good fit for our school; experience/exposure to osteopathic medicine.

ATSU—SOMA: What did you do during any gap years between UG and applying to medical school? What would make you an independent learner? Why do you want to be an osteopathic physician?

Dalhousie University: Why medicine. Strengths and weaknesses. Experiences that have shown them a certain aspect of medicine

VCOM: VCOM includes three essays as part of the Secondary Application:

What qualities do you feel you bring to VCOM that would enhance the overall climate of our college?

Osteopathic medicine is a distinct practice with parallels to allopathic medicine. Why do you desire to enter the field of osteopathic medicine?

There are many problems facing health care in America today. Describe what you feel are the most important and what you, as an osteopathic physician, would do to help find the solutions.

We also offer a fourth essay that is directed toward our re-applicants:

Did you submit an application to VCOM last year? If so, please explain how you improved your application.

Ohio State: We ask three essay questions:

In your own words, define altruism and provide an example (or two) of when you exhibited altruistic behavior.

Articulate your understanding of social justice versus advocacy for social justice.

Describe one or more experiences where you collaborated or worked as part of a team with people of different racial, ethnic and/or socioeconomic backgrounds and/or belief systems than your own. What impact did this experience(s) have on you?

State University of New York Upstate: Not applicable.

University of Manitoba: Heritage. Commitment to community.

University of Miami: Why they want to attend medical school at the University of Miami Miller School of Medicine?

What writing tips would you offer to your applicant pool?

ATSU—Kirksville College: Proof; Don't use jargon; Explain your experiences clearly; Don't use too many "I" statements (sounds conceited); If cutting and pasting, be sure the school name is correct; Use examples as illustrations for your characteristics—don't just tell us you are this and that type of person.

ATSU—SOMA: Make sure to shadow a DO & show your passion for DO. Get plenty of community/volunteer service, especially to underserved populations. Make sure to keep competitive GPA and don't take MCAT more than three times.

Dalhousie University: Check for grammatical and spelling errors. Make sure the essay flows well so that the person reviewing and scoring does not have to work so hard for the information.

VCOM: Write from the heart. Be careful not to make the statement too choppy after edits (this often occurs when the initial statement is over the size limit). Try not to write a creative writing essay.

Ohio State: Provide insight into who you are as a person that is not available in other parts of the application. Whatever you decide to write about, provide some discussion as to how this would make you a caring physician.

SUNY Upstate: Please do not have run-on sentences or use a quote as the intro to your personal statement—I don't care about Robert Frost, I want to know more about you. Please be sure to spell physician correctly, if you really want to be one. Spend a great deal of time proofing your essay. Do not rely only on spell check, but please use it. If it doesn't look like a person put a great deal of time, thought, and energy into their application, the admissions committee won't be inclined to do so.

University of Miami: Be organized and to the point. Don't add fluff. Being an effective communicator is an important skill for physicians to have. Show us that you are an effective communicator.

Which grammatical mistakes make you cringe?

ATSU—Kirksville College: Run-on sentences; too many "I" statements; incorrect use of homonyms.

ATSU—SOMA: Confusing "your" and "you're." Not knowing where to put the apostrophe (i.e. before or after the s). Simply not proofreading in general with stupid mistakes makes me cringe.

Dalhousie University: Simple spelling mistakes should never happen.

VCOM: Poor spelling and punctuation.

Ohio State: Improper use of verb tenses.

University of Manitoba: Essays are assessed by an independent panel.

University of Miami: Spelling. See the wrong school listed in an essay where someone forgot to change it.

What do you not like to read in a personal statement or essay?

ATSU—Kirksville College: Don't use this as a creative writing assignment or be metaphorical—say what you mean and don't leave us guessing the meaning of your essay. Use the space wisely.

ATSU—SOMA: A long drawn-out story, keep the "story" part short and sweet.

Dalhousie University: Long excerpts about research findings that become complicated and difficult to follow and honestly tell us little about the actual applicants

University of Miami: I like to feel the passion the writer has for a career in medicine. Make it interesting to read because I have to read several hundred this week!

What do you love to read in a personal statement or essay?

ATSU—Kirksville College: Personal journeys that created the motivation for medicine; What drives them toward osteopathic medicine; Illustrative examples to display their character.

ATSU—SOMA: A life changing event or really good medical situation they've experienced personally.

Dalhousie University: Love to read about a personal life story and for the applicant to demonstrate how their insight saw them through it. Also how it led them to medicine as a profession. Humility and honesty about whom they are and what they have to offer medicine.

VCOM: With regard to our secondary application essays, I love to read why the applicant is applying to VCOM.

Ohio State: The Admissions Committee enjoys reading the responses of applicants whose true passion for helping people and genuine interest in medicine shine through no matter the topic.

SUNY Upstate: Personal stories about applicants, what makes them unique, what sets them apart from the other applicants, what they are passionate about.

University of Miami: That an applicant already understands the challenges and rewards of being a member of the medical profession

What bores you?

ATSU—Kirksville College: Mundane accounts of the same things in their application—a regurgitation of their resume. Name dropping—I hate that. In depth descriptions of their research (many of us reading the files are not researchers).

ATSU—SOMA: Applicants who are children of doctors and how they followed mom or dad around in the clinic.

Dalhousie University: Facts, one-line statements about them without really providing a picture of who they are and what they might bring to our school/ program.

VCOM: We prefer not to read personal statements that are written in a creative-writing format; we want information displayed in a more factual and heartfelt manner.

Ohio State: Talking about how great our college is or repeating information found in print or on the Web is not useful to us.

State University of New York Upstate: Don't try to impress upon us what a genius you are. Confidence is good, but overconfidence can be a turnoff. Let your experiences and achievements speak for themselves. View the essay as our chance to get to know you as a person and as a future physician.

University of Miami: "I want to be a doctor because I want to help people." "I can't think of anything else I would want to do."

What experience would you like students to write about more often?

ATSU—Kirksville College: Their motivation for WHY they want to be in a profession that helps people in the more difficult of circumstances. How they will persist and press on when things are difficult.

ATSU—SOMA: I like to hear about something they learned or saw on a medical mission trip.

Dalhousie University: Personal/life lessons.

VCOM: Why they want to practice medicine, what field they are considering post-graduation, and international clinical experiences.

Ohio State: Any experience in which the student was actively involved, exhibited altruistic behavior, or grew as a person.

University of Miami: The epiphany they have had about medicine. Some of the amazing experiences and people they have met so far. Stories about overcoming adversity.

What topics are risky? When do such topics work?

ATSU—Kirksville College: Name dropping-never works; Disgusting descriptions (love of blood and guts in a very detailed description)—never works; Very in depth description of personal illnesses—may work when explaining large gaps in background, but can be risky in evaluating whether this could be something that could reoccur and take the applicant out of school permanently; Sexual identity—works when it is a part of your journey description or how it applies to medicine. Does not work when it is just a fact thrown out there for no reason. The evaluators want to see relevance for everything in the file toward medicine. If left with no info for why that is relevant, it just dilutes the file with irrelevant info. Achievements that are unrelated to medicine with no corollary to tie them together.

ATSU—SOMA: Speaking about their sexual orientation or religion is risky in the statement. If they want to work with this particular population as part of their life work then it can be okay in the statement but not just as an 'fyi'

Ohio State: Occasionally, some applicants sound as if they are making excuses for poor grades, MCAT scores, etc. These explanations can be effective when there were circumstances that they were able to overcome. Other risky topics include adversity such as an abusive relationship, substance abuse, a dysfunctional family, etc. If these issues have been dealt with and overcome, they can be effective topics.

SUNY Upstate: Sometimes students will talk about, let's say, having been captain of their volleyball team or something totally unrelated to the field of medicine and, by the end of the essay, you're left wondering why this information was included at all. Think about the point you're trying to make and be sure that your message is conveyed to the reader. Also, avoid blanket statements and generalizations about people and certain professions. You never know who will be sitting on the Admissions Committee and what their career path has been.

While not a topic, using humor can be risky. If it's used correctly, it can make your essay more creative and interesting. More often than not, however, you come off as silly, which leaves the reader questioning your sincerity and maturity.

University of Miami: When the applicant is the patient. When they complement this experience with other clinical experiences.

Which topics would you advise students to avoid addressing?

ATSU—Kirksville College: Very in depth personal conditions or super gory infatuations with aspects of medicine.

ATSU—SOMA: Religion, sexual orientation, politics, views on health care reform (in some circumstances, if they are taking a political sway one way or the other).

Dalhousie University: Often religious and or political ones can cause some difficulty as they may cause a bias depending on the person reviewing and scoring the essay.

Ohio State: We would not want to restrict a student from addressing a topic which he or she felt compelled to write about since all information provided is used to assess whether or not the student is a good match for our program.

University of Miami: Personal health issues. Essays that have no direction or purpose that do not allow you to know very much about the applicant's motivation or enthusiasm.

What's an example of a ridiculous achievement that you've seen referenced in a personal statement or essay?

ATSU—Kirksville College: Father, Husband (Ironically, I have never seen women list Mother/Wife as an achievement); PhD in Hard Work; Talking of all the marathons they've completed (honorable, but what is the relevance to medicine??).

ATSU—SOMA: I can't think of any off-hand.

Dalhousie University: Donating blood five, ten etc. times.

Ohio State: Unless a student is simply trying to fill an application with activities and achievements, they list achievements that they feel are important.

SUNY Upstate: "At age four I was reading human anatomy books for fun . . ."

University of Miami: Co-Captain of the High School Chess Team.

INSIDE THE ADMISSIONS OFFICE

Do you have an overall mission statement that you follow when looking at personal statements, essays, and applications in general?

ATSU—Kirksville College: Yes. We look at our University mission statement when evaluating applicant information to find students whose backgrounds and motivations best match our institution.

ATSU—SOMA: We don't necessarily require the essays to meet our mission but we do look at the entire application as a whole when considering our mission.

Dalhousie University: No.

VCOM: Yes. The mission of the Edward Via College of Osteopathic Medicine (VCOM) is to prepare globally minded, community-focused physicians for the rural and medically underserved areas of Virginia, North Carolina, South Carolina and the Appalachian Region, and to improve human health especially of those most in need.

Ohio State: Ohio State performs a holistic review of the application file.

SUNY Upstate: We truly see the personal statement as the one place where we really get to know the student, the one place where they become more than just their numbers—it is our opportunity to see who they are and what they are all about.

University of Miami: How much do I know about the applicant's motivation, enthusiasm, perseverance, and character after reading the essay. How effectively did the applicant tell the story.

How many personal statements do you and your staff receive? How many secondary essays? How much time do you spend reading each application? Each personal statement and essay?

ATSU—Kirksville College: For just our one medical program (we have dental and biomedical sciences programs that we also review files for admissions), we received 4400 last year. Out of those primary applications, we received approximately 3000 secondary applications. Reading a single application can take around fifteen minutes, depending on the depth of the information/letters of recommendation/etc. Personal statements and essays—one to five minutes each.

ATSU—SOMA: We receive over 5000 primary applications and about half of that number return their secondary applications, from there another 1000 would be considered a prescreen reject b/c not meeting our minimums to come to interview so we read about 1500 essays (for SOMA). We spend a couple minutes on reading them.

Dalhousie University: Each applicant must complete the personal essay, we receive approximately 1000 applications annually. To thoroughly review an essay it will take anywhere from fifteen to thirty minutes.

VCOM: This year we will receive almost 5,000 primary applications. We read the personal statement for all primary applications. We anticipate receiving over 2,500 secondary applications. Our secondary includes three essays. We spend 10–20 minutes on each application during a review session.

Ohio State: About 4,000 personal statements and about 5,800 secondary essays (we have three essay questions on our secondary application and we receive about 2,900 secondaries each year). On average we spend 5–10 minutes reading each application, including the personal statement and secondary essays.

SUNY Upstate: Each AMCAS application has a personal statement, which we read; last year there were 3,800. We do not require secondary essays. Each application is reviewed at least twice and we do a thorough screen each time. The time varies—some can take 15 minutes to read and others can take half an hour.

University of Manitoba: Twenty-five; varies.

University of Miami: Four thousand Secondary Applications, each with four to six essays. I spend two to three hours a day for six months reading. Forty members of the Admissions Committee will also be reading as the evaluate and rank each applicant.

What work experience do you require from the people reviewing applications? Are there any particular qualities that you look for in a reader?

ATSU—Kirksville College: Internal training for all people who are reading files/interviewing applicants/sitting on Admissions Committees; Admissions training. College degree. Readers need to be good with grammar, English, writing, communication skills.

ATSU—SOMA: The Admissions Counselors are the only ones reading and reviewing applications. All will have experience in recruitment, education and admissions.

Dalhousie University: Admissions committee members participate in a brief workshop to provide a review of what to look for, how to score, etc.

VCOM: In general, we restrict application review to senior administration. These individuals include our President, Dean, Vice President for Student Services, and Director of Admissions.

Ohio State: Previous admissions experience is essential. Fairness, compassion, and the ability to read between the lines are a few of the qualities that are useful.

State University of New York Upstate: Training and admissions experience.

University of Manitoba: First Nations, Metis and/or Inuit background.

University of Miami: Senior faculty member of the medical school. At least three years of Committee experience.

Do you use an academic or other index initially to sort applications into "for sure," "maybe," and "long shot" piles? If not, how do you do your initial sorting?

ATSU—Kirksville College: We have a multi-dimensional rubric for sorting. It is not based on one aspect alone, with the exception of GPA minimums.

ATSU—SOMA: We have solid candidates that we automatically move to invite to interview, some risky or borderline candidates will move to a queue for a second look with our academic committee which consists of faculty who review the file and make a decision. Those we reject get moved to a queue but have one more pair of eyes on them one last time before they get the reject letter.

Dalhousie University: Applicants must meet the academic criteria in order to proceed to next step in process.

VCOM: Yes. We place a strong emphasis on the science GPA. We work with a minimum of 3.0 but our average science GPA is 3.5. We closely screen all applicants with a science GPA under 3.3.

Ohio State: We use a combination of grades, test scores, and experiences to sort applications into "invite to interview," "possibly interview," and "do not interview" groups.

State University of New York Upstate: We used to use a matrix that sorted applications based on GPA and MCAT scores, but now we review each application by hand once it is complete.

There are so many variations in applications—e.g., lower MCATs with a really high GPA from an Ivy League institution, inconsistent MCATs, grad work and post-bacc course work, low verbal scores for ESL students; I worried about fairness. Reviewing each application by hand makes it more consistent.

University of Miami: Yes. Three piles: interview, don't interview, interview only if space allows.

What steps do you take to recognize and prevent plagiarism? Do you have an institutional policy regarding plagiarism?

ATSU—Kirksville College: There is an institutional policy. We do not have a software program at this time to recognize it. If we suspect it, we investigate.

ATSU—SOMA: We ask the applicant on the application if they've ever been reprimanded academically and expect them to be truthful about plagiarism. Typically if they have a past history it's not likely they will be invited to interview, we are quite strict on this.

Dalhousie University: No.

Ohio State: It would be very difficult to know if someone plagiarized his or her personal statement or essay responses. If it were discovered that any part of an application was plagiarized, it would be taken very seriously. Our students are required to sign a medical student honor code and conduct themselves in a professional manner.

University of Miami: Plagiarism is an immediate rejection. We use commercially available scanning software to detect prior publication of more than an unreferenced sentence or two.

If you have not already explained this, what is the process that each application undergoes, from receipt to decision? How many hands does it pass through on the way?

ATSU—SOMA: Primary application received, secondary application received. Entire app reviewed by an admissions counselor and typically reviewed by the faculty in academic committee for a second look, so the average applicant will get two sets of hands on the application before a decision is made.

ATSU—Kirksville College: Pre-Screen (one person). Pre Screen Committee for Interview Decision (four people). Interviewers (three people). Admissions Committee for final decision (seven people). Admissions Wait List, if applicable (two to four people).

Dalhousie University: Applications are reviewed first to ensure they meet the minimum academic criteria. If they do they proceed to be reviewed by the admissions committee and to have their supplemental form and essay scored. These scores are added to the academic scores along with their interview scores to arrive at a total score. The total score is used to rank order applicants and to then offer positions. An essay and supplemental form will pass through a minimum of two hands and a max of eighteen depending on the first set of scores generated by the two members of the admissions committee.

VCOM: When we review an AACOMAS application, we look at three categories of information—requirements, academics, and extracurricular activities. With regard to requirements, we want to ensure the applicant has completed or will complete their undergraduate degree before matriculation; that the applicant has completed or will complete the course requirements before matriculation; and that the applicant has a recent MCAT score (within the last four years). If the requirements have not been met, we send notification that we will be unable to proceed with the application for the current cycle. If the requirements have been met or will be met before matriculation, we look at the academics. We want to ensure that the GPA meets our minimum. If the minimum GPA has not been met, we send notification that we will be unable to proceed with the application for the current cycle. If the minimum GPA has been met, we take a closer look at the GPA and MCAT score. We review the academic and nonacademic portions of the AACOMAS application concurrently because we feel the extracurricular activities are just as important as the academic background. For a candidate to be competitive, it takes a range of nonacademic activities that speak to his or her interest in becoming a physician. We are not particular about what form these activities take. However, it is important that these activities reflect the candidate's passion for medicine and capacity for studying. Candidates who present a competitive AACOMAS application will be invited to submit a secondary application. Note: Not all of our candidates receive this invitation. Once the application is complete, we screen the application again to determine whether or not the candidate will be invited to campus for an interview.

Ohio State: When verified applications are received from AMCAS electronically, an e-mail is sent from our admissions office to the applicant providing them with access information to a personalized status page and the secondary application. From this status page, the applicant can track receipt of reference letters and view their application status in real time. Applicants are notified through the status page of their invitation to interview (if applicable) and of the Admissions Committee decision. The page is interactive, which allows the applicant to: confirm or reschedule an interview date; accept an offer of admission or withdraw; or accept or decline a scholarship award online. Applications are reviewed upon receipt of the AMCAS application, the secondary application, and MCAT scores, and pass through about four or five sets of hands. Applicants are invited to an on-campus interview about one month in advance of their scheduled date. Interviewed applicants receive an admission decision within two weeks of their interview date.

University of Manitoba: Admissions office to panel; recommendation from panel to Admissions. Panel conducts an interview. Composite score also includes referee letters.

University of Miami: Prior to interview; filtered by Admissions Office Staff, reviewed by the Admissions Dean and three faculty members prior to invitation to interview. Once interviewed, reviewed by thirty members of the Admissions Committee for a final disposition.

THE INFLUENCE OF THE ESSAY

If you have an applicant with lower numbers (MCAT and GPA) but a great personal statement, what do you do? If the personal statement is unimpressive but the student's grades or MCAT scores are great, what then? Is it possible for a personal statement to change your mind about a candidate? And what kind of influence can secondary essays have?

ATSU—Kirksville College: If the personal statement and secondary essays are strong, but everything else is weak, it won't make a difference. However, if an applicant is borderline, it can shift toward the side of offering an interview. However, we look at everything, including LORs.

ATSU—SOMA. The personal statement would need to have some major flaws (something controversial or just bad grammatically) in order for it to be the deciding factor of not to bring a candidate. If it's just boring that won't stop us from inviting someone to interview. If it's fantastic and yet the GPA/MCAT is low, unfortunately it likely isn't going to be the deciding factor to bring someone, their numbers do count and even if they are very articulate it doesn't mean they will get invited.

Dalhousie University: All components are scored provided the applicant meets our minimum stated academic criteria. Once all components of an application are scored we "z-score" each component to ensure it is weighted according to is overall score value. This means that one high scored component cannot make up for a low score on another component.

VCOM: We place a strong emphasis on the science GPA as it is the best predictor of performance in our program. We do utilize the personal statement to learn about the candidates' passion for medicine. The personal statement and secondary essays can sway our decision to invite a candidate in for an interview.

Ohio State: If one part of an application is weak, we review the rest of the application materials to determine if the student will be invited to interview or not. There have been some instances where applicants wrote about inappropriate topics in the personal statement, which caused our Admissions Committee to believe they were not appropriate for our program. Responses to secondary essays can have a similar influence; they are used to provide additional information not found elsewhere in the application.

SUNY Upstate: Yes, I think that the personal statement can have a huge impact on an admission decision, both positive and negative.

University of Miami: We are looking for students who are smart and who are effective communicators. With 8000 applicants, once you find and identify a major problem, you move on to the next applicant.

How is your decision affected by a perspective or opinion (expressed by an applicant in a personal statement or essay) with which you categorically disagree? What happens if you find the content offensive?

ATSU—Kirksville College: Everything is weighed in terms of fit to mission. If the individual does not have the personal motivations and experiences that fit our mission of service, then they would be weeded out. We do value diversity and do NOT look for like-mindedness, but the professionalism of the individual in expressing their individuality and opinions would be weighed.

ATSU—SOMA: I've disagreed many times with the content of a personal statement, that in no way deters me from inviting a candidate to interview. They have the right to their opinion.

Dalhousie University: The admissions committee members review the file together; the applicant name is blinded from the file.

VCOM: All communications should show a well-thought-out point of view. We will likely not penalize a candidate for having an opinion that we merely disagree with. However, if we find content in a personal statement or essay offensive or unimpressive, then that can prevent a candidate from receiving an invitation for an interview.

Ohio State: If an interview is granted, more questioning will occur to determine how the student would handle situations in a patient care setting. They would most likely not be invited to interview if the content was more than a difference of values.

SUNY Upstate: One applicant stated that "people are only sick because they choose to be." The thought of someone one day treating patients with this belief is scary. If your grades and MCATs are borderline, this only makes one more reason not to consider you further.

University of Miami: Opinions within reason are not judged if the applicant can support their opinion. If the content is morally questionable, the applicant will not be interviewed. For example, "This country needs to stop wasting health care dollars on taking care of the elderly" or "If a patient is stupid enough to smoke or take drugs, we should not provide medical care." Judgmental or prejudicial opinions will not get you an interview.

The low GPA/MCAT score explanation: When is this necessary? Unnecessary? How often does this change your mind? (Have you ever received any ridiculous explanations that you'd like to share?

ATSU—Kirksville College: We want to see why they had dips in their curricular experiences, or if something affected them negatively. We like to know what happened and how they persevered to come out of it positively. The applicant's honesty is valued.

ATSU—SOMA: I wouldn't put a lot of emphasis on low scores in an essay. It can be addressed if they want but not the focus of the entire thing.

VCOM: Because we place such a strong emphasis on the GPA, we look for the candidate to provide an explanation for a low GPA. Reasonable explanations include: working full-time during college; a traumatic event or serious illness; the illness of a family member; or the birth of a child. We do not appreciate candidates who blame their performance in a class on the professor, or candidates who do not take appropriate personal responsibility for weaknesses.

Ohio State: It could be useful if there was an unusual dip in grades or if there was an unusual incident during the MCAT exam administration. One low grade does not necessarily need to be explained. Rarely do explanations for grades or MCAT scores change the Admissions Committee members' minds—the interview typically brings out other strengths and/or weaknesses; grades and MCAT scores are a part of the total application presented.

State University of New York Upstate: I think it is absolutely necessary to put something somewhere if you need to explain your scores. The last paragraph of the personal statement or a separate note to the admissions committee works fine for me. I just think it is really important for the student to clarify the reasons why something might be "off"—please don't leave what was going on in your life at that time up to my imagination or the imagination of twenty admissions committee members!

University of Miami: If a person has an MCAT/GPA that is within a reasonable range of our current average, it will be acceptable. There is a point with both academic metrics that below which an applicant will have great difficulty with the first two-years of medical school. The applicants clinical, research and life experiences, and motivation for a career in medicine are better predictors of who will be a great physician than MCAT/GPA are.

GENERAL APPLICATION QUESTIONS

If an element on the application is marked "optional," is it truly optional? If a candidate opts not to complete that part of the application, is his or her candidacy weakened?

ATSU—Kirksville College: We do not have any optional areas.

ATSU—SOMA: No, but we don't have anything optional.

Dalhousie University: Their candidacy is not weakened. We have removed most of these areas mostly because applicants were always completing them even if they had nothing further or necessary for their application to add.

VCOM: We do not include any optional portions on our application.

Ohio State: If applicants do not complete "optional" questions, their candidacy won't be adversely affected. Not completing other parts of either the AMCAS or secondary application denies us essential information, which could impact the outcome.

SUNY Upstate: Yes, it is truly optional—it makes no difference to me.

University of Miami: Optional is truly optional. Don't make up fluff.

Do applicants send extra material to you? If so, which materials are helpful? How much is too much?

ATSU—Kirksville College: Sometimes students sent updated academic records, updated experiences, etc., and all that gets loaded into their overall file. We don't like to see more than four or five Letters of Recommendation, or a bombardment of updates. An update or two is no big deal. Other than that, I would wonder how prepared they were to submit their file to begin with.

ATSU—SOMA: Often candidates will send an update to their resume which might include recent research, work or shadowing. An email is fine, it is added to their file. We don't need additional LOR's unless it's from a DO and they didn't have a DO letter originally. Don't send a bunch of LOR's we don't need.

Dalhousie University: Applicants are asked to only send official transcripts which are placed in their files. All other materials are not retained and either returned to the applicant or recycled confidentially.

VCOM: We only require two letters of recommendation—one from a premedical committee or science faculty member and one from an osteopathic physician. Some applicants also submit letters from supervisors, academic advisors, or allopathic physician mentors; we welcome these recommendations.

Ohio State: Yes. Information updating their application between the time they submit the AMCAS application and the time of the interview is helpful. Sending grades at the end of each term and complete manuscripts of research is not necessary.

State University of New York Upstate: Yes, additional information can be sent, but it can get out of hand. A letter of recommendation from someone that the applicant shadowed, a supervisor, or an advisor is helpful, but a letter from a doctor that did your surgery when you were nine is not helpful. Also, please do not send videotapes, DVDs, CDs, 3" e-ring binders, or complete manuscripts—an abstract is fine. I do encourage applicants to send updated information in, particularly if they are interviewing in the spring and they submitted their AMCAS application the previous summer.

University of Manitoba: No.

University of Miami: Updates three to six months after original submission are useful if significant addition experience has occurred.

Do you regard or consider candidates who fulfilled their premedical requirements via a post-baccalaureate program rather than a premedical curriculum in college differently? If so, how? Is it beneficial for a student to complete premedical requirements within a particular channel? If so, which is preferable?

ATSU—Kirksville College: Students that do a post-bacc usually have a reason for doing so, so we want to know what that is. Poor undergrad grades, change of career, etc. We prefer they take upper level courses and take their pre-reqs more recently, if possible.

ATSU—SOMA: No, there is no preference if someone did a post-bacc or decided to go the medical route after completing their BS in something completely different. Often this makes for a more mature and interesting candidate but we want to see why they chose to take the medicine path. A post-bacc is often necessary even for those who started out as pre-meds in UG because they didn't do so great, so we recommend it.

VCOM: We do not regard candidates who fulfilled their premedical requirements via a post-baccalaureate program differently. In fact, we offer a post-baccalaureate program for students who might need to enhance their premedical coursework. Our program comes with a guaranteed offer of admission into the following years medical school class if certain academic and non-academic qualities are achieved.

Ohio State: We do not regard applicants differently.

University of Miami: Students who fulfill their premedical requirements in a post-baccalaureate program because they are changing directions in their life are looked at more positively than students who performed poorly in college with the requirements and then take a post-bac year to bring up their GPA. In these situations we really heavily MCAT score to help us determine if the student has mastered the required sciences or not. The traditional pre-med channel is preferred but not required. Approximately 25 percent of the last several classes have been non-traditional students.

Do you find that students with a particular major (biochemistry, for example) are particularly well prepared for the challenges of medical school? If so, which major(s)?

ATSU—Kirksville College: Science majors do tend to struggle less than non-science majors, simply because they would have had a much broader exposure to the sciences. However, there is not a major that tends to do better.

ATSU—SOMA: Yes, Biology, Physiology, Biochemistry, Chemistry are usually well-prepared with a variety of science courses.

Dalhousie University: We do not have specific course or degree prerequisites

VCOM: We do not hold any preferences regarding our candidates' undergraduate major. Consequently, for the Class of 2009 admissions cycle, we added an additional six hours of science as an entrance requirement. We feel this will better prepare our candidates, regardless of their major, for our medical school curriculum.

Ohio State: We don't. A strong science aptitude, regardless of major, will prepare students for the medical school curriculum.

University of Miami: In my opinion, biochemistry and cell biology are the two biological sciences that best prepares a student for the first two-years of medical school.

Does coming from a specific, underrepresented-in-medical school field (French, for example) help someone? Hurt someone?

ATSU—Kirksville College: Not hurt or help. As long as they are prepared to do hard, rigorous sciences, any major is fine.

ATSU—SOMA: It won't hurt them if they have a lot of science coursework along with their other major. If they only have foreign language or say psych classes and then did just the minimum pre-reqs for med school then yes it hurts them, we want to see a minimum of fifty-five science hours above and beyond the pre-reqs.

Dalhousie University: No.

Ohio State: We view these students as bringing much-needed diversity to the class.

University of Miami: We value diversity and recognize that correcting under representations in medicine is both a goal and societal responsibility of the medical school.

How are nontraditional applicants viewed by the admissions office? What questions might you ask yourself while reading a nontraditional student's application that you wouldn't ask while reading a traditional student's application?

ATSU—Kirksville College: They are very well accepted because they tend to have a much less idealistic view of the world and the working environment than traditional students. I usually ask what experiences they have had that have helped them be prepared to go into medical school, especially after being out of school for a while (if courses were not too recent)?

ATSU—SOMA: No bias or preference for non-traditional. Again, we just want to see their pathway to medicine, why they are choosing this route later in life, etc. We've had many nontraditional students matriculate to SOMA.

Dalhousie University: Non traditional applicants must do a very good job selling themselves and convincing the committee that they know what medicine is about and the demands of the profession.

VCOM: We accepted a number of nontraditional applicants into our program this year. If a candidate has been out of the classroom for several years, we want to ensure that he or she is prepared for our curriculum.

Ohio State: Nontraditional applicants are viewed similarly as the non-science applicants—they will bring a different level of diversity to the class. We try to determine how long they've been interested in a career in medicine. Is this a recent decision with no experience to back it up? What is their motivation?

University of Miami: We like non-traditional students. They bring maturity and experiences that usually we do not see in students right out of college. We look at the experiences the non-traditional students have had and who this may add to their practice of medicine in the future.

Do you have a descending degree of importance that you assign the different application requirements? Is the MCAT score, for example, the most important measure of ability? Where do the personal statement and essays fall?

ATSU—Kirksville College: No. Everything is weighed as a piece of the whole application.

ATSU—SOMA: GPA is typically most important, then MCAT, then clinical/volunteer hours (including community service). The essay isn't a top factor in their measure of ability.

Dalhousie University: We are looking for a balanced student with solid grades and continued and a variety of extra curricular involvement. The components of our application are scored somewhat equal across the board but the interview does hold the most weight.

VCOM: We first consider the science GPA, then the essays, then lastly the MCAT.

Ohio State: We do not rank or assign percentage values to the different parts of the application.

State University of New York Upstate: I would say that grades and MCAT scores account for the largest part (about 65–70 percent) of each decision, followed by the personal statement, then extracurriculars—clinical, research, and service experiences.

University of Manitoba: MCAT must meet eligibility requirements but pool is not ranked with this score unless not recommended by Panel.

University of Miami: In descending order with all being important: Clinical, life, research experiences, then MCAT/GPA, then letters of recommendation, then communication skills, then personal statement, then leadership, then community service and societal involvement.

If you had the option of doing away with the AMCAS (or ACOMAS) personal statement, would you? What about secondary application essays?

ATSU—Kirksville College: No and no.

ATSU—SOMA: I would be okay if they did away with the personal statements on the primary application; they all tend to say the same thing anyway. I do like our secondary essay questions that are specific to our school, however. I would keep those.

VCOM: We heavily weight the personal statement and essay responses. Thus, we would not support a decision to eliminate these portions of the applications.

Ohio State: Absolutely not! Although we change the secondary essay questions periodically, we will continue to use them to obtain additional information not found in other parts of either application. We use the personal statement and secondary essay questions to assist us in gaining insight into the applicant's thought processes, motivation, and commitment to a career in medicine.

State University of New York Upstate: No—I really value the personal statement. To me, it is the only place where the applicant truly becomes more than their "numbers." I want to learn something about the kind of person they are, what they are passionate about, what they value, and how they came to the decision to pursue medicine as a career. We do not require an additional essay.

University of Miami: I would not do away with the essays. They are critical assessments of communication skills and allow the applicant to express their desire and motivation for a career in medicine.

OFFICIAL DISCLAIMER!

Our editors aren't asleep on the job.

The following personal statements and secondary essays appear exactly as they did for medical school admissions officers. We only changed the layout so that the essays fit on the pages of this book. Because we have not edited the essays, you may find errors in spelling, punctuation, and grammar. We assure you that we found these errors as well, but we thought it would be most helpful for you to see what the admissions officers saw—not what they could (or should) have seen. We recommend that you carefully proofread your own personal statement, but should you miss an error, take comfort in the fact that others (accepted applicants, even!) sometimes did too.

—

Chapter 8

REAL PERSONAL STATEMENTS AND SECONDARY ESSAYS

ADAM JOHN DEFOE

After college, Adam worked on an inpatient chemical dependency unit at a hospital in Minneapolis for nearly two years. During that time, he also volunteered with the University of Minnesota EMS squad.

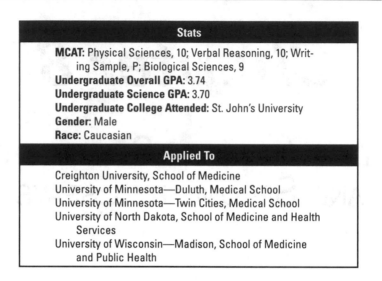

Stats
MCAT: Physical Sciences, 10; Verbal Reasoning, 10; Writing Sample, P; Biological Sciences, 9
Undergraduate Overall GPA: 3.74
Undergraduate Science GPA: 3.70
Undergraduate College Attended: St. John's University
Gender: Male
Race: Caucasian

Applied To
Creighton University, School of Medicine
University of Minnesota—Duluth, Medical School
University of Minnesota—Twin Cities, Medical School
University of North Dakota, School of Medicine and Health Services
University of Wisconsin—Madison, School of Medicine and Public Health

AMCAS Personal Statement

I believe I started on a quest to become a medical doctor long before I entered higher education. Visits to the family doctor always brought a sense of awe, as I was interested in learning about the human body. I can clearly remember my eagerness in fourth grade while learning the major bones of the human body. In high school I had the same interest in the sciences, and the idea of being a doctor was rolling around in the back of my mind. This idea has been reinforced in a number of ways throughout the years, both directly and indirectly.

Starting with the present, I am currently employed as a Psychiatric Associate at Fairview-University Medical Center. I work primarily on the Adult Chemical Dependency Inpatient Unit, but I also have experience on other behavioral services units. This position has allowed me to experience a variety of mental health disorders and treatments. I work directly with patients and medical staff, which has provided insight into working in a hospital setting, as well as continuous improvement in my interaction skills with patients and medical staff. Most importantly, this position allows me to help people on a daily basis, while utilizing the knowledge I attained as an undergraduate.

On my quest to gain medical experience, I attained certification as an Emergency Medical Technician. I learned much in the training, which included an ambulance ride along and shadowing in the Emergency Room. I have since put this training to use by volunteering with the University of Minnesota Emergency Medical Services. This team of EMT's provides emergency medical service to university events such as hockey games. Thus far, being a part of the team has been rewarding and has provided some insight into another aspect of medicine.

Next, I enlisted the guidance of Dr. Richard Johnson, a radiologist practicing in my hometown of Devils Lake, ND. My experience with him was quite rewarding. Dr. Johnson taught me about his profession as well as giving me a tutorial in radiology. He even lent me books to read and learn from for the duration of the shadowing experience. I also had the opportunity to see instruments such as a CT scanner and ultrasound in operation. I walked away from this experience with a newly found interest in medicine.

My undergraduate career was spent at St. John's University in Collegeville, MN. My time there served as preparation for medical school, both academically and personally. I believe I was able to mix both my interests and pre-med requirements into an appropriate major and minor, all the while laying a good foundation for medical school. While at times the class load was challenging, I feel I effectively managed classes, on-campus employment, and other priorities. Through on-campus employment and involvement in Taekwondo I was able to cultivate my leadership skills, which I think are important for any profession. Along with leadership, the liberal arts education I received at St. John's fostered my critical thinking. Through the classes I took and through extra-curricular activities, like Student Congress, I am able to effectively research and examine both sides of an issue before reaching a decision. I value this critical thinking ability, especially as questions of medical ethics become increasingly important.

An experience I had that indirectly reinforced my decision to become a doctor is one I had a few years ago. I was given the opportunity to visit the mission of Father Jack Davis in Chimbote, Peru. Chimbote is a large, poverty-stricken city, but Father Jack is doing all he can to help the poor there. While working with Father Jack I experienced first hand the lives of the people there. The living conditions and lack of adequate health care really made me examine life in the United States and think about what I wanted to do with my life. I walked away from my trip to Peru with a new compassion for people and just a general desire to help. Hopefully someday I will be able to return to Chimbote and help the people there even more.

Finally, I would like to share an idea purported by Dr. Roger MacDonald, a traveling country doctor who practiced in northern Minnesota for many years. As a closing thought in a radio program he stated that the medical profession has a place for all types of personalities. I agree with Dr. MacDonald and think that my own personality would easily blend into the profession.

If I am invited to join the class of 2009 I know there will be a difficult, but rewarding road ahead of me. I look forward to the challenge, now more than ever, after having been out in the "real world" for a while. Working full time has served to strengthen my work ethic and feed my desire to learn. These things are evident in my undergraduate career as well, and I hope to apply the same hard work, dedication, and commitment to medical school.

See page 252 to find out where this student got in.

ALEXANDRA PAUL

As an undergraduate, Alexandra's second major was in a subject not typically seen among pre-meds: Spanish. She was a varsity athlete for four years and was also head coach for a local high school crew team. Additionally, Alexandra was able to complete some basic science research in cystic fibrosis at Rainbow Babies and Children's Hospital in Cleveland. Alexandra made the Dean's List all four years of college and was he recipient of the Robert M. Fuller prize for the greatest promise of a successful career in chemical research. During her senior year, she was elected to Phi Beta Kappa and Sigma Xi.

Stats
MCAT: Physical Sciences, 11; Verbal Reasoning, 11; Writing Sample, N; Biological Sciences, 12
Undergraduate Overall GPA: 3.98
Undergraduate College Attended: Union College
Gender: Female
Race: Caucasian

Applied To
Dartmouth Medical School
Georgetown University, School of Medicine
Harvard University, Harvard Medical School
John Hopkins University, School of Medicine
SUNY Upstate Medical Center
Tufts University, School of Medicine
University of Pennsylvania, School of Medicine
Yale University, School of Medicine

AMCAS Personal Statement

Every time I look down at the blue bracelet with the initials S.J.L. on my wrist I am reminded of the tragedy that occurred a little over a year ago. It seemed like the perfect end to the rowing season. My boat had just won bronze medals, competing against 54 other colleges, in the Varsity Women 4+ event at the Dad Vail Regatta, the biggest college regatta in the United States. We were standing near the finish line to watch the rest of that afternoon's races before heading back home.

As the next race approached the finish line, the crowd went wild. The Boston College Men Lightweight 8 crossed the line first over four full seconds ahead of the second place boat. As soon as the boat crossed the line however, the two-seat, Scott Laio, collapsed and passed out into the bow of the boat. Initially, everyone thought that he was just lying down from exhaustion, after the physiological equivalent of sprinting a mile. However, we saw the bow seat attempting mouth to mouth resuscitation but Scott remained unconscious. I was dumbstruck and couldn't believe what I was seeing. I became full of frustration, knowing that there was nothing I could do from where I was and honestly most likely nothing more my CPR certification could have done than was already being attempted. I could not intervene to save this young student's life and was overcome by a painful helplessness.

I was also confused. How could this happen? Could this happen to me? I had just pushed my body through 3 grueling 7+ minute races in 24 hours. Originally, it was presumed that Scott died of a heart attack but a later autopsy showed that there was no sign of a heart attack, no blood clots and no cardiomyopathy. Toxin screens also came back negative. I recently heard Scott's pediatrician, Dr. Ali Loveys, speak at the most recent US Rowing Coach's Convention and she said that they have determined that modern technology was just not capable of finding the cause of death. The strong desire I felt to help Scott and the empathy for his friends and family reaffirmed my belief that medicine is the right field for me.

Like Scott, I am a rower. What exactly does this mean? It means 9 months of sweat and pain, 9 months of blisters, 9 months of morning practices and missing out on late nights my friends can't seem to stop talking about. Nine months which lead to only six 7-minute races in the spring.

But rowing also gives me the opportunity to set a goal and then prove to myself that I am capable of achieving it. My drive and determination in rowing extends to my life in general. I have a strong desire and I am driven to be a physician. I believe that the decision to enter the medical field cannot be external; it must come from within not because someone else thinks it is the right career choice. I want to be a physician. I see accidents or tragedies and I feel an overwhelming need to help anyone who is suffering. I am also fascinated by the things the human body is capable of and have a strong desire to understand the molecular mechanisms that are occurring in the body at all times.

The cult of rowing, as my non-crew friends have so aptly termed it, does not disappear when one leaves the country. While I was abroad in Seville this past winter, I found a rowing club and began sculling on the Guadalquivir River. The national sculling team also trains there and everyday when I went out on the water, the US Champion Women's Sculler passed me effortlessly. Instead of becoming disillusioned, I relished the opportunity that this situation provided me. Every day I went out on the water and tried to push a little harder, tried to make it just a little more difficult for her to catch up to me. Although It's probably safe to say that to her, passing me on the last day was just as effortless as passing me on my first day on the water there, I was very pleased with my improvement in the single.

Certain things in my life take priority and similar to rowing, I searched out the opportunity to shadow an ophthalmologist, Dr. Juan Rubliales-Bellido while in Spain. This experience not only allowed me to use my Spanish in a clinical environment but also gave me the opportunity to compare the medical systems of the United States and Spain.

Before leaving for Spain I made the difficult decision to leave the Leadership in Medicine Program. This program allows students to obtain an MBA in addition to a BS and gives guaranteed acceptance to medical school. As a high school senior I knew that I wanted to be a physician and I could not let a guaranteed acceptance pass by. However, my research and clinical experiences have helped me come to the conclusion that as a physician, I want to be in the clinic with patients instead of isolated in an office crunching numbers. Sure, If I had stayed in the program I would still be a doctor, but would I be the best doctor that I could be? While giving up a guaranteed acceptance is never easy, I believe that I made the right personal choice. Management is not where my interests lie and I felt that continuing to pursue a degree in this field would not only make me unhappy but would also hinder the development of my clinical skills. My internal drive, passion for learning and compassion makes medicine the perfectly suited field for me.

See page 252 to find out where this student got in.

BASHIR HAKIM

Bashir has been an e-board member of both the pre-medical and Muslim Students' Associations at Michigan State University. He has also been involved with Big Brothers Big Sisters since 2007, and volunteered and done research in hospitals throughout his four years at MSU.

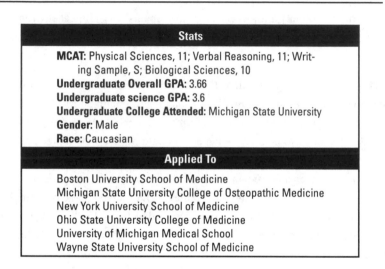

Stats

MCAT: Physical Sciences, 11; Verbal Reasoning, 11; Writing Sample, S; Biological Sciences, 10
Undergraduate Overall GPA: 3.66
Undergraduate science GPA: 3.6
Undergraduate College Attended: Michigan State University
Gender: Male
Race: Caucasian

Applied To

Boston University School of Medicine
Michigan State University College of Osteopathic Medicine
New York University School of Medicine
Ohio State University College of Medicine
University of Michigan Medical School
Wayne State University School of Medicine

AMCAS Personal Statement

The game of football is a game of struggle, a battle of wills and grit unlike any other. It is a game of constant ups and downs, anxiety and excitement. Yet, the forty eight minutes spent playing the game is only a fraction of what decides the outcome. It is the constant struggle off the field, in the weight room, in the film room analyzing previous games to identify shortcomings and review strategy, and on the practice field implementing game plans that decides the winner long before the game is played. It is the preparation off the field that makes all the difference. It is the melting pot of different players understanding each person's role in coming together to work as a single unified team that determines the outcome. During my high school years, I was fortunate enough to play on the football team, and the lessons learned in that experience will help me as a physician and throughout life. The discipline, the work ethic, and the leadership skills that I obtained playing football better prepared me for a life of responsibility and dedication to my craft. To be successful meant giving it your all and working as hard as humanly possible to achieve your goal. The core process for success in medicine is no different. It is the preparation and effort and desire to succeed that determines one's success long before one's first step into a hospital or medical school. The experiences that I have attained throughout my years in high school and Michigan State University both between the hash marks and the book covers have helped me become the individual I am today and hopefully a successful physician tomorrow.

A football team is composed of a wide array of players, all of whom seek the same goal, unified by those select few who stand out, the players who work harder than everybody else, those who are always the first on the field and the last to leave. These select few often elevate a team from mediocrity to extraordinary, through leadership, effort, respect and compassion towards their teammates and coaches. The same can be said for the medical field. Serving as a leader in organizations at Michigan State University has helped me become a better leader and person as well. As an executive board member of both the Muslim Students' Association and the Pre-Medical Association on campus, along with my "teammates"—my fellow executive board members—we have worked together and succeeded in achieving goals. As Social chair of the Muslim Students' Association, I worked with the rest of the executive board to organize dinners, educational seminars, social events, and other activities aimed at increasing awareness on Islamic issues and to aid in promoting diversity on campus. As treasurer for the Pre-Medical Association, I helped organize events to increase education on admissions to medical school and the practice of medicine, and the organization brought various physicians and admissions officers from several medical schools to speak on their experiences and tips on how to gain admission into medical school. As Vice President of both organizations next year, I will continue such work. Such experiences have helped me grow into a leader and a person others can depend on and trust. As a physician, I expect these qualities will help me in working with my fellow doctors and nurses in order to achieve the goals set out for us the moment we step in the door on our first day of residency: to save lives and maintain health.

As an emergency room research assistant at Ingham Hospital in Lansing, MI, I encountered a wide range of patient pathology as well as a host of physicians with different personalities and approaches to patient care. Not surprisingly, the physicians who spent more time with patients informing them kindly and respectfully of their medical problems and what they need to do to be healthy had the most satisfied patients. While seemingly obvious, these two qualities are often lacking in many of our physicians. That experience showed me how the compassion they exhibited towards their patients was contagious. My experience as a big brother for Big Brothers Big Sisters similarly showed me the importance of compassion, respect, and kindness.

Eating lunch and sharing experiences and advice with Morteda, my little brother, made for wonderful experiences that will help me in the future as a parent and as a physician who sees patients for the beautiful human beings they are, and sees the workplace as a place of healing and just not trauma and pain.

The knowledge and skill necessary to become an excellent physician is immense, yet it is the input of each individual physician that determines the final outcome of their careers. In a football game with forty seconds left on the clock, it is the team, the individuals who have worked the hardest and sacrificed the most who will come out on top. Those physicians who strive to continuously improve their book knowledge and personal skills, the physicians who work tirelessly to better know their patients, to be better individuals through their work and experiences, will undoubtedly become the best. Through my experiences and years at MSU, I am confident I am ready to become one of these physicians.

See page 252 to find out where this student got in.

BRANDON DEVERS

Brandon worked two summers at the National Institutes of Health (NIH) and conducted research at the National Institute for Neurological Disorders and Stroke (NINDS), where he was awarded the Exceptional Summer Student Award. After his sophomore year, he worked at the National Human Genome Research Institute (NHGRI). He also played varsity football for four years, volunteered as a tutor for Horton's Kids, and coached a youth basketball team.

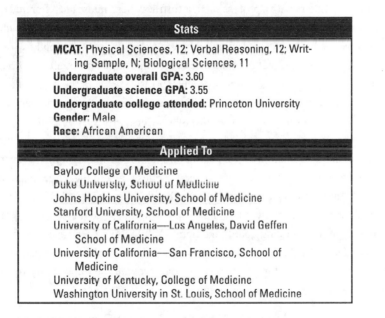

Stats

MCAT: Physical Sciences, 12; Verbal Reasoning, 12; Writing Sample, N; Biological Sciences, 11
Undergraduate overall GPA: 3.60
Undergraduate science GPA: 3.55
Undergraduate college attended: Princeton University
Gender: Male
Race: African American

Applied To

Baylor College of Medicine
Duke University, School of Medicine
Johns Hopkins University, School of Medicine
Stanford University, School of Medicine
University of California—Los Angeles, David Geffen School of Medicine
University of California—San Francisco, School of Medicine
University of Kentucky, College of Medicine
Washington University in St. Louis, School of Medicine

AMCAS Personal Statement

When I was twelve, riots broke out in my city after a white police officer shot and killed a black teenager. I remember my parents waking me up around midnight to inform me that they had to leave immediately and did not know when they would be back. It was my responsibility to watch over my younger siblings, wake them up in the morning, feed them breakfast, and make sure that we were all ready for our carpool to school. I can still picture my parents emerging from downstairs clad in full riot gear. They were wearing bulletproof vests, carrying guns, and each had a protective helmet in hand. That was the first time I remember thinking to myself that I may never see my parents again. While I was overcome with this dread and confusion, I also knew that I had three younger siblings who were depending on me. That experience not only taught me the value of responsibility, but also engraved in me a deep respect for life. Not only was I twelve and facing the fact that my parents could die at any moment, I also came to the realization that my parents were actively putting their lives at risk to protect the lives of others. This was very inspiring and it influenced my views on life, personal interactions, and civility. I believe that this and similar early experiences not only helped shape me into the person I am today, but have also led in part to my interests in medicine, especially my desire to help others.

While my early environment and experiences instilled in me an interest in serving more than just myself, my later experiences with medicine linked this desire to serve and help others with a profession that fulfilled these interests. After undergoing shoulder surgery, I was invited to shadow the surgeon who had operated on me for a week to observe his rounds and surgeries. I remember the anticipation I felt dressing up in nurse's scrubs and stepping into the operating room. Although I observed surgeries repeatedly for three straight days, I never lost interest in the experience. I was captivated by each surgical procedure and the explanations that accompanied them. Yet, the most rewarding experience throughout the week was visiting the patients afterwards in the recovery ward. Just being a part of that experience and witnessing the joy and appreciation of the patient and his or her family upon recovery was amazing. I also noticed how adamantly the families thanked the surgeon and that he knew each family member's name. I believe that this type of personal interaction and the establishment of a trustworthy relationship with the patient and his or her family are imperative in practicing quality medicine. While this experience exposed me to the direct and individual service a doctor can provide for his or her patients, later experiences also showed me that medicine can provide the opportunity for service on a more global level in a group oriented setting.

This past summer I worked at the National Human Genome Research Institute (NHGRI). It was exiting to be at the forefront of genomics research during these times of rapid discovery, insight, and technology development. I was especially interested in projects and meetings concerning gene discovery and therapy directed towards improving medical treatments for a variety of disorders such as cystic fibrosis. While the experience itself was rewarding and educational, I was also impressed by how brilliant and interesting the people I was working for were. Yet, what impressed me the most was how they all worked together. Furthermore, although I was the least experienced member of the group, they all listened intently to my opinions and suggestions during meetings and small conferences. While being an athlete has always taught me the value of teamwork, this experience taught me its importance and applicability in the real world. I believe this concept of teamwork is critical in the medical profession. While each doctor is intelligent and possesses his or her own personal skills and talents, the advancements in health care that we enjoy today did not stem from one or several different individuals working alone. Instead, they reflect the vast network of health professionals working together to gain insight and knowledge from one another with the common goal of improving medicine and health care in general. As a doctor, I would strive to establish networks and consult with other physicians, as this interaction is invaluable from both a health care and academic standpoint. Thus, my experience at the NHGRI helped to reinforce my value of teamwork and further define the type of medicine I want to practice. Although these two experiences exposed me to two distinct sides of the medical profession, they both taught me that the primary interest of the medical field is the service of others. These experiences, among others, resonate strongly with my interests and goals, which were engrained in me at an early age. It is important to me that I am able to lie down each night and know that I have actually helped someone and improved the quality of his or her life. This may occur through direct patient care or simply through the establishment of a worthwhile doctor patient relationship.

See page 252 to find out where this student got in.

CAELAN JOHNSON

As an undergrad, Caelan did psychiatric neuroimaging research. She graduated with general honors and with departmental honors from her school's Neuroscience and Spanish departments. During her post-baccalaureate year, she worked a tutor and volunteered at a pediatric hospital. The following year she worked as a pediatric dental assistant.

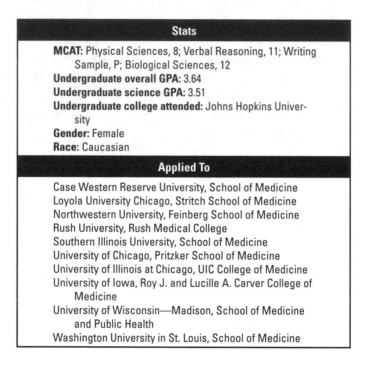

Stats

MCAT: Physical Sciences, 8; Verbal Reasoning, 11; Writing Sample, P; Biological Sciences, 12
Undergraduate overall GPA: 3.64
Undergraduate science GPA: 3.51
Undergraduate college attended: Johns Hopkins University
Gender: Female
Race: Caucasian

Applied To

Case Western Reserve University, School of Medicine
Loyola University Chicago, Stritch School of Medicine
Northwestern University, Feinberg School of Medicine
Rush University, Rush Medical College
Southern Illinois University, School of Medicine
University of Chicago, Pritzker School of Medicine
University of Illinois at Chicago, UIC College of Medicine
University of Iowa, Roy J. and Lucille A. Carver College of Medicine
University of Wisconsin—Madison, School of Medicine and Public Health
Washington University in St. Louis, School of Medicine

AMCAS Personal Statement

My inspiration to pursue medicine came from an aunt who completed an MD/PhD when I was in grade school. She visited us often and spent hours describing the remarkable things she learned. Now, as a retinal surgeon and mother of four, she illustrates the joys and challenges of balancing a family with practicing medicine. As an adult, I see her path as something for which numerous experiences in my life have prepared me: academic, cultural, work- and family-related, and others. I put a lot of thought into pursuing medicine, and am extremely motivated to become a physician. The field of medicine integrates many of my academic and personal interests, such as human biology, anthropology, and helping people understand and address issues regarding health and living.

The art of communication has always intrigued me. I spent my childhood in culturally diverse areas of Wisconsin, Illinois, and Ohio, and I continue to have a deep desire to learn how other cultures communicate. I enjoy poetry, in both English and Spanish, and editing, and I have received literary honors and awards for excellence in both Spanish and English. More importantly, however, I view communication as an essential tool for problem-solving. Through various jobs, travels, and life experiences I have noted that improved communication not only solves problems but can preclude them as well. After completion of my two months at Escuela Internacional in Salamanca, Spain, I decided that I want to incorporate Spanish fluency into my career. I would love to work with the largely underserved Midwestern Hispanic population in a healthcare setting, to help improve the quality of their care.

The development of the brain has also interested me; because I have taught, counseled and observed children, I have considered the fields of child psychiatry, pediatrics, and pediatric neurology. From the age of fifteen, I worked with children at a day camp in Illinois. By my fifth year there, I ran the camp when the Director was gone, took charge of disruptive campers, and interacted regularly with parents, who can be the most challenging aspect of working with children. I dealt with discipline problems and learned about diplomacy in delicate situations, reprimanding without adding to the problem, and motivating kids to behave. My recent experiences shadowing the attending physician on the schizophrenia service at the Johns Hopkins Hospital showed me that some of the same problem-solving skills I utilized at camp are essential in medicine. This year I will continue to interact with children and parents as a dental assistant in a pediatric practice in Illinois.

Through my work with children, I have come to see the importance of education in everyone's life. Assisting in a Spanish class at Baltimore City College High School and volunteering at Mt. Washington Pediatric Hospital helped me realize my ideal role would be a mix of teacher, social activist, and healthcare provider: a physician. I found that I was less interested in teaching kids about a specific subject than in making sure they knew how to deal with other people, make good decisions in life, communicate with those around them, and take care of themselves. I also discovered that I couldn't ignore my love of Neuroscience. During the year I focused on Spanish, I still read every brain-related article I could find and really missed my science coursework. It was while studying in Spain that I resolved that the best way for me to pursue my interests in Spanish and Neuroscience and meaningful interaction with people would be through medicine. When I returned to Baltimore, I renewed my double major status, and have thoroughly enjoyed courses like psychopharmacology and general biology.

As a part of the Neuroscience curriculum, I worked on a few studies as a research assistant doing volumetric analysis of structural MRI data at the Johns Hopkins University School of Medicine. What I love most about the systems approach to the brain is that it ties back into how we communicate, on numerous levels. Each element of communication, such as emotion, speech production, word recognition, sensory cues, and cognition has its own area, but they are all connected, and the information must be passed on to the body so that it can respond appropriately. The communication between physician and patient is analogous to that between the brain and the body in that the physician must effectively convey her knowledge for the patient to use and benefit from it. I want to be a physician in order to use my knowledge of language and science to creatively help people deal with their health and life issues. Medical school will give me the education I need to achieve this goal, and the opportunity to continue to grow in my understanding of others and myself.

See page 253 to find out where this student got in.

CAROLYN HAUS

After graduating from college, Carolyn worked at the Mayo Clinic in Rochester as a Transfusion Laboratory Technologist, where she performed compatibility testing and prepared blood and blood products for patients. With the Mayo MOST Program, she gave presentations promoting healthy lifestyle choices at local elementary schools. After a year at Mayo, she began working for BioLife Plasma Services, where she administered health screenings to donors and assisted them through the process of donating plasma. While preparing for med school, she took part in several volunteer activities and shadowed physicians.

Stats
MCAT: Physical Sciences, 10; Verbal Reasoning, 10; Writing Sample, N; Biological Sciences, 9
Undergraduate Overall GPA: 4.0
Undergraduate Science GPA: 4.0
Undergraduate College Attended: University of South Dakota
Gender: Female
Race: Caucasian

Applied To
Creighton University, School of Medicine
Mayo Clinic College of Medicine, Mayo Medical School
University of Minnesota—Duluth, Medical School
University of Minnesota—Twin Cities, Medical School
University of North Dakota, School of Medicine and Health Services
University of South Dakota, School of Medicine

AMCAS Personal Statement

I heard a click as the overhead page system came on, "Trauma team to the ER, stat." Those simple words were enough to cause my heart to pound. I gathered my supplies and sprinted to the emergency department where I saw a team of doctors, nurses, and other medical personnel already forming. The doctor in charge explained, "We have a female involved in a motor vehicle accident arriving by helicopter in approximately five minutes." Before I knew it, a stretcher was wheeled into the room, and I heard, "Let's get an ABG drawn now!" I swiftly pulled on gloves and assembled a syringe. As I approached the patient, I could hardly tell I was looking at a young woman. Her face was blood splattered and embedded with shards of glass from the windshield. I deftly felt for a pulse, but nothing. Finally, I found a pulse, albeit faint. I smoothly positioned the needle and breathed a huge sigh of relief when I saw the welcome flash of blood fill the syringe hub. I had just successfully handled my first emergency situation as a clinical laboratory science intern. With my role complete, I observed as the doctor finished stabilizing the patient to prepare her for emergency surgery. I was awestruck by his incredible poise, in spite of the intensity of the situation, and the manner in which he demonstrated genuine empathy as he later comforted the patient's family.

I always had a passion for becoming a physician, but this moment truly pinnacled my desire to pursue the dream. When I had the experience of actively participating in saving the life of a young woman, I felt an overwhelming sense of fulfillment. In this situation, I recognized that I possessed what it takes to remain calm and focused during a critical situation and to work compassionately, as part of a team, to assist in saving a life. I realized that I could actually make a difference.

Even before this experience, I was diligently forging the path to becoming a physician. My first step was shadowing a family practice physician. After spending time in a family practice setting, I felt further gravitated toward the profession and inspired by the doctor's display of compassion to each patient he interacted with. One experience, involving an elderly couple, was particularly influential for me. A gentleman, accompanied by his wife, was being seen for a routine checkup to monitor his diabetes. Instead of rushing through the follow-up appointment, the physician took the time to thoroughly address the concerns of both the patient and his wife. Moreover, the doctor understood that traveling was difficult for the couple so he personally ensured that the gentleman could be scheduled for all his necessary tests that day, thereby avoiding the need for a return trip. At the conclusion of the appointment, the physician even walked the couple through the medical center to their next appointment. This is the type of doctor I aspire to become. I want to be there for my patients and their families, not solely as their medical doctor, but also as someone to lend a helping hand.

Upon entering college, I progressed nearer my goal of becoming a physician. I deliberately selected my undergraduate major of medical technology because it assured me extensive patient contact and relevant clinical experience. During my clinical laboratory science internship, I had the opportunity to play an active role in patient care. Through my internship, I also discovered my inherent ability to thrive in high pressure situations, such as the trauma case. Aside from completing a demanding internship at the top of my class, I sought out a part time job as a hospital phlebotomist so I could interact to a greater extent with patients. As a phlebotomist, I further realized I possessed the ability to comfort and gain the trust of even the most apprehensive patients.

Upon completing my internship, I advanced toward my aspiration of becoming a physician by accepting a position in Transfusion Medicine at Mayo Clinic. Not only did this experience provide me vital clinical experience, it also presented me with numerous emergent situations, where patients' outcomes hinged on my ability to rapidly prepare blood and plasma products for transfusion. I found these "stat" situations particularly valuable because they provided me the occasion to function in a leadership capacity by communicating directly with the patient's primary physician and prudently monitoring inventory levels to avoid exhausting supplies of rarer blood types.

Now, as I find myself in the final stretch of preparation for medical school, I am a laboratory technologist at Altru Hospital in Grand Forks, ND. This job has brought me yet closer to my goal by allowing me increased responsibility and a greater impact on patient care. Moreover, I have further explored my interest in medicine through additional physician shadowing experiences, and I have continued my tradition of volunteering. At the culmination of these experiences, I am confident in my ability to relate to patients with true compassion, to be a leader and a teacher, and to enter medical school with the enthusiasm that will enable me to develop into an admirable physician by working as a true advocate for the patients I intend to serve.

See page 253 to find out where this student got in.

CHRISTINA AHN

Christina graduated with distinction from Stanford University and was initiated into the Phi Beta Kappa Society. She gained valuable research experience through projects in organometallic chemistry as well as in an internship at a local pharmaceutical company, Roche Bioscience. Outside of medicine, she served as a pit orchestra conductor and was the principal violinist in the Lagunita Piano Trio, which performed at the Bing Concert Series at Stanford Hospital, among other venues. She was also a featured soloist on the soundtrack of the animated short film "Cat Ciao." In addition, Christina was an active volunteer spending time in the ER, abroad in Haiti caring for children, and at the Arbor Free Health Clinic at Stanford University. When time allowed, she also tutored underprivileged children.

Stats

MCAT: Physical Sciences, 14; Verbal Reasoning, 11; Writing Sample, Q; Biological Sciences, 11
Undergraduate Overall GPA: 3.8
Undergraduate Science GPA: 3.8
Undergraduate College Attended: Stanford University
Undergraduate Graduation Year: 2003
Gender: Female
Race: Asian

Applied To

Columbia University, College of Physicians and Surgeons
Duke University, School of Medicine
Johns Hopkins University, School of Medicine
    Harvard University, Harvard Medical School
Stanford University, School of Medicine
University of California—Los Angeles, David Geffen School
    of Medicine
University of California—San Diego, School of Medicine
University of California—San Francisco, School of Medicine
University of Michigan, Medical School
Washington University in Saint Louis, School of Medicine

AMCAS Personal Statement

It was the busiest time of senior year when the director of Stanford Latter-day Saint's production of "Fiddler on the Roof" approached me about potentially conducting the pit orchestra. Although I was swamped already, I decided to conduct because I knew I would regret it if I didn't try it. Conducting was amazing—I distinctly remember the feeling of the dark wood of the baton in my hand, and tracing out patterns in the mirror to practice the movements. I remember changing tempos incorrectly and laughing with the rest of the orchestra as we ended in cacophony. And I remember the darkened hush of the full auditorium at the start of each performance as a lone violin played a lilting melody at my command.

I knew I would regret it if I didn't try it. These words not only described my decision to conduct, but also my journey to realizing that I wanted to become a doctor. In high school and college, I was fascinated by organic chemistry—how one could start with A, B, and C, simple molecules, and end up with D, a branching, complex molecule that could be a potential pharmaceutical. Dr. Dave Smith taught me in a chemistry class and suggested that I apply for a summer position at Roche, a pharmaceutical company in Palo Alto, CA. Intrigued, I took him up on his offer. Under his supervision, I learned how to attach side groups to a simple precursor molecule, how to purify products from each reaction, and how to analyze each intermediate compound. In the end, I synthesized nine potential drugs for osteoporosis for the company. I really enjoyed the intellectual challenge and the potential future benefit of my research, but I was interested in medicine and wanted to give it a chance.

Then my advisor brought up the possibility of my going to Haiti. At first, I thought she was out of her mind. But after several months of debating, I knew volunteering there was the perfect opportunity to get clinical experience while helping others. When I arrived in Haiti, I saw shoeless young children picking through garbage on the roads and dozens of crazily painted pick-up trucks called tap-taps crammed with people. Almost immediately, I was surprised and humbled by the people. One Haitian boy taught me how to paint. Another taught me that "Ki-jun oi-ye?" is "How are you?" in Creole. I had thought I would be the only one giving and teaching, but instead they were teaching me.

I also realized in Haiti the energy demands of physicians when I volunteered at Mother Teresa's Clinic for Young Children and Babies. The children at this clinic were abandoned or in need of medical care. All of the children showed signs of malnutrition, their ribs making ridges in their dark skin. Every day, I fed bananas to the older children and creamy mash to the younger ones. I changed diapers and held countless children in my arms. There was a lot of work to be done, but knowing that I was helping even in such a small capacity gave me endless amounts of energy. From this experience, I knew that I wanted to help others in need and had to be in a profession that I could be passionate about.

To explore my interest in medicine further, I participated in SCOPE (Shadowing for Clinical Opportunities and Premedical Experience). Every week, I spent an eight-hour shift in the emergency room helping the doctor I was assigned to with his work. There, I saw amazing technique: one doctor did a successful spinal tap on a convulsing woman. I also saw horrible tragedies—a man went into cardiac arrest because of a blood clot in his brain, leaving him a vegetable, while his two daughters cried in the corner of the operating room. In the ER, life and death coexisted— and yet, through it all, the doctors used their skill to help people regain their health. And the fact that they tried—and I knew then that I wanted to chance to try—is what matters.

This year, I am exploring my commitment to medicine by doing clinical research at the San Francisco Veteran Affairs Hospital on spinal cord injuries. Dr. Bobby Tay and I are currently trying to reverse some of the damage from spinal cord injury with a cell death inhibitor and are testing it on mice. We do spinal cord surgeries for the experiment, and I remember one surgery I did vividly—quickly slicing through the pink muscle to expose the white spine, snipping away both sides of the butterfly shaped bone, and picking out the bone shards leaving a square window. There it was— white soft tissue, the spinal cord—and one thin red blood vessel running vertically down the middle. My first perfect laminectomy. I couldn't help grinning like an idiot—it was that satisfying.

After the end of each performance of "Fiddler on the Roof," I was a multitude of emotions—happy, proud of my orchestra and bone weary. But I was buoyed by the knowledge that the best was still to come—the exit music after the bows. Free from restrictions given by singers, dancers, producers and directors, we flew, transforming tempered marches into a pounding race. The escalating tempo of our music gave me energy that I didn't know I had—and I see now all at once how the driven passion of the ER doctors, the Haitian babies warm in my cradled arms, the beauty of a perfect laminectomy are all signals of what can be done, what can happen, what one can learn, if one is unafraid to try—and I am excited to find what my future holds.

See page 253 to find out where this student got in.

COLLEEN KNIFFIN

Colleen volunteered for a year with a medical service organization in Africa before attending college. While in school, she continued to work in the medical field and held a job as a patient care technician at a local hospital. She also oversaw a campus-wide mentoring program, organized an annual conference on volunteer service, and ran freshman orientation.

Stats

MCAT: Physical Sciences, 11; Verbal Reasoning, 10; Writing Sample, S; Biological Sciences, 12
Undergraduate overall GPA: 3.77
Undergraduate science GPA: 3.70
Undergraduate college attended: Wheaton College (IL)
Gender: Female
Race: Caucasian

Applied To

Baylor College of Medicine
Loma Linda University, School of Medicine
University of California—Davis, School of Medicine
University of California—Los Angeles, David Geffen School of Medicine
University of California—San Diego, School of Medicine
University of Illinois at Chicago, UIC College of Medicine
University of Minnesota—Duluth, Medical School
University of Minnesota—Twin Cities, Medical School
University of Southern California, Keck School of Medicine

AMCAS Personal Statement

I remember waking that morning to the rooster's crow just as the sun peaked over treetops of the rain forest. By that time, the small Ghanaian village was already bustling with activity as people left to work in the cocoa fields. I fumbled in the folds of my mosquito net until I found the opening and slid my feet onto the cold cement floor. Locating some clothes stacked on the floor of my perpetually dark mud hut, I dressed quickly and made my way to the mission compound, greeting each villager along the way with "Daayo" ("good morning" in Twí).

I soon found the doctor that I was shadowing during my two month stay in the village (the second portion of a five month program with the medical non-profit organization, Mercy Ships). Dr. Gurling introduced me to a young African who had stepped on a thorn a week earlier. Following his tribal practice, the boy had packed the large wound with mud, leading to an infection. Dr. Gurling, who needed to see other patients, asked if I would care for the boy. I gathered antiseptics and knelt down to clean the wound. Between winces of pain, the patient flashed me beautiful smiles of gratitude. I fought back tears of joy as he hugged me when I finished. If the doctor or I had not been there to help, the boy's foot would have become dangerously infected. My tears flowed from the knowledge that I had given a gift that the boy may not otherwise have received—health.

There is something significant about providing healthcare. Even more extraordinary is offering health to those who would otherwise be helpless. Someday, whether by traveling again to a small Ghanaian village or by volunteering weekly in an inner city clinic, I want to be involved in giving health to those in desperate need. Obtaining that ability is one thing that greatly excites me about becoming a physician.

From another experience with Mercy Ships, I can recall the lines, a thousand people long, on the pier next to the hospital ship. During this screening week the Africans would wait for days hoping to get a doctor's appointment. Had that ship not been there, many would have suffered to their death. But, because a handful of doctors used their vacation time to volunteer in Africa, those otherwise hopeless people were given health. I want to be involved in that type of medical work.

There are many other ways to bring relief to suffering and desperate people. Doing social work or lobbying for the underprivileged offer good alternatives. So then, "Why medicine?" you may ask. "Why accrue a huge educational debt and dedicate many years in medical training?" I struggled with this question for a while myself and, after much introspection, have formulated two answers.

First, my passion for providing desperate people with healthcare is conveniently supported by both my aptitude and affinity for scientific study. Throughout high school and college biology and chemistry classes have been my most rewarding and enjoyable academic pursuits. I love the sense of achievement when I finally understand how a complicated chemical reaction progresses. While my classmates are preparing to graduate from college and "been done with school", I feel I have only sipped from the ocean of information that I want to learn. There is so much to know about the structure and function of the human body.

Second, through my hospital work experience I witnessed the profound emotional effects that can be made on people by simply healing their body. I remember realizing this during one night in particular. I was bathing an elderly woman who was very sick and quite delirious. As I changed her diaper I recall wondering why I was at a job where so much of my work was not even comprehended by those I was helping. It smelled bad. I was tired. I wanted to go home. A few moments later, however, as I rubbed lotion into her feet, the elderly woman opened her eyes, grasped my hand, and gave me that same unforgettable look that I had seen on the African boy. She smiled because I had tended for her physically and, being near death, she cared about her health above all else. The gleam in the woman's eyes, however, also revealed that through my corporeal touch, I had ministered to her emotionally as well. At that moment I realized the strong impact that one can have on people, emotionally as well as physically, who are desperate for medical attention. This experience confirmed my desire to provide healthcare above any other type of social service.

I recognize that I hold lofty ideals of serving those who would otherwise receive no care. However, these dreams are also balanced by a comprehension of the difficult realities of medicine. Through my job at the hospital I learned that overnight shifts are not easy. There is endless paperwork. Decisions need to be quick and correct despite stressful conditions. And most importantly, patients do not often offer the "grateful African boy" smile.

These truths, although they have not frustrated my dreams, have caused me to realize the amount of discipline, dedication and unshakable vision that will be required to achieve my goals. I am ready for the challenge.

See page 254 to find out where this student got in.

DAN NAYLOR

Dan volunteered for two-and-a-half years on a research project that examined the relationship between a "Western"— i.e. high sugar, high fat, low fiber—diet and the chronic low-level inflammation characteristic of a number of disease states. He also worked for a year at a lab that focused on iron absorption and metabolism research. At school, he was a member of the University of California Marching Band for four years and achieved many leadership positions within the group. He was also a leader in the music program of a religious fellowship for a year. He shadowed a local pediatrician for a semester and worked at the biosciences library on campus.

Stats

MCAT: Physical Sciences, 11; Verbal Reasoning, 10; Writing Sample, Q; Biological Sciences, 14
Undergraduate overall GPA: 3.46
Undergraduate science GPA: 3.38
Undergraduate college attended: University of California—Berkeley
Gender: Male
Race: Caucasian

Applied To

Boston University, School of Medicine
Case Western Reserve University, School of Medicine
Dartmouth College, Dartmouth Medical School
Drexel University, College of Medicine
Duke University, School of Medicine
George Washington University, School of Medicine and Health Sciences
Georgetown University, School of Medicine
Harvard University, Harvard Medical School
Johns Hopkins University, School of Medicine
Loma Linda University, School of Medicine
New York Medical College
New York University, NYU School of Medicine
Northwestern University, Feinberg School of Medicine
Oregon Health & Science University, School of Medicine
Pennsylvania State University, College of Medicine
Stanford University, School of Medicine
Thomas Jefferson University, Jefferson Medical College
Tulane University, School of Medicine

University of California—Davis, School of Medicine
University of California—Irvine, College of Medicine
University of California—Los Angeles, David Geffen School
   of Medicine
University of California—San Diego, School of Medicine
University of California—San Francisco, School of
   Medicine
University of Chicago, Pritzker School of Medicine
University of Michigan, Medical School
University of Vermont, College of Medicine
University of Southern California, Keck School of Medicine
Vanderbilt University, School of Medicine
Yale University, School of Medicine

AMCAS Personal Statement

The shrill sound of the whistle echoed through the tunnel, and nervous anticipation quickly turned to excitement as we rushed onto the field. After hours of practice learning and refining the skills necessary to put on a dazzling performance with the University of California Marching Band, I finally high-stepped into Memorial Stadium for the first time, and was suddenly surrounded by tens of thousands of fans. The long, exhausting days of training and a spirit of dedication to the university showed their value in a performance that left those in the stadium cheering with pride and appreciation.

I devoted countless hours over the next four years to this entirely student-run organization. I served through numerous leadership roles, involving everything from leading musical rehearsals and interacting with big financial donors at fundraising events, to performing first aid duties such as bandaging light wounds and calling 911 for band members in life-threatening situations. On a campus of over fifteen times the number of people living in my rural hometown, the band was an effective way to develop a sense of belonging. However, the transition to college was less successful than I had hoped. I found myself caught up in the new experiences of living with hundreds of people my own age, band-related commitments and a part-time job. With so many distractions, my grades suffered, and I ended my first year frustrated but motivated to improve. That summer, I excelled in my organic chemistry class, and having convinced myself that I could do well, I renewed my long-developing interest in becoming a physician. I decided to pursue a major in molecular and cell biology, and focused on learning more about the profession.

There is no single event in my life that I look back on and say, "This is when I decided to become a doctor." Though my mother is a clinical laboratory scientist, neither of my parents is a doctor, and they never specifically suggested that I become one. For me, the decision has been more gradual and natural. I've always loved investigating the world around me: I happily caught lizards in the front yard at five years old, and was looking at blood smears under my mom's microscope at age ten. During middle and high school, my reading interests centered on a number of books about veterinarians, neurosurgeons, and the deadly Ebola virus. More recently, I've confirmed my ability to think scientifically, perform detailed procedures, and produce accurate results in collaboration with other scientists during my internship and employment in a nutritional genomics laboratory at Children's Hospital in Oakland, California. We are attempting to elucidate the connection between a poor diet and low-level inflammatory conditions such as childhood obesity, diabetes, arthrosclerosis, and possibly even cancer. My own work consists primarily of observing gene expression in the tissues of mice chosen from inflammation-prone genetic backgrounds and fed a variety of unhealthy diets. Through this study, I hope to see evidence of an increase in inflammatory mediators brought on by the bad diets.

As a complement to my scientific interests, I've always been drawn to care for and motivate others. This has been most evident in my work with children at summer day camps in the eight years before college, during which I rose to become a senior leader in the last three years, and my people-oriented leadership in the Cal Band. I have also begun supporting and encouraging others with my interest in music, playing the guitar and singing at my church. It has been a natural, more personal extension of my ability to lead others than was expressed through the Cal Band. I have led musical worship regularly now for the college and high school groups, and for the adult religious services, attended by hundreds of people.

Hoping to acquire some grasp of the trials doctors face every day in the practice of their scientific and relational talents, I recently shadowed a pediatrician over the course of a semester. I became more clearly aware of the breadth of a doctor's responsibilities: the long days, extensive paperwork, and the daily confrontation with the heart-tugging trials of human life. And I resolutely accept them, because from the very first visit with this doctor, I began to see just how rewarding the profession can be.

"Dr. Wolffe" was a huge man with a heart to match. I followed him down the silent hallway into the examination room for the first time, and there sat a young Latina mother gently cradling her child, only a few weeks old. The doctor's evident confidence in his years of training and his commitment to medical science, complemented by his ability to truly care for someone, showed their value in the trusting smile on the face of that young woman. This and every other visit helped me realize that my lifelong attraction to the medical profession does not arise from a grand vision to rid the world of cancer or childhood obesity. Rather, it is my intention to use my growing knowledge and skills in concert with my concern for others to fight such problems, one person at a time.

See page 254 to find out where this student got in.

DEEPIKA RAO

Deepika followed her passion for human rights and International health to Thailand, where she studied malaria and tropical medicine for a year. She also spent a year researching blood coagulation at a medical school and is a trained EMT. When not spending time in hospitals, Deepika is an avid traveler and performs Indian Classical Dance.

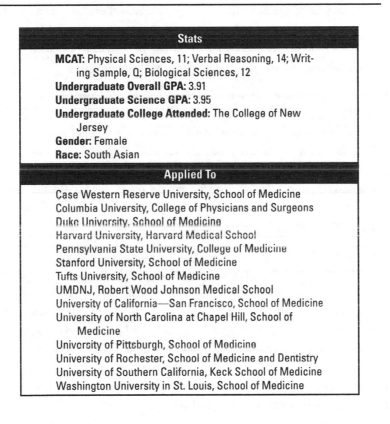

Stats
MCAT: Physical Sciences, 11; Verbal Reasoning, 14; Writing Sample, Q; Biological Sciences, 12
Undergraduate Overall GPA: 3.91
Undergraduate Science GPA: 3.95
Undergraduate College Attended: The College of New Jersey
Gender: Female
Race: South Asian

Applied To
Case Western Reserve University, School of Medicine
Columbia University, College of Physicians and Surgeons
Duke University, School of Medicine
Harvard University, Harvard Medical School
Pennsylvania State University, College of Medicine
Stanford University, School of Medicine
Tufts University, School of Medicine
UMDNJ, Robert Wood Johnson Medical School
University of California—San Francisco, School of Medicine
University of North Carolina at Chapel Hill, School of Medicine
University of Pittsburgh, School of Medicine
University of Rochester, School of Medicine and Dentistry
University of Southern California, Keck School of Medicine
Washington University in St. Louis, School of Medicine

AMCAS Personal Statement

In the Indian dance form Bharatnatyam, the dancer is whole and yet divided. She is part musician, part storyteller, part athlete, part divine. She must be graceful and powerful, conscious of every angle of her body but entangled in the dance, alert to the rhythm but lost in the music. She is a thousand paradoxes, and yet she is as complete and beautiful as the human body itself. Twelve years of training has taught me dedication, discipline, and tested my determination. A lifetime as a dancer has opened me to all the experiences that have shaped the steps of the art that is my passion and my future: medicine.

A physical consciousness was born of my training – an understanding of the joining and limits of tendon and bone, a fascination with the workings of this beautiful, familiar, yet mysterious body. Through this awareness, I have developed a deep passion for science - especially medicine.

When the staff at the Medical Center at Princeton's ER realized my interest in doctoring, they took interest in me as well. I learned the basics of suturing and sterile technique, of chest X-rays and EKGs. I watched a team of doctors and nurses push a chest tube through a young man's intercostals as they reinflated his left lung, and was amazed at the beauty of their work. Like a well-coordinated dance, their synchronized movements flowed with the ease and grace of practiced precision.

One evening, screaming drew me to a curtained cubicle where doctors and nurses surrounded a scared little boy with a gash in his forehead. Without thinking, I held his hand and began singing nursery rhymes, trying to distract him from the suture. He tried to sing with me, between shrieks, and when the nurses freed him he threw his little body into my arms and clung tightly until his mother came. The emotions that went through me are hard to describe, but the happiness I felt in that moment I can never forget. I realized that the healing power of medicine is the ability to bond with and comfort another human being.

Later, my research with Dr. S on blood coagulation furthered my love of science, and I gained more than research experience. Under his guidance, I learned to dissect journal articles, to design experiments, to write papers, and to be proactive, knowledgeable, and aware. During this time, I was also able to join residents and attendings on morning and grand rounds in the ICUs of NJMS. Amidst the yawns and coffee cups of those morning sessions, I carefully studied the injuries and treatments of the patients, and later brought to Dr. S my questions about sepsis and multiple organ failure. I saw patients place their lives in the hands of these doctors, and I saw the doctors' expertise and worthiness of that trust.

But gritty experience has also taught me that even doctors are sometimes helpless: against disease and insurance policies – and patients themselves. During the long nights I shadowed Dr. A in a pediatric ER, I learned what it is to be helpless. I failed to convince a teenage girl to change her dangerous sexual habits, despite her syphilis. I watched teen mothers dump their screaming, sick children in a cubicle and escape to the cafeteria. For the first time, I confronted the fear of losing a patient as we rushed to the bedside of a young man who coded. And through all this I could see the depth of compassion and understanding in Dr. A and her colleagues, and I admired their dedication.

I could see this dedication in the malaria wards of Bangkok as well. I had chosen to go to Thailand because I had completed the requirements of my undergraduate Biology degree in two years, and wanted to explore my interest in tropical medicine: a field woefully neglected in the United States but one that is central to international health. I created internships with Bangkok's Faculty of Tropical Medicine to study different aspects of the field – parasitic and viral disease, vector control, drug resistance. I worked in labs where research had an almost immediate impact on treatment methods in wards and rural areas. I attended classes and seminars with Ph.D. students and practicing physicians from around the world. I spent hours in the malaria wards, where every bed was occupied by a sick and bewildered villager. There, I saw how medicine and its practitioners, like art and its performers, transcend all social, cultural, and linguistic barriers.

Like dance, medicine has the power to connect different people, just as my experiences in the different cultures of Asia and the Middle East will help me to better understand my patients. Doctoring is the only profession where the entirety of one's career is dedicated to another's well being, and it is the only profession in which I can find the intellectual challenge, honor, and moral satisfaction I seek.

I have watched the physician's art in motion but have yet to learn the steps, to practice them, to perform them. The qualities I admire most in a dancer are those I admire most in a physician, and those I would like to see in myself: a keen understanding of and respect for the body; maturity, discipline, and honor; sensitivity to what is not obvious; empathy and communicativeness; skill honed by practice, a fighter's spirit – and complete commitment to the art.

See page 255 to find out where this student got in.

DREW JOEL SCHWARTZ

Drew competed internationally as an equestrian in three-day eventing and had a leadership role with Relay for Life. He conducted two years of independent research, three semesters of which were in organic synthesis, for which he received a scholarship from the North Carolina American Chemical Society. He also received a biochemistry fellowship to work in microbiology.

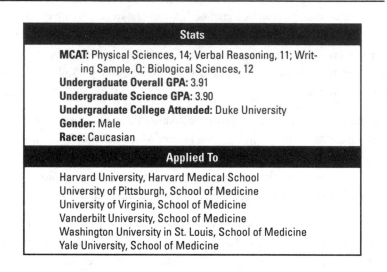

Stats
MCAT: Physical Sciences, 14; Verbal Reasoning, 11; Writing Sample, Q; Biological Sciences, 12
Undergraduate Overall GPA: 3.91
Undergraduate Science GPA: 3.90
Undergraduate College Attended: Duke University
Gender: Male
Race: Caucasian

Applied To
Harvard University, Harvard Medical School
University of Pittsburgh, School of Medicine
University of Virginia, School of Medicine
Vanderbilt University, School of Medicine
Washington University in St. Louis, School of Medicine
Yale University, School of Medicine

AMCAS Personal Statement

I remember in May of this year watching empathetically as Barbaro uncomfortably galloped on three legs attempting to reach the finish line at the Preakness. Many fans shared in the disappointment and profound sadness of a champion's misfortune, but I understood in a way many could not. In the fall of 2004 I was competing in the national championships of three-day eventing, the equestrian triathlon and most dangerous horse-related sport. During the most demanding phase of cross-country, my horse and I miscommunicated. I fell off, crashing to the ground. I could feel a sharp pain in my knee, but I had to continue. I willed myself to keep going, to keep fighting, just as Barbaro did. I threw myself back on my horse using only my right leg and pushed on. I struggled against the pain and finished the difficult, championship-level course, collapsing on my horse. The competition was not over, though, because the final phase still loomed. The next morning my knee was the size of a grapefruit, and I could not straighten my leg. My horse and I navigated the final phase of show jumping and we completed the national championships. But, just completing did not satisfy my grand expectations. I had trained so hard for so long and had expected to place very highly. But like Barbaro, my dream would go unrealized due to injury.

The best professionals cared for me. Each day of physical therapy during my convalescence was more challenging than the one before, but the doctors assured me that soon I would be able to ride again. Nevertheless, I felt handicapped. My knee affected my friends as well. At the North Carolina state fair, I asked my friends if we could leave early because of the pain. I became overwhelmed with frustration. Eventually, I found it easier to sit in the dorm by myself, allowing my friends to have fun without me. Although this was the most difficult time of my life, it afforded me ample time to re-evaluate.

After some time sulking in my dorm room, I realized that I was not as paralyzed by pain as I thought. I could change this feeling, maybe not for me, but possibly for others in similar situations. It was in this time of adversity that my life goal became aiding others in similar struggles. I did not want others to feel the pain of unfulfilled potential and handicap as a result of an injury or disease. I wanted to give others what my doctors gave me--a second chance. I thought back to high school to the first time I had considered medicine. The sage advice of my mentor at the time, Mr. Epperson, made me realize that I wanted to be a doctor and aid others just as I was aided.

Mr. Epperson captivated me with both the subject and delivery of his A.P. chemistry and neuroanatomy lectures. At the end of each neuroanatomy class, I had more questions than before the lecture started. He fostered my love of science, encouraging me to investigate further. We would talk for hours about our shared fascination with the brain and chemistry, about which we could not learn enough. To foster this curiosity, he gave me Harold Klawans' book Defending the Cavewoman. Klawans described his patients presenting with various neurological problems, and he crafted each case story to inspire suspense and encourage the reader to conjecture about the problem. This book provided me the first glimpse of the joy and art of medicine. I wanted to investigate problems and discover solutions just as he did.

Sitting captive in the dorm room, my thoughts drifted from those high school conversations to my passion: my eight-year history with horses. Recalling the long hours of work to become an international competitor, I wondered if the same character traits I developed then could aid me as a physician. Each day, my horses required over three hours of training and care. Although it was difficult to maintain schoolwork, friendships, hobbies, and other sports, I dedicated myself to my horses. I prioritized being successful and maintaining healthy horses over normal high school activities. Some weekends we drove over five hours to competitions while others I had riding lessons to maintain progress in the sport. With this time commitment, I had to develop time management skills. There was little free time after finishing horse chores, soccer, and homework, but the lack of free time did not bother me. Instead, I focused on the horses because I loved them. The sport I loved most required hard work and dedication, much like a career in medicine. I felt assured that I had the discipline necessary.

All of these thoughts crystallized my desire and resolve to become a doctor. While not the first time I considered medicine, this was the defining moment when I knew I needed to be a doctor. Since then, I have dedicated myself to the pursuit of medicine by experiencing patient care as a patient advocate in the hospital, shadowing a primary care physician, and participating in medically-related extracurricular activities. Barbaro will never win the Triple Crown, and I will never win the championship, but I now have a more important goal in mind--helping others overcome medical obstacles in the pursuit of their dreams.

See page 256 to find out where this student got in.

DUSTIN Y. YOON

Dustin published seven papers as an undergraduate; served as a Trauma Resuscitation Volunteer at University of Maryland Shock Trauma; worked and as a teaching assistant in the chemistry department and was appointed to the Academic Ethics Board Committee at Johns Hopkins; made Omicron Delta Kappa Honor Society and Dean's List; and received a Howard Hughes research award and the Fogarty International Fellowship Award. He also worked as a softball coach and the director of a youth summer camp.

Stats
Undergraduate overall GPA: 3.79
Undergraduate college attended: Johns Hopkins University
Major: Public health, biotechnology
Degree earned: BA, MS
Gender: Male
Race: Asian

Applied To
Case Western Reserve University, Cleveland Clinic Lerner College of Medicine
Drexel University, College of Medicine
George Washington University, School of Medicine and Health Sciences
Georgetown University, School of Medicine
Johns Hopkins University, School of Medicine
Thomas Jefferson University, Jefferson Medical College
University of Maryland, School of Medicine
University of Pennsylvania, Perelman School of Medicine
University of Rochester, School of Medicine and Dentistry
Vanderbilt University, School of Medicine
Yale University, Yale School of Medicine

AMCAS Personal Statement

I never knew that someone could cry without shedding tears. It seemed so unnatural to me. Yet there I was witnessing a mother and her baby both crying, but too dehydrated and weak to shed tears. The woman was desperately clinging to her three-month-old son who was dying of kwashiorkor. She looked at us with the belief that we were miracle workers evident in her eyes. After an exchange of clicks and intonations in Xhosa, the translator said, "She says, 'I do not want to breastfeed my baby because my breast milk is poison; my first child died because I fed her my breast milk.'"

This was the bleak situation we saw upon our arrival in the village hospital of Umtata, South Africa, 20 miles from any known source of running water. But I was not a miracle worker. I was not even a health-care professional. I was merely a college student trying to comfort this mother and gently debunk her belief that an evil spirit was living in her breast milk. Convicted to answer her desperate call for help, I nervously clasped her gaunt hands and talked with the translator. I soon realized that even a vast amount of medical knowledge could not have swayed this mother's mind. Despite this, my team was blessed with the opportunity to describe the nutrients in her breast milk to her. After an hour of seemingly fruitless labor, we finally convinced the mother to breastfeed her son. On that day, we got a small taste of what performing miracles was really like.

My desire to become a doctor has always existed with a two-fold purpose: to teach, and heal, the sick. Growing up, I wanted to become the world's best teacher. I was amazed at the power that teachers possessed to make a difference in their student's lives. In middle school, I first developed strong social skills and the passion to teach the underserved. Every week, I accompanied my mother to Korean nursing homes, where I taught English and washed out the eyes of the elderly. These individuals had so much wax in their eyes that they could no longer see properly. My fervor to teach prompted me to become a Teaching Assistant in the Chemistry department at Johns Hopkins, where I won the school's teaching award. Lecturing to a group of 90 students at a time, I witnessed the importance of clear and effective communication when presenting new ideas. What I had once learned in the classroom became the crux of my lectures and lab meetings. Principle became practice.

My enthusiasm, however, was not limited to the classroom, but expanded into the clinical and spiritual settings as well. After serving as a public health assistant in South Africa, my desire to practice medicine in socially disadvantaged communities was re-affirmed. I volunteered in the Episcopal Migration Ministry at the Baltimore Resettlement Center where I helped African immigrants obtain visas, employment I-9 eligibility records, and receive health tests to ensure their political asylum status. However, this was not enough to satiate my hunger to serve. My spirituality became a priority and guiding force that conferred a deep sense of peace and happiness in my life. I ardently involved myself with the ministry at church where I became the Youth Director, a bible study teacher, and the praise band lead guitarist, all of which required not only leading by words, but also by example.

It was during this time that I decided to spend a year in the division of pediatric neurology at Johns Hopkins as a laboratory technician. I researched the pharmaco-genetics of Tourette Syndrome (TS) with the goal of finding an association between the genetic variations in dopamine/serotonin receptors and the etiology of TS. It was in this laboratory and clinical setting that I witnessed the debilitating effects of TS in children and the desperate need for medical research.

By involving myself in teaching, medical research, and public health work I have cultivated a passion to utilize the gifts that I have been bestowed upon. But when I interacted with the elderly or the sick mothers in Africa, I always wished I could do more than hold their hands. Someday, I hope to go back to that village hospital in Umtata, not as a timid young man, but as a confident and promising miracle worker-- in the guise of a doctor.

Turn to page 256 to see where this student got in.

EDDIE SILVER

Eddie shadowed an orthopedic surgeon the summer before his senior year and was involved in one of the doctor's research projects. He also played on the varsity tennis team and intramural basketball team and worked at a Hillel Soup Kitchen.

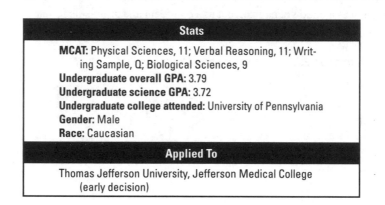

Stats
MCAT: Physical Sciences, 11; Verbal Reasoning, 11; Writing Sample, Q; Biological Sciences, 9
Undergraduate overall GPA: 3.79
Undergraduate science GPA: 3.72
Undergraduate college attended: University of Pennsylvania
Gender: Male
Race: Caucasian
Applied To
Thomas Jefferson University, Jefferson Medical College (early decision)

AMCAS Personal Statement

I want to dedicate myself to the study of medicine because I have a very strong interest in health, nutrition, and rehabilitative and preventative medicine, and believe that there is no better way for me to contribute to society. Over the past few years, the reading I have most enjoyed includes the latest medical and nutritional research, as well as issues in medical sociology. There is nothing that I would find more worthwhile than studying and practicing medicine.

Attending college in West Philadelphia has afforded me a glimpse into the vast economic disparities that plague our communities. As a director of Hillel's Sunday Night Soup Kitchen, I spend time with economically and socially disadvantaged individuals each week, and have experienced first hand the correlation between economic well-being and health, which has been thoroughly illustrated to me as a Health and Societies major at Penn. Volunteering at the soup kitchen has been both an educational and motivating experience. I have learned about some of the medical issues that face the working and non-working poor, including nutritional deficiencies, child health care needs, and prescription coverage problems. While it has been rewarding to participate in this food distribution program, I believe it would be even more satisfying to directly impact people's lives as a physician. I want to study medicine because of the dire need for quality health care for the economically disadvantaged, and hope to be a part of a generation of physicians who work towards lessening health and social disparities.

I credit my initial interest in health and nutrition largely to my passionate desire to succeed in sports. The abuse I have done to my body as an athlete made me a permanent fixture in my orthopedist's office throughout my high school and college athletic careers. My freshman tennis season in high school was over before it ever started due to hamstring tendonitis. After a frustrating year without tennis, I hit the courts as a sophomore determined to improve my game. That spring I had a successful campaign at number one singles, and spent every Saturday and Sunday working on my game for several hours a day. By the time I played the first national tournament of the summer, I had so thoroughly weakened my ankles that an awkward landing on my foot after an overhead attempt left me with two fractures and ligament damage in my left ankle. After a vigorous summer rehabilitation process, I again made it back to the courts, this time with such determination that I achieved my best national junior singles ranking of 138.

My college tennis career has only reinforced the reality that my body was not meant for hitting tennis balls eighteen hours a week. Each year I played through pain, and each summer I rehabilitated a severely weakened rotator cuff and a chronically inflamed biceps tendon. I credit my interest in fitness, strength training, rehabilitative medicine, nutrition, and my own resolve (some might say stubbornness) for my ability to compete in a sport for which my body was not designed. My experience as an athlete has reinforced my belief in the healing power of medicine. I also believe that this experience has helped me to develop my resolve, which should enable me to become a patient, understanding, and dedicated physician.

In the past, I combined my passion for tennis with my desire to help improve the lives of others through my involvement in Arthur Ashe's wheelchair tennis clinics. Helping this group learn to play tennis was most satisfying, and I became more optimistic about the ability to heal the body, mind, and spirit. After my sophomore year in college, I learned about the lives of children suffering from juvenile rheumatoid arthritis, as a counselor at Camp Victory. These experiences reinforced my desire to help others overcome their physical limitations and pain.

This summer I have become even more committed to pursuing a medical career. Volunteering in the Section of Orthopedic Surgery at St. Christopher's Hospital for Children, I have watched my own pediatric orthopedist, Dr. Pizzutillo, and his partner, Dr. Herman, care for children debilitated by hip disease and scoliosis. Observing the very physician who repeatedly expedited my return from injury, and helping him document a study of growth plate ankle fractures in children has been especially interesting.

Please give me the opportunity to gain access to the medical knowledge that will enable me to help narrow the health divide plaguing our country, and assist my future patients in enjoying life to the fullest extent possible.

See page 256 to find out where this student got in.

ELIZABETH KIM

Elizabeth was able to get an early start on med school by taking several first year medical courses while in the Georgetown University Special Masters Program in Physiology and Biophysics. In addition, she has been heavily involved in her church through helping to plan church-wide events, leading and counseling junior high and high school students in the youth group, being involved in evangelical and campus outreach, and teaching at Vacation Bible School. She also plays the violin in chamber music groups and has worked as an MCAT instructor and a high school and college-level science teacher.

Stats
MCAT: Physical Sciences, 11; Verbal Reasoning, 8; Writing Sample, Q; Biological Sciences, 14
Undergraduate Overall GPA: 3.4
Undergraduate Science GPA: 2.9
Undergraduate College Attended: University of California—Berkeley
Gender: Female
Race: Asian American

Applied To
Albany Medical College
Drexel University, College of Medicine
Eastern Virginia Medical School
George Washington University, School of Medicine and Health Sciences
Loma Linda University, School of Medicine
Loyola University Chicago, Stritch School of Medicine
New York Medical College
New York University, NYU School of Medicine
Pennsylvania State University, School of Medicine
Rosalind Franklin University of Medicine & Science
Saint Louis University, School of Medicine
Tufts University, School of Medicine
Tulane University, School of Medicine
UMDNJ, New Jersey Medical School
University of California—Davis, School of Medicine
University of California—Irvine, College of Medicine
University of California—Los Angeles, David Geffen School of Medicine
University of California—San Diego, School of Medicine
University of California—San Francisco, School of Medicine
University of Illinois at Chicago, UIC College of Medicine
University of Maryland, School of Medicine
University of Pittsburgh, School of Medicine
University of Toledo, Health Science Campus
University of South Florida, College of Medicine
University of Southern California, Keck School of Medicine
University of Washington, School of Medicine
Yeshiva University, Albert Einstein College of Medicine

AMCAS Personal Statement

The brilliant spotlight cast itself as the sweat beads on my nose glistened in the light. We had rehearsed countless hours for the opening night of the UC Berkeley Symphony. Hertz Hall, seating nearly 700, was packed as the concert had been sold-out days in advance. It was the first time in the university's history that a recording of the symphony would be sold, and it was being broadcasted live over a popular radio station. Any accident or mistake could ruin everything for the group. Inhaling deeply, I reminded myself that I am and have always been a performer-- pressure drives me to focus and excel. It is this very quality, I believe, that has carried me through the challenges of balancing the demanding but rewarding schedule preparing me for the medical field.

Having been born at a county hospital at no expense to my then-destitute parents, I was cognizant at an early age of how much I wanted to give back to the needy community as a doctor. Thence began my life-long pursuit to become a physician. That desire brewed until high school, when I chaired the World Health Organization committee at my school's Model U.N. conference. After discussing health issues for an entire weekend and coming up with mock resolutions, I realized that these resolutions would never be put into effect unless there were people willing to volunteer their lives to improve society's worst health problems. That wake-up call further established my commitment to the field of medicine. Since then, my reasons have been solidified and my unrelenting zeal for the field continues to shape my present.

Identifying an ability to deal well in emergencies, I volunteered at the Children's Hospital Emergency Department where I was able to witness the manifold responsibilities of a physician. Interestingly, the insights I gained while spending those midnights in the E.R. were quite contrary to my initial appetite for technical medical skills and knowledge. Yes, learning suture techniques and assisting surgeries in minor ways excited me, but more so, I valued the meaningful connections with patients and their families. I got to put a rub-on tattoo of a roaring lion on a boy's arm, bringing unanticipated delight and strength to him despite his suffering. I put a consoling arm around a sobbing mother to assuage her worries. I remember reading a bedtime story to a critically-ill, six-year-old friend when her mother left her alone at the hospital that night. I treasured making that positive and noticeable difference, realizing that even the little things speak with a bold voice: Hey, I am here and I care.

This voice echoed in my heart most clearly when I had the short opportunity to meet residents of the Elmwood Convalescent Hospital. During visits, I befriended Grandpa Bill. Though emaciated, bedridden, and fed intravenously, Bill, with his physical atrophy but overwhelmingly conquering spirit, changed my life. We spent one particular Valentine's Day telling jokes in Spanish and I listened to his harmonica rendition of Brahms' Hungarian Dance. But the next time I came to visit Bill, the nurses told me that he was no longer with us. After reflecting, I felt privileged to be a part of Bill's life. It was different to know that there was nothing I, or any doctor or nurse, could do to save him from the clutches of death other than to be there for him during his lonely hours. I hope Bill knew that I was there and I cared.

I have always believed that true sacrifice is when one does not receive personal benefits. Thus, my chief end of becoming a doctor is not to feel accomplished at the end of a long day; I do predict hard times when I will be heartbroken and disappointed. Rather, my desire stems from knowing that I will have something uniquely invaluable to share often: my knowledge, caring support, and words of hope. Whether halfway across the world on medical missions or with the underprivileged a few blocks away, my personal conviction is that becoming a doctor is a significant life decision committed to serving others even before serving myself.

Through the Georgetown Special Masters Program, I have engaged in the academic rigor of pursuing a medical education and have confidence that this is not an unrealistic lifelong dream, but something for which I have the competency. Through teaching and mentoring youth and experience in leading peers, I have learned how to guide with humility and alacrity. Through involvement in church and my personal spiritual growth, I am constantly striving for the integrity of character that such an influential career demands. Through my employment experiences, I have developed interpersonal skills in dealing with strangers, those with special needs, and individuals of ethnically diverse populations. Finally, through my involvement in musical performance, I have learned how to manage panicked situations under the spotlight and the importance of unified teamwork so that 700 occupied seats and some radio listeners could hear a ravishing performance of Brahms' Symphony No. 4. I am genuinely grateful for each of these life experiences, for they have led me to this point in my life where I feel more prepared than ever to enter the medical field.

See page 256 to find out where this student got in.

ERIC RANDOLPH SCOTT

As an undergraduate, Eric participated in bioethics, philosophy, and interdisciplinary academic organizations. He volunteered at a local hospital, worked for the American Cancer Society, and worked with a mentor in the field of oncology. His was on several Dean's Lists, a member of Phi Beta Kappa, and a part of UVA's Echols Scholars Program. He took full advantage of his summers by doing laboratory research and taking summer classes. One summer, he studied comparative bioethics in London. He also participated in religious organizations, intramural sports, and political organizations.

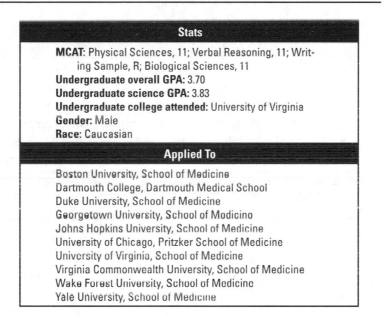

Stats

MCAT: Physical Sciences, 11; Verbal Reasoning, 11; Writing Sample, R; Biological Sciences, 11
Undergraduate overall GPA: 3.70
Undergraduate science GPA: 3.83
Undergraduate college attended: University of Virginia
Gender: Male
Race: Caucasian

Applied To

Boston University, School of Medicine
Dartmouth College, Dartmouth Medical School
Duke University, School of Medicine
Georgetown University, School of Medicine
Johns Hopkins University, School of Medicine
University of Chicago, Pritzker School of Medicine
University of Virginia, School of Medicine
Virginia Commonwealth University, School of Medicine
Wake Forest University, School of Medicine
Yale University, School of Medicine

AMCAS Personal Statement

The world is a harsh place. That is a position I think is indisputable. We all have challenges and obstacles we must overcome. Taking difficult classes, competing with your friends for precious few high grades, or overcoming shyness to approach faculty for recommendation letters. These are obstacles for many people. They are mere trivialities, however, with the proper perspective. The true struggles are those that threaten one's very life and well-being. Nature forces us to face countless difficulties each day; among them epidemics affecting multitudes, bodies wasting away leaving helpless loved ones, or the death of a child–the most innocent of us all. The suffering caused by these natural processes would certainly be sufficient, but there are also those sufferings inflicted on man by man. Combined, these evils can seem overwhelming. I believe it is each man's task to stem this tide of pain in whatever way they are capable.

I cannot claim that the origin of my desire to be a doctor is to help other people. I grew up in a hospital; my first memories are of doctors and hospitals. I had acute lymphoblastic leukemia, and was in and out of the hospital throughout my childhood. Many of these memories are not vague recollections of events, but vivid impressions of emotions–fear, pain, happiness, relief, and hope. For whatever reason I came out of this experience asserting that I wanted to be a doctor, a position I have maintained to this day. The ambition to be a doctor is not one that is discouraged by those around you. It is not hard to see why people are reluctant to leave the medical track, even when they find they are not suited to it. I do not believe I have remained in the track merely out of habit, however. In fact, I think it is almost miraculous the degree to which medicine is what I now desire to do.

My motivation now comes from several perspectives. The first is the pursuit of knowledge. Frankly, I love to learn and participate in the process of discovery. Science, history, literature, mathematics, and politics can all hold my attention. I do not think, however, there is anything more marvelous or contains more mysteries than the human body. Medicine allows me to pursue my desire for scientific knowledge. During my undergraduate years I have also developed a passion for philosophy. Chief among my interests in philosophy is ethics–how we should live our lives. The field of medicine is one that presents (and will continue to present) unique and serious issues that require answers. These problems are not merely abstract, but are faced daily by practitioners and must be answered to set social policy. I have a strong desire to participate in the dialogue to answer these questions. Finally, I have experienced the good that medicine can do. From my experiences as a patient, volunteer, and observer of medical professionals I have a sincere appreciation of the burden placed on a physician. Every visit a doctor makes in a day can dramatically change a life. Each visit is an opportunity to do good, however, and improve someone's quality of life. I cannot imagine a more gratifying life than doing such good on a daily basis.

There have been times I have questioned my resolve to be a physician. The most significant of these, I believe, occurred while I was studying in London. In an off-hand remark the head of admissions to St. Thomas medical school questioned the British policy of accepting students into medical school at the age of eighteen. She reflected: "Sometimes I wonder if what we're doing is right. We're taking our brightest, most creative students and turning them into human computer terminals." This affected me a great deal. I think she gave voice to a concern I had in the back of my mind. Is medicine just about memorizing and regurgitating at the appropriate time? Might a profession in academics be better than being an over-priced reference book? Having given the question thought I think the answer is no. The ideal practice of medicine is not reducible to diagnosis and distribution of drugs. Rather, proper care requires someone to care for the patient. Having experienced prolonged care I am confident the human aspect is not trivial. Receiving medical care can be a very scary thing, and any comforting can reduce the inevitable fear and anxiety. A kind look, pleasant small-talk, or the development of a trusting friendship can each help alleviate distress. A human being who cares is necessary for such relationships to occur, however.

Lastly, I want to be a doctor because I think I would be a good doctor. Despite my other motivations I do not think I could enter a profession that I could not excel in. I have the sincere belief I will be a good doctor, however. I believe I have the analytic and communication skills critical for success. Likewise, I have a temperament and a sympathetic outlook that I think are conducive to long-term success in the medical profession. I believe that to squander ability is wrong. I believe it is a moral imperative to use one's gifts in the proper ways. The medical profession is a proper way to harness potential. Though idealistic, I envision the good doctor as a model human being—using his reason to assist his neighbor in combating evils of the world. This is a vision I would like to have of myself.

Fundamentally the medical profession is based on healing and the reduction of suffering. I believe no other profession has an ethos as noble as that of the medical field. It is an ethos I could envision holding for my entire professional career. Likewise, I am motivated not only by the ends of medicine, but the means as well. The scientific and moral aspects of medicine are things that excite me. I think a good doctor should also understand why they hold their ethos, or they do not hold it at all. The justification for having such a creed is that to heal and relieve suffering are goods, some of the greatest goods men are capable of producing. To argue for the legitimacy of the state Thomas Hobbes claimed that a state of nature would be "solitary, poor, nasty, brutish and short." I believe life can still be that way for many. It is the moral task of each of us to try and eliminate that life not only for ourselves but also those around us. Those in the medical profession are uniquely qualified to aid this goal. By facilitating health, medicine facilitates man's growth, creation, and achievements. I hope I am given the opportunity to participate in such accomplishments.

See page 257 to find out where this student got in.

GEORGE ISSA

George was a volunteer at the Gwinnett Sexual Assault Center, an organization devoted to helping sexually abused children with their recovery, and worked as a Resident Assistant at the University of Georgia for three years. A recipient of the EHS Faculty Outstanding Senior Award, George has taught MCAT, GRE, SAT and PCAT courses for a test preparation company.

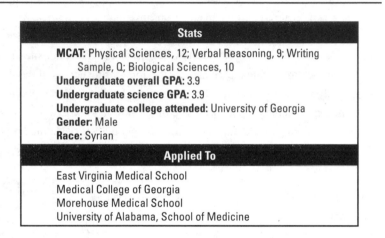

Stats
MCAT: Physical Sciences, 12; Verbal Reasoning, 9; Writing Sample, Q; Biological Sciences, 10
Undergraduate overall GPA: 3.9
Undergraduate science GPA: 3.9
Undergraduate college attended: University of Georgia
Gender: Male
Race: Syrian

Applied To
East Virginia Medical School
Medical College of Georgia
Morehouse Medical School
University of Alabama, School of Medicine

AMCAS Personal Statement

I still remember her name, Danielle. She was eight years old and had been sexually assaulted by her neighbor. Talking to a child about his/her sexual abuse was one of the most difficult experiences I have gone through, but it was my job when I volunteered at the Gwinnett Sexual Assault Center. Listening to Danielle tell me about her experience was heartbreaking. I vividly remember the details of her horrific incident and the pain she had suffered. Yet, despite her ordeal, she once told me, "I know it's not my fault and that I am still a good person. I just want to grow up and not let this happen to others." At that moment I realized that this eight year old girl had more courage, confidence and wisdom than I could only hope to have some day. Her attitude towards life was an eye opening and inspiring moment that has forever ingrained within me the desire to help those in need.

This desire has led me here, to Athens Regional Hospital where I am waiting my turn to apply for a student volunteer position. As I look around, I realize how many people share my aspiration of entering the medical profession. I arrived one hour in advance to the registration time, and yet I am already number 22 on the waiting list.

Everyone here must have their own reasons for pursing one of the most difficult careers in the world. I assume that some of the underlying motivations include the desire to help others, to make a good living, and to be respected within society. However, it is amazing how the last of these three motivations far exceeds any other profession. Numerous public service careers are available that do not require nearly as much education as a doctor. There are also many occupations that can accumulate financial security that far exceeds that of a physician, but I do not know of many professions that are as respected. Doctors are not only those who treat the ill, they are also great humanitarians and well rounded in all aspects of life. This is a level of honor that is not reached by many but that I strive to achieve.

My decision to pursue a career in medicine originated from several years of personally suffering from severe cystic acne. My three brothers and I all had acne, and while we received the aid of many doctors during our teenage years, I do not believe that they acknowledged the severity of the condition. I feel as though they merely saw teenage acne as a minor case in human development. Although it is not a life threatening condition such as diabetes or cancer, acne can have a great emotional impact on the life of an individual and it has left one of my brothers with permanent facial damage. From then on, I decided that I would become a dermatologist focusing on the treatment of acne and other diseases that cause both physical and emotional scarring. I am also considering entering a MD/PHD program so that I can conduct research to help find cures for various skin diseases.

Even though my current field of interest is dermatology, there are many aspects of medicine that fascinate me. Growing up with various health ailments has made me curious about the function of the human body. From having acne, acid reflux disease, a lazy eye and being lactose intolerant, I have always wondered what makes one human body so different than the next. While I do understand the basic principle of many diseases, I would like to learn more about how they are treated and the ways diseases could be healed in the future. There are many fields in the medical profession and I know that my years at medical school will direct me towards a specialty best suited for me.

One of the motivating factors in my career choice has been my aspiration to work hard and achieve the excellence my older brothers have reached. The large age gap between my brothers and I created three close friends that I truly admire. From the endocrinologist, the dentist and the neurobiology professor at Stanford; my brothers have studied relentlessly, made many sacrifices, and have each achieved their dreams. I know that the path I have chosen is arduous, but whenever life gets tough, I think of my brothers whom I have always looked up to for guidance. Visualizing their accomplishments gives me the strength to push through even my most difficult endeavors.

I began this essay at the hospital, but unfortunately could not finish it there. It turns out that I must postpone my volunteering due to a positive TB skin test. Although I am unable to volunteer at the hospital this summer, I plan on doing so starting my senior year and for the remainder of my time prior to medical school. I have since had a TB chest scan in which doctors have determined that I do not have active TB and have prescribed me to take Isoniazid for nine months. Medicine, science and volunteering have been fields that I have always enjoyed. I know that working at the hospital will only reassure me of my decision to pursue this career, and, as a doctor, I will strive to serve my patients not only as a healer but also as a friend.

See page 257 to find out where this student got in.

GWENDOLYN RIDDICK

Gwendolyn was the valedictorian of her high school graduating class and went on to study at East Carolina University. There she was both on the Dean's List and part of the school's Honors Program from which she graduated Magna Cum Laude.

Stats
MCAT: Physical Sciences, 7; Verbal Reasoning, 7; Writing Sample, 0; Biological Sciences, 7
Undergraduate Overall GPA: 3.7
Undergraduate Science GPA: 3.6
Undergraduate College Attended: East Carolina University
Gender: Female
Race: African American

Applied To
Edward Via Virginia College of Osteopathic Medicine

AMCAS Personal Statement

I have selected to pursue a career in the field of medicine because I have a keen desire to rid the world of plagues and diseases through scientific breakthroughs and discoveries. I have always had the desire to help others. Throughout my high school years, I volunteered at the local nursing home, tutored my classmates in math and science, and engaged in community service projects.

My volunteer experience, at the nursing home, gave me the initial inspiration to become a physician. It was an honor and a privilege to serve the elderly patients and to see a smile on their faces when I arrived and departed from the rehabilitation center. I took pleasure in assisting the nursing staff with the patients. I encouraged the patients through singing, conversing, reading, and offering a helping hand. I yearned countless times of one day discovering new medicines and medical treatments that would help alleviate the discomforts that attaches to aging.

My grandfather's diagnosis of leukemia in 1995 motivated me to learn more about medicine. During that time, I didn't fully understand the disease's state and its medical complications. In the hospital's lobby area, I read pamphlets about leukemia and was fascinated with the medical terminology in the brochure. As I continued to read about leukemia, I became additionally interested in how the disease's condition impacts the human body. After my grandfather's death in 1996, I was determined to study medicine and its effects on the physical body.

Also, the birth of my daughter, Aniya Riddick, in November 2001 greatly influenced my educational pursuits. Unexpectedly, I became a single teenage mother during my last year in high school. I was determined to succeed academically because of others who were in like situations. I studied harder and challenged myself by taking advanced classes such as Calculus, Honors Physics, and Advanced Placement English. Also during this time, I served as the senior class President, Vice President of the Student Government Association, and Vice President of the Beta club. At the end of the year, I was recognized as Valedictorian of my high school class. This achievement was the initial plateau of new beginnings for my educational desires and pursuits.

I am determined to receive a medical degree from Edward Via Virginia College of Osteopathic Medicine. After completion of a residency program, I plan to practice medicine in a rural and medically undeserved area. I plan to specialize in gynecology and/or obstetrics. The Virginia College of Osteopathic Medicine will provide me with the opportunity to engage in scientific research. This will allow me to improve the health of all humans globally. To achieve these goals, I realize that I have to become knowledgeable, compassionate, enthusiastic, altruistic, and dutiful.

In closing, I am passionate about providing help and support to others in their time of need; this inspires me to become a physician. A career in medicine will give me the opportunity to provide a service to the public through the diagnosis and treatment of illnesses, diseases, and infections. I have decided to study medicine for a number of reasons: the contributions that can be made to the community, the knowledge and lifetime learning in the profession, the opportunities to work in different communities, and the patient interaction.

See page 258 to find out where this student got in.

HANNAH BROTZMAN

Hannah worked in her school's Community Service Office throughout all four years of college, and also completed an internship at a local hospital. Vice president of her sorority, Hannah completed two years of basic science research in a biochemistry lab and won a few awards for leadership, as well as for her writings on philosophy.

Stats
MCAT: Physical Sciences, 13; Verbal Reasoning, 9; Writing Sample, Q; Biological Sciences, 9
Undergraduate Overall GPA: 3.9
Undergraduate Science GPA: 3.95
Undergraduate College Attended: Lehigh University
Gender: Female
Race: Caucasian

Applied To
Albany Medical College
Boston University, School Of Medicine
Brown University School of Medicine
Dartmouth Medical School
Emory University School of Medicine
Georgetown University, School of Medicine
Ohio State University, College of Medicine
Tufts University, School of Medicine
University of Pennsylvania, School of Medicine
University of Vermont, College of Medicine
Wake Forest University, School of Medicine

AMCAS Personal Statement

"Prove that you exist," said the short, zealous intellectual leaning over my desk. It was my first philosophy class, and as a freshman I was daunted by Dr. Levine's inquisition. Fast-forward to the present. As a senior majoring in philosophy, I have come to anticipate and even appreciate such difficult questions. As a student of philosophy, I am confronted with questions that have challenged thinkers for millennia, and have learned that even the simplest philosophical question requires a thorough and well-reasoned response. Case in point: after three years of studying philosophy, I still have difficulty "proving" to my ethics professor that stealing, and even murder are necessarily wrong. Studying philosophy has taught me that questions are often more complex than they appear. I have also come to recognize that philosophy, like life itself, is about pursuing that which is right, good, and true. For me, aspiring to become a physician is about contributing to the common good--and doing so in a way that matches my innate aptitudes and interests.

Studying philosophy, particularly ethics, has strengthened my interest in becoming a physician. This interest, however, was piqued long before I read a single word of Plato's Republic. When I was twelve, my family moved from a rural Illinois farming community to a much larger city in Missouri. There, my parents took me to a pediatrician for the first time. My new physician was enthusiastic, warm and welcoming--quite unlike the cold-handed, syringe-wielding family doctor I had grown up with. Whereas I'd previously dreaded doctor visits, I now found myself altogether unafraid of upcoming appointments. I would even "attend" when one of my brothers was ill, eagerly yammering off various symptoms and imagined diagnoses. As a result of my pediatrician's patient encouragement, a seed of interest in medicine was planted.

Like my childhood pediatrician, I am interested in, and drawn to children. As a college freshman, working in my school's Community Service Office, I designed and implemented a new service program to combat hunger among the area's poorest citizens. (To my surprise, I learned that the average age of a homeless person in the area was nine years old, and that many of the city's poorest children ate only two meals per day.) In an attempt to address this problem, I began leading groups of Lehigh students to prepare weekly dinners at a local Boys & Girls Club. Initially, our efforts were met with some resistance. Many of the parents did not want to accept charity, and there was palpable tension between the "rich" Lehigh students and their less-fortunate neighbors. With a little persistence, however, our efforts proved fruitful. Soon, the children were lining up to feast on the meals we eagerly served. Moreover, some of the parents began stopping by for a meal, or to express appreciation. By the end of my freshman year, Kids' Café had grown into a daily program, and through the ongoing support of Lehigh volunteers, continues to this day.

As an aspiring physician, I look forward to the opportunity to continue positively impacting others. Although it is impossible to know precisely where a career in medicine will lead me, I have already begun to formulate a vision for my career. I imagine working closely with patients, providing an empathetic and supporting environment in addition to medical expertise. An incident that took place during my semester-long medical externship last year more precisely illustrates the type of doctor-patient relationship I hope to avoid as a physician. During my first day in the Obstetrics/Gynecology department at St. Luke's Hospital in Bethlehem, I was shadowing a resident in charge of prenatal visits. The patient was a nineteen year-old woman, newly married and pregnant for the first time. She and her husband were visibly ecstatic, hanging on the resident's every word and fully expecting to hear that their baby was healthy. When the ultrasound revealed that their baby did not have a heartbeat, however, their smiles gave way to sudden disbelief and anguish. Without a word, the resident bolted from the room to find a specialist, with me in tow. I am sympathetic to the resident's lack of composure, as well as the impulse to seek expert help. Yet, I am struck by how insensitive and unsympathetic we must have appeared to this young couple. As a physician, I would one day hope to demonstrate the kind of empathy, compassion and support needed when dealing with such difficult circumstances. No small feat, I am sure.

I am attracted to the field of medicine because I believe it affords the opportunity to impact others in practical and meaningful ways. Although the idealist in me wants to save the world en masse, I am reminded that the world is, in fact, made up of individuals who must be understood and helped one person at a time. It seems to me that medicine, like other service professions, is at least as much about understanding and improving the human condition as it is about employing one's scientific expertise. John Stuart Mill admonished others to strive for "the greatest good for the greatest number." It seems to me that medicine is a fine place to begin answering such a challenge.

See page 258 to find out where this student got in.

JACQUES COURSEAULT

Jacques has worked a variety of jobs, including an Emergency Medical Technician volunteer, a personal trainer, a college athletic trainer, a CPR instructor, and a construction superintendent. While at Tulane University, he received Psi Chi Honors in psychology, created an organization called "Men of Color," and published articles on psychology.

Stats
MCAT: Physical Sciences, 8; Verbal Reasoning, 8; Writing Sample, Q; Biological Sciences, 10
Undergraduate Overall GPA: 3.95
Undergraduate Science GPA: 3.45
Undergraduate College Attended: Tulane University
Gender: Male
Race: African American

Applied To
Baylor College of Medicine
Duke University, School of Medicine
Emory University, School of Medicine
Johns Hopkins University, School of Medicine
Louisiana State University, School of Medicine
Medical College of Georgia, School of Medicine
Morehouse School of Medicine
Northwestern University, Feinberg School of Medicine
Saint Louis University, School of Medicine
Stanford University, School of Medicine
Tulane University, School of Medicine
Wake Forest University, School of Medicine
Washington University in St. Louis, School of Medicine

AMCAS Personal Statement

Volunteering as an Emergency Medical Technician has confirmed the fact that I am destined for a career in medicine. I have experienced many situations that have allowed me to witness the differing sides of medicine. In a single night I was the hero who helped a girl suffering from an allergic reaction and the opponent who had to restrain a patient that had overdosed on crack cocaine. I felt the relief of a post-ictal seizure patient who was revived from an IV and oxygen, and at the same time witnessed how adequate healthcare was not always provided to the less affluent. My passions are in both feeling the joy of being at another's aid, and also in contributing to improve the healthcare system through research.

I would be an asset to the field of medicine because I have many qualities and skills that are required to be a successful physician. My strongest quality is my very diverse background. My experience has taught me how to communicate with many different types of people. As an EMT, I have realized that you cannot relate to everyone the same way, including patients. Some are definitely easier to work with than others. Adjusting to these differing personalities has never posed a problem for me because I always strive to first understand, and then be understood. Working with a team, or on a one-on-one basis with another person is much more enjoyable to me than working independently. The many resources and experiences that others can contribute are invaluable. I look forward to working side by side with other doctors to provide a patient with the best multi-faceted approach to improving their health. In addition, my diverse interests include reading poetry on open mic night at the local coffee shop, putting at the nearest golf course, or even enjoying the latest opera at the local theater.

Thinking critically is an aspect of life that never intimidates me. I have the knowledge, skills, and confidence to approach situations from many different perspectives. My critical thinking skills are polished everyday when I need to decide how to manage my time, what type of treatment to provide for a patient, or which workout regimen to prescribe to one of my clients. A routine day does not fulfill me; give me a challenge and I will conquer it.

I will always have an undeniable passion for the complexity associated with the human body. One day I will understand its mechanism, but will never fully grasp the amazement of its structure and function. In addition, the technology and the advancements of medicine will always keep me on my toes. I want to learn how to take that ACL out of a cadaver and transplant it into the knee of the local high school all-star. There is not a single interest in my life that excites me more than learning about the human body.

Another quality that should be present in a physician is being able to work under pressure. Physicians are faced daily with cases in which the symptoms might not correlate exactly to a certain diagnosis. Pressure is indefinitely increased when a patient is rightfully demanding to know what might be causing their discomfort. I experienced a similar situation, at the age of 17, working as a superintendent in construction. The job involved replacing all of the drywall in a public school, which opened in just a few days. Everything was running smoothly until I fully inspected the work that our sub-contractor was doing, and realized that it was not up to par. In fact, it was completely dangerous. With the school opening in just a few days, I had to come up with a solution. After relaying the situation to my Project Manager, I realized what needed to be done and placed it into effect. Not only did I prevent schoolchildren from being endangered, but I also saved the company from a potentially huge loss. Knowing that I have a deadline to meet, and that others can be affected by my actions keeps my performance at its peak.

A future in medicine will fulfill every desire and demand that I require in a career. I need to be able to work with others, think critically, study the human body, and work diligently under pressure. Because religious faith and family are important parts of my personal life, I desire a career which affords me the opportunity to professionally express myself. For example, ethical considerations are of utmost importance in a physician's life. The same ethical principles can also be applied to my devotion of family. Sure there are other careers that could fulfill some of these needs, but only a career in medicine can meet all of these demands. Therefore, I am not only choosing to be a physician, the career has called me.

See page 258 to find out where this student got in.

JILL HUDGENS LEE

*Jill participated in several medical mission trips to Kenya. She
was also a member of her school's Division I soccer team.*

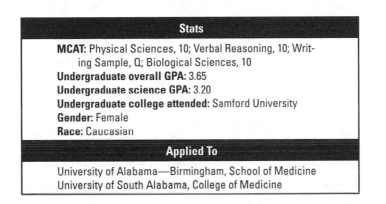

Stats
MCAT: Physical Sciences, 10; Verbal Reasoning, 10; Writing Sample, Q; Biological Sciences, 10
Undergraduate overall GPA: 3.65
Undergraduate science GPA: 3.20
Undergraduate college attended: Samford University
Gender: Female
Race: Caucasian
Applied To
University of Alabama—Birmingham, School of Medicine
University of South Alabama, College of Medicine

AMCAS Personal Statement

It was January 2003, and there was a long line of people outside our humble clinic in Mombassa, Kenya. Although the temperature had risen over 100 F, and the humid air made it difficult to breathe, the people continued to line up with hope in their eyes that they would be able to see an American doctor and receive free medicine. As I observed the crowd, I noticed a young woman cradling an infant in her arms. Immediately, I was drawn to the placid nature of this little one. As I walked closer to the woman, I noticed the baby in her arms was undisturbed by the intense heat, virtually motionless-too motionless. My experience on the maternity ward of a hospital at home had taught me enough to know that something was wrong with this baby. Immediately, I led the mother through the line of people and into the clinic. My father was inside examining a patient, but when he caught a glimpse of the distress in my eyes, he rushed over to take a look at the infant. As he examined him, I tried to offer comfort to the worried mother. Even though my father and I did not speak this woman's language, our faces said more than our words ever could. As my dad looked up to tell me that the child was deathly ill with diphtheria, I was unable to contain the sympathy that I felt for this mother. Tears flowed freely down my face as I told her, through an interpreter, that we would have to take her baby to the hospital in order for him to have a chance of surviving the illness.

During the time that I have spent in Kenya, I have found myself in many situations similar to one that I have just described. At times, I feel frustrated because of my knowledge of medicine at this point in time provides me with little ability to provide medical care to those who need it. However, assisting the medical professionals in many procedures and comforting and reassuring the patients made this volunteer experience my most satisfying yet. Providing free medicine and medical care to the underpriveleged people of Kenya, communicating compassion and concern for their welfare, and subsequently seeing their profound gratitude for our services has completed my understanding of why I want to become a physician. Not only will my interest in science and healthcare be satisfied, but a career in medicine rewards my interests in counseling and provides a deep sense of fulfillment for playing an integral role in the lives of others.

I have prepared myself to pursue a career in medicine in many ways. My volunteer experiences at Baptist Montclair Hospital and Children's Hospital have given me the opportunity to interact directly with patients. The medical missions trips I have gone on have also provided me with substantial contact with patients. I have volunteered at Easy Street Rehabilitation Unit, where I assisted physicians, physical therapists, and occupational therapists in patient rehab after strokes and surgeries. My internships with Dr. Duane Randleman in cardiothoracic surgery, Dr. Mary Louise Guerry-Force in pathology, and Dr. Maura Carter in neuropsychology, as well as my work-experience with my father in neurology have allowed me to view many perspectives in the medical field. As a physician, it is imperative that I demonstrate good leadership skills. The past three summers, I have served a leadership role at Kanakuk Kamps in Colorado, where I was allotted responsibility for counselors and campers, as well as planning daily activities for the camp.

Understanding that a career in medicine requires hard work, dedication, and time, I have further prepared myself for the rigorous demands by maintaining a busy schedule throughout my college career. I have consistently participated in athletics, volunteer activities, and extracurricular hobbies, while maintaining a rigorous academic curriculum. I have been successful with these activities because I budget my time among all of them.

See page 259 to find out where this student got in.

JIMMY LEE KERRIGAN

Jimmy was a member of Phi Beta Kappa, Alpha Epsilon Delta, Vanderbilt Student Volunteers for Science, College Scholars, president of Model United Nations, and lieutenant of training for the Vanderbilt Emergency Medical Society. He also served as assistant editor for his undergraduate research journal and a tutor in the Office of Disability Services at two separate state universities. In addition, he shadowed pediatric cardiothoracic surgeons, served as a research assistant and medical records clerk, and was the recipient of the Harold Sterling Vanderbilt and Toyota Community scholarship.

Stats

MCAT: Physical Sciences, 14; Verbal Reasoning, 11; Writing Sample, S; Biological Sciences, 13
Undergraduate Overall GPA: 3.99
Undergraduate Science GPA: 4.0
Undergraduate College Attended: Vanderbilt University
Gender: Male
Race: Caucasian

Applied To

Duke University, School of Medicine
Emory University, School of Medicine
Harvard University, Harvard Medical School
Johns Hopkins University, School of Medicine
Northwestern University, Feinberg School of Medicine
University of Alabama—Birmingham, School of Medicine
University of Chicago, Pritzker School of Medicine
University of Pennsylvania, School of Medicine
University of Tennessee—Memphis, College of Medicine
Vanderbilt University, School of Medicine
Washington University in St. Louis, School of Medicine

AMCAS Personal Statement

"Since he was knee-high to a grasshopper," is how my mother responds when asked how long I have wanted to be a doctor. While that is an obvious exaggeration, the truth is that from my earliest considerations of a career, becoming a surgeon has been my goal. I first came to this realization while sitting with my father at Shoney's after school in fourth grade, where it was part of our daily routine to share a pitcher of tea while recounting our day's experiences. It was also during those afternoons, however, that he would tell me stories about his life. I learned that he had been rushed to St. Thomas Medical Center in Nashville in 1986 with near-complete blockages in four arteries. Luckily, his bypass surgery was a success, which gave me the opportunity to know him personally. I immediately announced with all of the confidence that a fourth grader can muster that I, too, wanted to be a heart surgeon so that I could save people's lives.

On June 25, 1994, less than six months after realizing that I was lucky for him to still be alive, my father suffered congestive heart failure. His passing was quite a shock to my ten-year-old psyche, forcing me through the usual emotions needed to cope with such a traumatic experience. However, I came away from the experience with a deep-seated need to prevent this loss from happening to others, a desire to give people the opportunity to know their loved ones through an extension like the one that I had been given to know my father, years that were some of the most valuable of my life.

For my widowed mother to raise three small children on the income of a bank teller was challenging, at best; however, her life was made more difficult in August of 1998, when she, too, was sent to Centennial Medical Center in Nashville for an immediate triple bypass. She quickly recovered, although she had to find new employment because she could no longer endure the physical stresses of standing behind a teller window for eight hours at a time. Again, I saw an example of what good doctoring had given me: more time with my loved ones. However, a few years later, I was unfortunate enough to see what mistakes could do, as well.

Three years ago, my mother began complaining of lightheadedness and numbness in her left arm. After a series of tests, it was found that blood was being diverted from her brain to her left arm due to a blockage in her subclavian artery; therefore, she was referred to a cardiovascular surgeon who inserted a stent. However, my mother soon began complaining of shortness of breath, a symptom that the surgeon dismissed as a common result of the surgery. After consultation with a pulmonologist, she discovered that the left side of her diaphragm had been paralyzed during the operation. Although my mother has completed physical therapy and is now on medication to alleviate her breathing problems, she does not have full capacity due to what can only be described, in the professional opinion of her internist and pulmonologist, as a mistake. I see daily how this error has affected her, how she cannot enjoy the same things that she used to, things that she used to treasure before her mobility was limited by the slip of a scalpel. Because I have seen the effects of a physician's mistake firsthand, I have developed a desire to become the best doctor that I can to minimize my chances of erring so that I do no harm to my patients.

I was lucky enough to have the opportunity to shadow a pediatric cardiothoracic surgeon during my sophomore year of college. Meeting at 7 a.m., I usually followed her to the operating room, where she would repair an infant's ventricular septal defect or ductus arteriosus, operations that normally proceeded without incident. One morning, however, she was not in her office to meet me. I sat for half an hour after paging her before a surgical assistant peeked in, threw a set of scrubs at me, and told me to hurry to the O.R. I was tying my mask as I walked in to see a four-month-old in cardiac arrest, a fact apparent from the tone of the monitoring equipment. I stood to the side of the room as members of the surgical team performed chest compressions until an extracorporeal membrane oxygenation machine could be connected, but for those fifteen minutes before the child regained life, I felt utterly helpless - all I could do was watch. At that point, I became determined never to be helpless again. I took a CPR course, began working to bring an EMT program to my undergraduate campus, and rededicated myself to my dream of becoming a physician. There is no other career for me.

I can help myself. I cannot change my genes, which, as is apparent from my family history, are most likely flawed, but I can make lifestyle choices that will help me overcome the hand that Mendel dealt. Nevertheless, that only helps one person - me. That is not good enough. I have confirmed my childhood aspirations, and I know that I will be the person returning mothers to children and husbands to wives. That is why I am applying to medical school. If given the opportunity, I know that I will become the best doctor that I can be, allowing me to make a difference in the lives of others and preventing me from ever standing against the wall, helpless, again.

See page 259 to find out where this student got in.

MANSOOR KHAN

Mansoor was a member of the Stony Brook Honors College (from which he graduated Phi Beta Kappa), Editor-in-Chief of the university newspaper, and completed an honors thesis in Medical Anthropology on the topic of Patient Discrimination in the Emergency Department. He also founded and coordinated a volunteer mentoring program for middle school students with behavioral difficulties, studied abroad in Tanzania, and volunteered for three summers at Birch Family Camp for HIV/AIDS. Additionally, he served for two years as an EMT for the Stony Brook Volunteer Ambulance Corps and then worked as a nursing assistant in the Emergency Department of Stony Brook University hospital. He received a Howard Hughes Medical Institute Undergraduate Research Fellowship for his basic science research in a hematology laboratory and was part of the 2005 USA Today All USA College Academic Third Team.

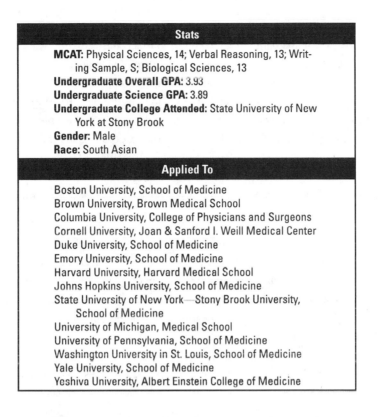

AMCAS Personal Statement

I could barely breathe. With Dustin's little arms wrapped tightly around my neck, I finally admitted defeat. "Hey buddy, let's hold on to the shoulders instead this time," I joked, marveling to myself at the unselfconscious laughter coming from the eight-year-old I was piggybacking. Dustin had been born paralyzed. Having never fully developed the use of his legs, he had to be carried through the woods by his camp counselor. Dustin played, laughed, wrestled and cried for his mother like every other camper. He was a normal kid, except for his paralysis—and the fact that he was HIV positive.

Many of the children at Birch Family Camp, a yearly summer camp that brings together volunteer counselors with inner-city families afflicted with HIV/AIDS, are HIV positive. I first volunteered there during the summer after my freshman year of college, and have continued every summer since. Birch Camp is a haven, a place where regardless of age, ethnicity, appearance, or (most importantly) disease status, every individual is treated like a human being. What amazes me most about the place is that there are no "cases" at Birch Camp, only people. Having seen the television shows and read the books that portray medicine as mechanized and dehumanizing—a profession in which a patient may be referred to as "the gun-shot wound in room three" or "the chest pain in shock trauma"—the Birch Camp approach has been eye-opening for me. I met physicians there—treating patients, caring for them, talking with them—who considered it both their job and their privilege to establish a warm rapport with each and every child and adult, and obviously took great pleasure in what they were doing. Their example rubbed off on the rest of us. Even those volunteers who initially lacked the maturity and compassion to embrace someone with one of the most frightening infectious diseases on this planet soon overcame their qualms. At Birch Camp, people really did come first. One's HIV status was an afterthought.

The experience of Birch Camp now permeates my view of medicine, and even of life. It made me think about how I could affect the lives of individuals around me in a positive way. In my sophomore year of college, I decided to try to put that realization into practice, and I began the JFK Mentoring Program, a volunteer effort in which undergraduates at Stony Brook University act as mentors, essentially big brothers and sisters, for students at nearby JFK Middle School. The program has since matured and has become quite successful. Three times a week, nineteen college students volunteer our time to ensure that the middle school children at JFK, whether they have behavioral problems, academic difficulties or language barriers, receive the attention they need. For us, these children are not just statistics, causes, or report cards. They are real, breathing, feeling human beings, and we have the opportunity to support them.

Looking back, I think Birch Camp and the JFK Mentoring Program prepared me for the experience that has influenced me the most powerfully thus far: a college study-abroad trip to Tanzania. There I saw inequality at its worst: bowlegged paupers asking for the tiniest scraps of food or bits of change; malnourished children vying for the opportunity just to touch the American foreigners, while flies buzzed around their scarred, bald heads; clinics so far from each other that HIV patients are too discouraged to seek treatment. Nearby, perched atop a steep cliff overlooking the vast landscape of East Africa, was an elegant and expensive hotel for rich tourists. For me, Tanzania personalized an understanding that had until then been merely academic. Poor Tanzanians weren't statistics called "Africans," living in a far-off continent; they were people. Tanzania provided me with a dramatic example of the profound disparities in health, education, and economic status present in this world.

As I continued to think about the possibility of a medical career, I realized that inequity no doubt exists even within the field of medicine. That is partly why, last year, I decided to study ethnic bias in the emergency room for my undergraduate

Honors Thesis. It came as no surprise to learn that even in my own country there exist disparities in health and access to health care between majority and minority populations served by the medical profession. Using an anthropological approach, my thesis examined patient perceptions about one kind of inequality, ethnic bias, in the ER, in order to help determine the mechanisms behind it. Perhaps if we can understand why we sometimes behave in a biased, prejudiced way, it might help eliminate this behavior.

To me, the idea of any kind of discrimination within medicine is unacceptable. The medical system must treat human beings, not just a "patient population." Hippocrates said it best. "It's far more important to know what person the disease has than what disease the person has." These words have rung true for me, in my view of medicine and the world around me, and I hope they continue to shape my future as a physician.

See page 259 to find out where this student got in.

MEGHAN ALLISON NESMITH

While still an undergraduate, Meghan shadowed doctors and took part in a clinical internship at Florida Hospital in Orlando. She also worked as a resident assistant and as a team leader for the Burnett Honors College for two years. In 2005, she was chosen to be a part of the President's Scholars Program, which sends 12 students to study abroad on a full scholarship for one term at the University of Cambridge. She also received The Order of Pegasus, an award based on academic achievement, leadership, community service, and university involvement, from the University of Central Florida.

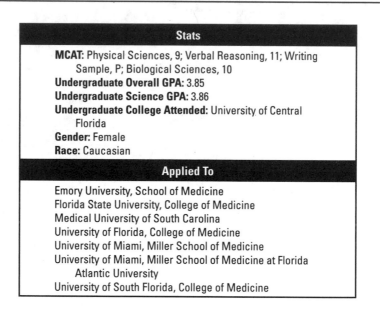

Stats
MCAT: Physical Sciences, 9; Verbal Reasoning, 11; Writing Sample, P; Biological Sciences, 10
Undergraduate Overall GPA: 3.85
Undergraduate Science GPA: 3.86
Undergraduate College Attended: University of Central Florida
Gender: Female
Race: Caucasian

Applied To
Emory University, School of Medicine
Florida State University, College of Medicine
Medical University of South Carolina
University of Florida, College of Medicine
University of Miami, Miller School of Medicine
University of Miami, Miller School of Medicine at Florida Atlantic University
University of South Florida, College of Medicine

AMCAS Personal Statement

Dr. Hill performs a laparoscopic hysterectomy, and dissects the uterus for me to see. Dr. Cole's patients hug her and tell me that I am learning from the best. A woman visiting a relative in Labor and Delivery tells Dr. Hill what a wonderful job he did delivering her baby a few years ago and how much she appreciated it. Dr. Dumois trusts me to help him remove a patient's stitches from his hand. Experiences such as these have solidified my desire to pursue a career in medicine.

Growing up, I have always had a strong love of math and science. These interests led me to pursue an education in mechanical engineering with a plan to study biomedical engineering. However, as I studied more in-depth engineering courses, I found that I no longer had the passion for the field that I previously had. I was invited to observe a graduate level biomedical engineering course in human anatomy, and this experience was fundamental to shaping the course of the rest of my life. Seeing the intricacy and beauty of the human body, and having the opportunity to aid in the dissection, sparked my awe of the human body and desire to understand its structure and function.

As a physician, constant interaction with patients, families, and other medical professionals is vital, making communication skills essential. As an extrovert, I love people; the presence of others fuels my motivation and drive. Helping others is my passion, whether it is with residents, freshman honors students, and in the future, patients. I briefly volunteered in a research laboratory, and this experience, although enjoyable, showed me that my interest in medicine is clinical and people-oriented. I ended my volunteering there when the opportunity arose for an internship at Florida Hospital.

The Clinical Internship at Florida Hospital had an extraordinary impact on my life, and I became absolutely positive that I would pursue medicine as a career. I had the opportunity to shadow a different phenomenal physician each week, both residents and faculty, in the Family Health Center. Each and every doctor excelled with their patients in his or her own way, and I learned so much from observing their different styles of caring for their patients. One pivotal experience was shadowing Dr. Cole, who specializes in geriatrics. Seeing the care with which she worked with the elderly patients was very moving, and I can only hope that one day I will be able to make as significant an impact on the life of someone else as she does. My favorite shadowing experiences have been the times I shadowed Dr. Hill. In the course of the first day I shadowed Dr. Hill in Labor and Delivery, I realized that being a physician was, more than anything, what I wanted to do with my life. Language is inadequate to describe the awe and amazement that I felt watching a baby delivered, seeing laparoscopic surgeries, or watching the interactions between patient, family, and physician. Watching Dr. Hill and other physicians work through a difficult surgery was incredible, and the intensity and exhilaration of the OR is something that I aspire to experience again. The energy and enthusiasm with which Dr. Hill cares for his patients is extraordinary; the kind, welcoming, and compassionate atmosphere he creates is one that I hope to emulate. Dr. Hill and all of the incredible doctors I have shadowed are extremely thorough, both in listening to and asking questions of their patients, and when explaining diagnoses to them. I learned so much watching them discuss charts and patient medical history; their meticulous attention to all details enabling them to accurately determine a diagnosis and treatment. Their dedication towards their patients, and their kindness and helpfulness towards me, demonstrated the qualities that I aspire to in my pursuit of a career in medicine and in life in general. My experiences are unparalleled, and through them, I have found my true passion in medicine.

Through the internship and shadowing, I have learned much about the medical field, and gained knowledge about medical school, residency programs, the daily activities of a physician, and clinical medicine. By keeping an open mind, I was flooded with knowledge about everything related to the medical field, and gained such an incredible perspective about working with patients.

I am drawn to medicine for its continuous challenges, new technology, and for my love of learning. I yearn to be a part of the growth in the medical field, and to learn my whole life, loving the challenges, and never becoming stagnant in my knowledge and experiences. Most importantly, as a physician, I will have the opportunity to make a positive impact on the quality of life for many people. To listen and understand my patients, to help them in every way my education and resources have taught me how, and to see them as more than patients, as the most precious human life- that is the gift that a career in medicine offers. Through compassion and care for each person, I hope to one day be the difference in their lives as Dr. Hill and Dr. Cole are to their patients. The greatest responsibility, the care of others, and for their loved ones, is my goal in life. To watch my patients grow, to share their lives, is my greatest ambition.

See page 262 to find out where this student got in.

MEKEISHA GIVAN

MeKeisha worked as an operating room assistant at Baptist Montclair Hospital in Birmingham, Alabama and shadowed physicians in a variety of fields. She also worked for Habitat for Humanity and volunteered for two years at Birmingham's Ronald McDonald House.

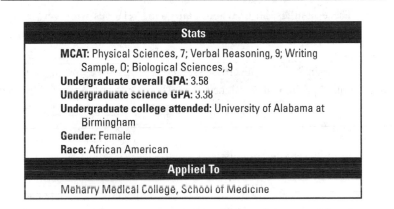

Stats
MCAT: Physical Sciences, 7; Verbal Reasoning, 9; Writing Sample, 0; Biological Sciences, 9
Undergraduate overall GPA: 3.58
Undergraduate science GPA: 3.38
Undergraduate college attended: University of Alabama at Birmingham
Gender: Female
Race: African American

Applied To
Meharry Medical College, School of Medicine

AMCAS Personal Statement

The black pill bugs slowly crept along the cardboard maze that led them on a predetermined journey. At the end of the straightaway, one of my seventh-grade students shined a flashlight on each of the small crustaceans, we hoped to teach the pill bugs to pick the left path over the right turn. After several trials—many of which resulted in the pill bugs rebelling and choosing the wrong path—the crustaceans began to follow the course that we had selected for the roly polies. This science project for the University of Alabama at Birmingham-Arrington Middle School Connection taught me perseverance, strength, and determination while also training me in the art of having patience with others. Furthermore, I learned that like the pill bugs, I also have a path to follow in order to complete my goals; this course is the path to a career in medicine.

Throughout college, I had certain medical experiences that enabled me to see the facets of medicine. Although these experiences often demonstrated both the positive and challenging sides of medicine, it was these inside views of the profession that piqued my interest. While in college, I took classes in addition to working at Children's Hospital, volunteering, and participating in other extracurricular activities. I have participated in the Alpha Epsilon Delta, Phi Kappa Phi, and Sigma Tau

Delta honor societies and been a member of the Orientation Leaders Team for my university. I have also attended the Summer Medical Education Program as well as the Joint Leadership Conference of the University of Alabama at Birmingham. I am a member of the Minority Scholars Program and participate in community activities with my church, Habitat for Humanity, and the Girl Scouts. One of my most meaningful activities—my work at the Ronald McDonald House—intensely shaped my perspective of medicine.

At the Ronald McDonald House, I performed chores for the families living at the home. These families, all of whom had young relatives who were patients at Children's Hospital, had to perform chores at the house in exchange for free room and board. At the time, my job at the Ronald McDonald House seemed like such an insignificant amount of work; nevertheless, I realized that sweeping, vacuuming, and other duties that I performed eased the stress placed on these families. Furthermore, this experience enabled me to realize the tremendous strength that families of the ill must exhibit.

During my first semester of college, I had to face many challenges as I adjusted to life at the university. In the months of August and September, my mother—the sole provider of our home—had to have both foot and heart surgery that had resulted from serious circumstances; it was at this time that I gained first-hand experience into what families of the sick deal with during times of illness. Because my mom was indisposed, I had to take on the responsibilities at home in addition to my duties related to school. Learning to manage my time was difficult; however, I persevered and made the Deans' List the following semester.

Although this trial greatly challenged my journey to becoming a physician, other tests were just as significant in my path to medicine; it was these tests that enabled me to better handle the later tribulations that I would face. Throughout life, I had to deal with the sicknesses of not only my mother, but other close relatives and friends. As a small child, I often visited the home of my grandmother and great-grandmother. During one visit to my grandparents' home, my great-grandmother went into shock. As my grandmother panicked, I calmly dialed 911 and requested that an ambulance be sent to the house. As the medics arrived, I watched in wonder as they carefully took care of my grandmother and healed her of her sickness. This experience opened my eyes to the wonders of medicine and strongly provoked my interest in the profession.

As a result of the many experiences that I had during my lifetime, I was able to experience the good, bad, and personal aspects of medicine. In my later years, the realistic features of the medical profession personally affected me; early on in my life, I learned the wonderful, life-saving side of medicine. It was this multi-faceted view of medicine that shaped my journey to becoming a doctor. While these experiences coursed the expanse of my lifetime, the journey truly began at the time of my birth. Although no one on earth knew of the physician that I would become, it was at the time that I took my first breath that I, like the pill bugs, had a path that was set into motion. My course is the path to becoming a physician.

See page 260 to find out where this student got in.

MICHAEL CURLEY

During his college years, Michael volunteered at an AIDS shelter in Madrid, Spain and worked on an ambulance serving inner-city St. Louis, Missouri. He also volunteered at a health clinic for uninsured members of St. Louis's Latino community. He was involved in Micah House, an academic, community service, and housing program that incorporated themes of peace and social justice in the urban community.

Stats
MCAT: Physical Sciences, 10; Verbal Reasoning, 10; Writing Sample, P; Biological Sciences, 11
Undergraduate overall GPA: 3.91
Undergraduate science GPA: 3.80
Undergraduate college attended: Saint Louis University
Gender: Male
Race: Caucasian

Applied To
Creighton University, School of Medicine
Loyola University Chicago, Stritch School of Medicine
Medical College of Wisconsin
Saint Louis University, School of Medicine
Tulane University, School of Medicine
University of Wisconsin—Madison, School of Medicine and Public Health

AMCAS Personal Statement

I was born into wealth. The youngest of five children raised on the income of a social worker, this wealth was that afforded to those fortunate enough to be born into a close-knit, supportive and loving family in which respect and sensitivity, education and service to others were deeply valued. The benefits reaped from this advantage molded my early personal growth, influenced my perspectives on others, encouraged me to explore, to risk, and to challenge myself, and to work to attain that which I value. Ultimately, it shaped me into the person that I am and will guide me in the pursuit of the person I strive to be.

Many of my earliest memories are of my siblings working diligently on their schoolwork at the kitchen table, of their investment in extracurricular activities, and of their involvement with community programs serving children and adults with cognitive and physical disabilities. With a natural tendency to imitate the behavior of those I admired, I developed a special love of learning, an interest in participating in a wide variety of activities, and an appreciation for the importance of working for the good of others with a spirit of compassion. These values were reflected in the effort that I invested in my schoolwork, the opportunities I took advantage of to develop my talents and leadership qualities and, in later years, by my work with some of the very individuals with autism, cerebral palsy and Down Syndrome that my siblings had enjoyed serving.

By the time I entered high school, my siblings' pursuit of college and graduate studies had taken them hundreds of miles from home, but we remained very close and their influence remained strong. With their support and that of my parents, I developed confidence to take on meaningful leadership roles in the arts, athletics, my school community, and employment. Theatrical performances provided me with an opportunity to develop strong communication skills; positions on the cross country and basketball teams impressed upon me the importance of physical and mental endurance as well as the critical nature of working effectively within a group; an opportunity to develop a classroom-based program celebrating student diversity taught me that one effective leadership tool was to encourage others to share the talents of which they felt proud; employment with children and adults with special needs stimulated empathy, patience, and creativity.

The lessons learned through these opportunities and my family experiences helped me to develop a personal philosophy regarding the value of human life and the importance of actively pursuing social justice. I was able to further investigate, develop and act on these beliefs as a student at Saint Louis University involved in Micah House, a community service and social justice program. An opportunity to study at Saint Louis University's Madrid, Spain campus allowed me to face new challenges such as utilizing my foreign language skills and adapting to and embracing a culture quite different than my own. While in Madrid, my dedication to volunteerism took me to the Ermita Del Santo AIDS Shelter. While further developing empathy and an appreciation for my own health, I witnessed and was touched by the intense resolve and love of life demonstrated by the shelter residents despite their serious health conditions.

Today I realize that the wealth stemming from my family, compounded over the years through the rich opportunities and experiences I have had, has formed my foundation. Qualities such as introspection, integrity, determination, compassion and maturity are the building blocks of this foundation, and are respected by my friends, acquaintances, teachers, work colleagues and those I have had the opportunity to serve. I look forward to the challenges ahead as I continue to develop the attributes, knowledge and skills necessary for me to fulfill my desire to be of service to others.

See page 260 to find out where this student got in.

MICHAEL FRANCO

Michael took time off from college to attend culinary school and worked at various high-end restaurants in Philadelphia. After returning to college, he volunteered at the emergency department of Cooper Hospital in Camden, New Jersey.

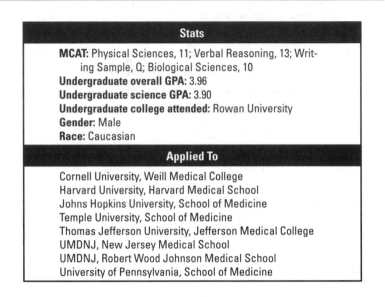

Stats
MCAT: Physical Sciences, 11; Verbal Reasoning, 13; Writing Sample, Q; Biological Sciences, 10
Undergraduate overall GPA: 3.96
Undergraduate science GPA: 3.90
Undergraduate college attended: Rowan University
Gender: Male
Race: Caucasian

Applied To
Cornell University, Weill Medical College
Harvard University, Harvard Medical School
Johns Hopkins University, School of Medicine
Temple University, School of Medicine
Thomas Jefferson University, Jefferson Medical College
UMDNJ, New Jersey Medical School
UMDNJ, Robert Wood Johnson Medical School
University of Pennsylvania, School of Medicine

AMCAS Personal Statement

It is around 7:00 o'clock AM, and the workday begins. Vegetables must be chopped, meat must be butchered and fish is to be filleted. Suddenly, without warning, it is noon; lunch is upon me. Orders line up in an endless stream. The temperature rises to a stifling, sauna-like level in front of the heavy, iron flat-top grills, and commands are being barked into my ear by a French chef who seems to think that the volume of his voice must be ten times that of the banging pots. In the kitchen of the French restaurant where I worked after leaving culinary school, the intensity level was always high. A delicate balance between speed and finesse was the rule, and sustained efficiency was paramount. The culinary world is still a field I truly enjoy; however, I always knew there would be a point when I would return to the academic arena and pursue my passion for learning.

Upon returning to college, medical school was not made my official target until relatively late. This decision did not come as an after-thought, nor as a result of procrastination. I had grappled with the idea of becoming a physician since the sixth grade; however, I always thought it to be beyond my reach. My notion of the medical school applicant was someone who was the child of a doctor (or at least the child of a college graduate), and someone from an upper-class family. I am neither. After much research, and with the support of the faculty at Rowan University, I was able to dispense with my misconceptions. Throughout my time in college, I had always maintained an excellent academic track record. Now, i just needed to be sure that a career in medicine was best for me.

To gain a better understanding of the medical profession, I obtained a volunteer research position with Cooper Hospital's Academic Associates Program. Working in the emergency department, I am able to witness doctors treating patients with ailments that range from serious traumas to the common cold. I see how the stress level increases with high patient volume. Yet the staff continues to provide quality care for the constant stream of sick and injured people. I appreciate the professional yet compassionate manner with which these doctors conduct themselves despite working long, strenuous hours. Working at Cooper, I see a similarity between my past work experience in restaurants and the emergency department. Like the French kitchen from which I came, a career in medicine would provide me with daily challenges that need to be overcome with proper organization, intensity and a wide breadth of knowledge. Unlike the kitchen, I am confident that my satisfaction with this profession would be far greater. Receiving thanks for serving a beautiful preparation of lamb is nice. However, there is much deeper meaning in receiving a smile from a previously tearful child who has had a laceration sutured and pain ameliorated.

Working as a physician will afford me the opportunity to harness my knowledge and skill to obtain substantive results. The idea that treating a patient with a medication, or with a specific operation can make a difference in the quality of a person's life buttresses my commitment to this path. I am confident that my education at Rowan University has provided me with the framework to succeed in medical school, and my years in the restaurant setting have given me a maturity that would not come with general college courses. Providing sustenance for a hungry diner comes with its own rewards; however, my need for scientific knowledge, and my desire to contribute to society can best be satisfied by embarking on a career in medicine. I know that upon obtaining my undergraduate and graduate medical training, I will be capable of fulfilling my potential as a physician as well as a compassionate human being.

See page 260 to find out where this student got in.

MICHAEL SOULE

Michael completed some basic science bench work before applying to medical school. During the year he was applying, he had already completed his EMS and was working doing some clinical activities. His work in an Indian NGO was also a plus. These experiences allowed Michael to gain exposure to what medicine is about (science, patient contact, healthcare structures) and figure out what he would like to focus on.

Stats
Undergraduate overall GPA: 3.9
Undergraduate college attended: Brown University
Gender: Male

Applied To
Harvard University, Harvard Medical School
New York University, Mount Sinai School of Medicine
New York University, NYU School of Medicine
Stanford University, School of Medicine
University of California—San Francisco, School of Medicine
University of Chicago, Pritzker School of Medicine
University of Illinois, College of Medicine
University of Miami, School of Medicine
University of Pennsylvania, School of Medicine
Yale School of Medicine

AMCAS Personal Statement

My core desire in life is to serve those who are underserved to the greatest extent of my ability. I have had many experiences living, learning, and working with people in neglected parts of society and have come to realize that I have some of the tools I need to do my life's work, but I am missing some crucial ones. I have worked with people in a care-giving capacity in which I was completely capable of getting the results I desired and others in which I found myself falling short.

In my work as a teacher, I have had a strong sense of being well equipped for working with those who society generally forgets. The summer after my first year at Brown, I worked as a teaching assistant at my high school. I taught a group that was an average racial and socioeconomic cross-section of the kids who didn't take honors classes as I had and who fall through the cracks of my school's system. I struggled through their apathy and unruliness and a weapon possession incident to creatively solve the problem of their lack of foundation in math. Many happily surprised faces turned to me when the final grades were posted. Several of my students passed who were sure they couldn't.

Thinking back, I asked myself, "How did I know what to do?" My answer came down to the fact that I had committed myself to understanding their life circumstances and acquiring all the teaching skills and I could to help these kids who don't usually get it. It felt wonderful to see the change I created so I kept teaching.

I taught a similar group of kids in Providence in a free SAT prep course. My math students posted amazing score increases. One raised his math score 330 points, the highest of any increase in the program. My students were shocked when my answer to their question, "Mr Mike, are you going to be a teacher?" was, "No." In answer to their inevitable, "Why?" I told them why I wanted to be a doctor.

I want to change people's lives for the better on the most fundamental level: their physical health. One's physical body is an incredibly important thing in this life and the preservation or restoration of health is one of the most incredible gifts that one person can give to another. There are countless people who need this service that only doctors can provide and I yearn to be able to give it. Educating the mind is essential, but is only fully effective when the body is healthy.

I have had some experiences with healthcare but in all of them, I was limited in my ability to have an effect on the lives of the patients. In order to become certified as an EMT in Illinois, one must do emergency room observation time. In the ER, I had an experience that cemented my desire to work with patients. An elderly man had fallen downstairs in his wheelchair and the paramedics left us with a baggie of his teeth and shreds of hair. He had almost been scalped. Far from being startled by his suffering, I found myself thinking only of what I could do to help him.

It was a busy night and I was left alone with him to clean his wounds and monitor his mental status. As I gently swabbed his head, checked his breathing, and talked to him, I saw the man slip slowly into incoherence. I got the nurse, he conferred with the doctor, and I was soon wheeling my charge to X-Ray. He held my hand the whole way and yelled when I had to leave him. I felt then that I wanted so much to have understanding to help him more than I could. I was helpless but inspired.

When I lived in India, I had constant reminders that I lacked some of the tools I need to do the work I long to do. Walking the streets every day, I wanted to do something to fight the destitution and illness I encountered at every turn. So, I volunteered at an AIDS care home. I worked on a project that tracked the patients' infections so as to better target their care. The files I worked with were hopelessly scrambled and admissions were disorganized. From my experience with patient files in EMS, I could show them how to track their patients efficiently to help eliminate some of the chaos in the records. While this was progress for the NGO and indirect help to the patients, I was stunned and silent when I stood next to the beds of the patients stricken with TB, HIV, drug addictions, and other afflictions. I had no great thing to give them but heartfelt wishes.

Eager to learn more and thus overcome my helplessness, I worked in a lab doing AIDS-related research. I gained an appreciation for the intensity of the micro-level work that goes into figuring out the virus' mechanism and how this gives rise to treatment. I then went on to do an independent study on AIDS in India and how NGOs like the one I worked in fit into the fight against this scourge. I gained a powerful understanding of the social and political aspects of the structural care that AIDS patients need. But I still lack the most powerful tools to make a difference.

In all of these experiences, I have found that I am not satisfied to just hold an oxygen mask or help the underserved from a desk or lab bench. I know what it feels like to positively influence someone's life using a comprehensive set of skills and a strong understanding of their situation in life. I feel that with a medical education I can create change in the most powerful way possible.

Secondary Essay

Michael used the following essay in his application to Yale University, School of Medicine.

Why Yale School of Medicine?

YSM's philosophy is two-pronged and resonates with who I am and the goals I seek to achieve. YSM pushes students to the limits of exploring what they want to explore and this ensures that they are in love with what they learn. When I was a youngster, I always wanted to play my own music. I was eternally frustrated that with my limited know-how on the cello, I could not manage to play what I felt so deeply in my heart. With time, good teachers, and a lot of practice, I started to be able to play that music, winning two concerto competitions and a composition award my senior year in high school. Throughout this process, I found my own way with many supportive teachers and a passionate view to guide me. The freedom I had made me love it even more, because it was my own drive that bore fruit. Brown's educational philosophy is a direct reflection of this same awareness that when people are supported and urged to pursue what is in their hearts, they excel. Yale's outlook is the same and I felt at home when I read "The Yale System."

My pre-med years at Brown were happily cooperative. Strangers helped me study for physics tests and I offered advice on organic chemistry to those in need. Rarely were test scores mentioned and even then, not competitively so. I was shocked to hear stories from pre-meds at other schools about the cutthroat tendencies of their classmates. It made me think, "If they can't help each other, how will they care for patients?" YSM also removes the obstacle of competition, replacing it with the fertile ground of a cooperative, supportive student body and faculty.

Both of these aspects were fundamental to my undergraduate experience and both are musts for my medical school because they create the perfect place to grow the seeds of the big ideas that I've been incubating.

During college, in addition to my scientific studies, I learned why some parts of the globe are more wealthy than others and how development functions. I was trying to learn how to change the reality of impoverished, vulnerable people through healthcare backed with an understanding of the flow of goods and social power. The thesis would give me the perfect opportunity to rigorously test and strengthen my ideas about how development and medicine mesh. The flexibility of YSM's fifth year would allow me to live abroad to gather data and experience. When I lived in India my junior year at Brown, I lacked some of the fundamental tools to understand what I was seeing and thus know how to really help. With the foundation of my clinical rotations, experience at the HAVEN clinic, and the background of three years of thesis work, I could return to India and have a strong framework to situate a growing understanding of what I can really do to change health realities there and thus draw on a greater array of beneficial action.

See page 261 to find out where this student got in.

MICHAEL YIP

Michael is a nationally-licensed EMT-b registered in Illinois. As an EMT, he worked for a private ambulance company and also as an emergency room technician. While in college, he was a member of the Division II men's ice hockey team, played on the ultimate frisbee team, and participated in many leadership roles within the residence halls. He has articles awaiting publication that involve his work in Arabidopsis and international relations research. He also conducted cancer research at the University of Illinois at Chicago, College of Medicine.

Stats
MCAT: Physical Sciences, 14; Verbal Reasoning, 11; Writing Sample, R; Biological Sciences, 14
Undergraduate Overall GPA: 3.98
Undergraduate Science GPA: 3.98
Undergraduate College Attended: University of Illinois at Chicago
Gender: Male
Race: Asian

Applied To
Baylor College of Medicine
Loyola University of Chicago, Strich School of Medicine
Northwestern University, Feinberg School of Medicine
Rush Medical College of Rush University
University of Chicago, Pritzker School of Medicine
University of Illinois at Chicago, UIC College of Medicine
University of Michigan, Medical School
University of Pennsylvania, School of Medicine
University of Wisconsin—Madison, School of Medicine and Public Health
Washington University in St Louis, School of Medicine

AMCAS Personal Statement

She is the mother of two children with a total of 5 grandchildren. She lives by herself in a house on the north side of Chicago. This is Ruth, a 79-year old patient with two hip replacements laying on a bed in the emergency room. I was the volunteer ER technician that day and, fortunately, was able to become acquainted with Ruth. Her most recent hip replacement appeared to be infected. She was in great pain and almost completely unable to move her left leg.

This was how we met. She was my pessimistic patient who was tired of hospital visits because, for her, they were only futile attempts to extend to her already fully lived life. Naturally, I could not stand to have a patient feel this way, and, thus, made it my objective to brighten her spirits by spending much of my time with her. It was not until after the CT scan and a visit to the vascular lab that she was admitted. By then, we had become well acquainted. She told me about her children and shared memories about her late husband. They were the joys of her life. She asked me about where I was from, what I do as a student and a volunteer, and even about my future aspirations. From our time together, she became livelier and even managed to smile through all the pain.

When we got her admitted to her room later that day, I asked the nurse for help to slide Ruth onto her new bed considering her minimal mobility and the amount of pain in her legs. However, when the nurse arrived, she refused to slide Ruth and insisted that Ruth could move to the other bed on her own. Shocked, I watched bitterly as Ruth slowly, and painfully, slid from one bed to another. During the excruciating experience, for both Ruth and me, I protested to the nurse repeatedly to no avail. She continued to insist that she could do it on her own. Unfortunately, protesting was all I could do as a volunteer. After what seemed like an eternity, Ruth made it to the new bed. From her facial expression, I could tell that she had reverted to being the pessimistic patient I had first met that morning. She was no longer the lively patient that she had been several minutes earlier. I left the room more frustrated than I had ever been.

This experience appalled me. I had never seen such a heartless display of patient care. It had occurred to me that medicine exists along a duality. Medicine is not just treating the symptoms or the patient's physical ailments. Medicine, practiced effectively, also requires the best patient interaction. It is imperative to treat the body and the soul of every patient. It was not enough to simply treat Ruth's extremities and inflammation because what good is her health if she has no spirit to enjoy it? Experiences that display poor patient care, like Ruth's, fuel my determination to be a doctor that can attack both of these sides of medicine.

I have already begun to explore both sides of this duality from my experiences in the medical field and even those outside of it. As an EMT-b, I have a head start on understanding the physical treatments of patients. I have been able to work both on a private ambulance and as an ER technician. These two positions have given me the unique opportunity to see a wide range of patients unavailable to most of the public eye. The nurses and veteran EMTs have taught me how to confront this duality by giving justice to both the personality and medical needs of a particular patient.

I have also learned the importance of behavior interactions outside of medically related experiences. As an Honors College tutor, I was in a program that offered tutoring for any undergraduate seeking help in classes. The program emphasized the necessity for good interactions between student and tutor. As a tutor, I needed to have very good interactions with other students, many of which are characteristic of a good health professional and doctor. Tutors need to be patient, encouraging, and give the student confidence that he or she will succeed.

In many ways, good patient interaction may lead to more effective medical treatment because they can lead to a better understanding of the patient and his or her condition. This constitutes the latter part of the duality. Medical school will provide me the necessary skills to combine with good patient interaction so that proper treatment can be administered. This knowledge, along with my motivation to administer the best patient care, will allow me to treat patients, such as Ruth, effectively. In this respect, I hope to treat patients, like Ruth, in a manner that would prevent the need for reoccurring doctor visits. It is my goal to understand my patients so that I can treat them as effectively as possible. This, I hope, will result in not only a lasting new bill of health, but also a smile, like the one Ruth gave me. My goal can only be accomplished with my continued development of good patient interaction and the necessary medical knowledge available to me through medical school. It is only with these skills that I will be able to treat my patients, address both sides of medicine, and achieve my goal.

See page 261 to find out where this student got in.

NAVID EGHBALIEH

As an undergraduate, Navid received many awards, including AMSA's The New Physicians 10th Annual Creative Arts Award, the Chancellor's Service Award, the American Cancer Society's Future ACS Leaders Award, and UCLA Bruinlife's Senior of the Year. During this time he also participated in many research opportunities, such as working in the Department of Neurobiology with Immunosciences Lab, Inc., while also examining a wide range of medical and cultural issues through articles he wrote and books he co-authored. He also worked with the Boys & Girls Club, St. Joseph Homeless Shelter, UCLA Federation Tutoring Program, and many other organizations.

Stats
MCAT: Physical Sciences, 12; Verbal Reasoning, 11; Writing Sample, S; Biological Sciences, 10
Undergraduate Overall GPA: 3.93
Undergraduate Science GPA: 3.80
Undergraduate College Attended: University of California—Los Angeles
Gender: Male
Race: Caucasian
Applied To
University of South Florida, College of Medicine

AMCAS Personal Statement

As an artist my continual search for a world-changing vision profoundly changed my own life one day. In a beachside parking lot stood hundreds of homeless people receiving free food and at the epicenter a line led to a doctor and his assistant. Following my astonishment with inquiry I learned that they were providing free medical care. A mother and three children timidly approached the doctor—I began sketching the interaction. The mother's abusive husband was shot in a drug deal, widowing her and forcing her onto the street with small children suffering from Post Traumatic Stress Disorder. The doctor's respectful compassion and ardent commitment allowed him to break down the patients' barriers to help them. I sketched the family while hearing their history, hopes and profound gratitude for the doctor. Since that day I have worked steadfastly toward becoming a physician. The dedication, passion, precision and intricacy required by medicine inspired my interests in research, education and volunteerism... all of which have prepared me well for the medical profession.

In moving toward a medical career I entered UCLA's Student Research Program and began work on child PTSD with Dr. Shelby—reflecting on the homeless family I sketched throughout research and publication. I examined children's linguistic and physical development standards to contribute to Dr. Shelby's coming book, in which she proposes that play therapy helps reverse the detrimental effects of children's traumatic experiences. Through this research I connected to a personal experience and found that my immense faith in modern medicine drives my desire to become a physician. Furthermore, I learned the value of research in modernizing and improving medicine. I took this knowledge back to the community by volunteering at the St. Joseph Homeless Shelter. I had a direct impact on the needing public by developing innovative health care modules to help educate the homeless about caring for themselves. These experiences, and my continued involvement in research projects with Dr. Gupta, a nephrologist, and with Dr. Vojdani, an immunologist, have revealed the medical field's capacity for change while strengthening my resolve to deliver better health care to the public.

My determination to reach out to those in need illuminated the importance of education. In 1998 I co-founded the Federation Tutoring Program, a non-profit tutoring organization for underprivileged, urban immigrant children. Today UCLA's Federation Club recruits talented students from UCLA and the Geffen School of Medicine. As director of these programs for the past five years I have cultivated my leadership abilities, organizational skills, and expertise in communication—essential attributes of a physician. I also learned valuable lessons about humanity that reemphasized my allegiance to benefiting the public. This led me to UCLA's education department to work with Professor Anderson as an Undergraduate T.A. and researcher. I designed individual instruction using the Gallup Organization's Strength Finder, an analytical survey that identifies students' academic abilities and limitations, and in turn enhanced my ability to understand and respond to people's needs. Comprehending, applying and disseminating knowledge and skills are both requisite and empowering in the medical field ...knowing this has surely nurtured me in my premedical education

Readiness for medical school meant coupling education and research with experience gleaned from occupational immersion. To fully prepare, I volunteered at UCLA Hospital to have primary patient contact as an escort. I found my greatest inspiration in Century City Hospital's Surgery Unit working directly with life-saving doctors. I was captivated as I observed and utilized the essential apparatus of medicine:

cooperation, compassion, energy, knowledge, and fortitude. I looked forward to my future as I participated in the phenomenal combination of the scientific world and humanity's intricacy.

Diversity and excellence—patent qualities of the profession I pursue—characterized my premedical experiences. My work ethic led me to receive alumni, student, administrative and national awards, while embodying the diverse cultures, socioeconomic classes, religions and motivations I am sure to encounter as a medical practitioner. By majoring in World Arts and Cultures I exposed myself to social divergence, while my Near Eastern Languages and Cultures minor strengthened the personal identity I bring to medicine. With Professor Bodrogligeti, PhD, I took graduate courses and participated in research to enrich my ethnic appreciation, preparing me to enter medical school with confident individuality. My many past roles have clearly prepared me for coming responsibilities. Research projects elevated my desire to seek innovative thinking; through education and teaching experience my dedication to aiding others grew; and as a hospital volunteer I acquired the ability to handle complicated circumstances with maturity, composure, and acumen. With each day I approach my role as a doctor…as a seeker, a healer, a teacher, a human being. Today the portrait of the homeless family I sketched encourages me each morning and night, promising a better future for those I am able to help.

See page 261 to find out where this student got in.

NIKUNJ NARENDRA TRIVEDI

When Nick was 16 years old, he founded a charity with his brother aimed at teaching CPR to their community. He participated in both clinical and wet lab research for four years, was published once, and presented those findings at a national convention. Nick served as the Assistant Director to the Pediatric AIDS Coalition at UCLA (PAC), the largest student-run philanthropic event west of the Mississippi. During his two years with the organization, PAC netted over $800,000 for the UCLA AIDS Institute, Project Kindle, Project Heartland, and the Elizabeth Glasier Pediatric AIDS Coalition.

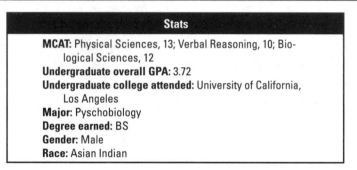

Stats
MCAT: Physical Sciences, 13; Verbal Reasoning, 10; Biological Sciences, 12
Undergraduate overall GPA: 3.72
Undergraduate college attended: University of California, Los Angeles
Major: Pyschobiology
Degree earned: BS
Gender: Male
Race: Asian Indian

Applied To
Brown University, Albert Medical School
Cornell University, Weill Medical College
Dartmouth College, Dartmouth School of Medicine
Drexel University, College of Medicine
Emory University, School of Medicine
George Washington University, School of Medicine and Health Sciences
Georgetown University, School of Medicine
Harvard University, Harvard Medical College
Mount Sinai School of Medicine
New York University, NYU School of Medicine
Northwestern University, Feinberg School of Medicine
Rosalind Franklin University of Medicine and Science
Stanford University, School of Medicine
Temple University, School of Medicine
Thomas Jefferson University, Jefferson Medical College
University of California, Davis, School of Medicine
University of California, Irvine, School of Medicine
University of California, Los Angeles, David Geffen School of Medicine
University of California, San Diego, School of Medicine
University of California, San Francisco, School of Medicine
University of Chicago, Pritzker School of Medicine
University of Illinois, College of Medicine
University of Pennsylvania, Perelman School of Medicine
University of Southern California, Keck School of Medicine of USC
Yale University, Yale School of Medicine
Yeshiva University, Albert Einstein College of Medicine

AMCAS Personal Statement

Flash back to June 15, 2003

When my mother receives a frantic phone call from our neighbor, she runs into the house next door, only to find my best friend's father lying face down on the floor next to the treadmill, in full cardiac arrest. The 911 operator tries to explain how to perform basic CPR, but terror, unfamiliarity, and a language barrier all get in the way. An ambulance arrives within ten minutes, but it is just too late.

I spent that awful evening with my best friend, which even now feels like one of the most difficult things I have ever done. Devastated by this sudden loss and exasperated by knowing that his death may well have been preventable, I struggled to understand what I should feel, and what I could do. I myself had learned CPR just a few months earlier, but why didn't anyone else know it that day, when it was needed? After many discussions with my family, we realized that this should be a call to action. Many of our loved ones--family and friends--were completely unaware of what to do in a medical emergency. So together, my brother and I created Shanti Charities, an organization focused on teaching CPR within our immediate community to individuals who may otherwise not be encouraged or motivated to learn it.

The course was free and lasted just four hours, but in that brief time I could try to encourage someone to make their life a bit better, perhaps through the class itself or perhaps through my discussion of healthy living habits. Many of our students struggled with English, but I welcomed the challenge. I felt inspired to see people who would never have learned CPR - an 80-year-old Gujarati woman doing this for her husband with a heart condition or an 11-year old boy who just wanted to make a difference - bending over a manikin to try to inflate its lungs. It was so encouraging to see these two, and many others, trying so hard to learn because it reminded me not only that our project was possible, but also that it was the right thing to do. Through the next six years, Shanti Charities went on to teach CPR to thousands of individuals with limited access in both the US and India. I can only hope that we inspired these people to see that they were capable of taking action in an emergency. As a physician, I hope to continue to inspire people not only in the case of emergencies, but also in every aspect of their lives to improve their health.

Even though I spent a lot of time trying to inspire others to action, I found myself feeling helpless when my own mother was diagnosed with cancer during my freshman year of college. After all, I didn't have the medical knowledge to impact her health using science. However, one especially helpless day, I was reminded of my own maxillofacial surgery for an overbite just a month prior. Even though my mom had no medical knowledge, her compassion and care were as helpful to my healing as my father's frequent reminders of what to do and when. So I decided I would take on the role of cheerleader, as she had done for me. It amazed me to see how my immature knock-knock jokes or even a simple smile turned her bad days into good ones, not just emotionally, but even in improving her nausea and fatigue.

Even more astounding to me was the effect the anticipation of a positive experience had on her physical symptoms. My mother's diagnosis came to us just after we had finalized the plans to visit India for a humanitarian mission and she was just as attached to the idea as I. We made an agreement: if her white blood cell count exceeded 3,000, we would go to India; if not, we would have to postpone the trip until next year. This goal helped her to fight through the tough days. When she was feeling especially sick and my usual antics weren't working, a simple "I know today isn't great, but think about it Mom. In four months, we can be in India making a serious difference!" motivated her to push herself and to keep fighting. When the date came for the final check, her count was over 4,000, and her doctors were astounded by her progress. Her achievement underscored for me the role that emotion plays in healing, and the importance of hope in making the patient feel better.

Continuing my schoolwork, helping my mom, and planning the humanitarian mission proved to be a very difficult balancing act. However, I discovered that being busy was something I really enjoyed. It kept me on task with all of my responsibilities and allowed me to be a more effective person. I now realize that I am not intimidated by what lies ahead, and I can't imagine dedicating my life to anything else. I want the personal interaction, the stress, the ups and downs, and everything in between because, for me, no other profession offers the opportunity to thrive in a challenging work environment, while simultaneously valuing empathy, the critical ingredient to keep us all well.

Turn to page 261 to see where this student got in.

REBECCA SHARIM

Rebecca was in the Pool Premedical Program at Lehigh University, which allowed her to hold summer internships and conduct research at the start of her sophomore year. She co-published two papers, presented research at two national conferences, and composed a senior thesis on stigma and liver disease. She was the recipient of multiple academic awards, including the George Lemmon Award for Research and the Contribution to Student Life Award. She was a 2005 Donald T. Campbell Social Science Research Prizes Finalist.

Stats
MCAT: Physical Sciences, 10; Verbal Reasoning, 9; Writing Sample, R; Biological Sciences, 9
Undergraduate overall GPA: 3.98
Undergraduate science GPA: 3.98
Undergraduate college attended: Lehigh University
Gender: Female
Race: Caucasian

Applied To
Temple University, School of Medicine (applied early decision)

AMCAS Personal Statement

"Never be a doctor if you're going to have any loans to pay back." "Don't do this to yourself." "You'll never have a family if you go to medical school." "The two worst jobs in America belong to physicians and teachers." Without even soliciting their advice, physicians noticed my "Pre-medical Volunteer" nametag, and immediately approached me with words of discouragement. I participated in a volunteer summer internship at St. Mary Hospital in Langhorne, Pennsylvania, following my sophomore year of college, in an effort to gain more experience in the medical field and solidify my lifelong desire to become a physician. Throughout the eight weeks, I spent mandatory hours in both the Emergency Room and the Operating Room, made contacts with physicians in specific areas of interest, and spent time shadowing them. In addition, each of us in the program attended weekly business meetings in which administrators of the hospital and local physicians spoke to us about their particular positions and experiences. Unlike the many years of high school I spent volunteering at a hospital and a nursing home, where

I was limited to carrying around food trays and refilling cups of water, I was able to gain hands-on and more intimate experience. Initially uneasy at the site of the blood gushing into plastic sheets draped around the orthopedic surgeon's patient in the OR, it took only a few days to grow accustomed to the images on the television screen during a laparoscopic procedure and the shocking way the neurosurgeon drilled into the patient's brain. By the end of the internship, I was ready to begin my junior year and the application process, with a newfound confidence in my abilities and chosen path. No longer shocked by the procedures or stresses I witnessed, I was only amazed at the lack of encouragement I received, and these quotes still ring sharply in my ears whenever I envision my future. However, instead of discouraging me, the experience only inspired me to pursue my goals further. After that summer, I learned that nothing would deter me from my plans, and that I could still say with conviction that this is what I want to do with my life, despite however much negative feedback I may receive.

As a member of Lehigh University's newly created Pre-medical Pool Scholar's Program, I have been given a variety of opportunities. Despite my strong affinity for the sciences and mathematics, I have always had a keen interest in a liberal arts education. Whenever I am not studying for an organic chemistry class or completing the science requirements, the ultimate treat is to read a good novel, take a religion or literature course, pursue artistic endeavors, or sit down at the piano, which I have been playing for fifteen years. Coming from a diverse family, with parents from different cultures and religious faiths, sociological issues stemming from these types of differences have always intrigued me. Having the opportunity to do additional research has been a wonderful experience for me. I knew that I did not want to spend my elective research in a laboratory, but rather wanted to focus on more personal concerns of medicine. Working with Dr. Lasker, a medical sociologist, has been an eye-opening experience. Together, we study the emotional side of diseases, rather than the biological. We have worked on and completed several projects that study the biomedical, socioemotional, and organizational aspects of concern for individuals with Primary Biliary Cirrhosis. My research focuses on one online support group for these people, and together, Dr. Lasker and I have identified different areas of concern. As an aspiring physician, this research has helped me to recognize the compassion and emotional support that patients desire and physicians should offer. In August 2005, Dr. Lasker and I will travel to San Francisco to present our research at the annual conference of the Society for the Study of Social Problems. We will travel to Washington, D.C. again in November to present this research at the annual conference for the American Public Health Association. I am also looking forward to the upcoming year, in which I will interview patients with different forms of hepatitis and learn about the stigma they experience. This will culminate in a senior year thesis and presentation, as a part of another honors program, the College Scholar Program, of which I am a member. My research has been an inspiring marriage of two of my interests, medicine and socioemotional issues, and through it I have learned valuable lessons about the impact that physicians can have on the mental health of patients.

I also recognize the importance of proper listening, guiding, and teaching, learned through six years of employment. I work full time every summer as a Teaching Associate at a private tutoring center in Morrisville, Pennsylvania. Opened as a center for educational therapy, this space now serves a wide variety of students, each with lessons tailored to their personal needs. My growth there has been invaluable. It has given me the opportunity to work with children and adolescents on a one-to-one basis, proving to me the power of cooperation and discovery. I am able to directly influence my students, whether they are exceptional learners, or simply need personal attention, by illustrating to them not only the mechanics of reading, writing and math, but also the sheer joy of accomplishment. I am a people person and cherish the moments I spend with others. Through this experience at the tutoring center, I have learned that I also value sharing the benefits of education through instruction. One of the lessons I have learned is how important it is for a physician to be a good listener, a patient teacher, and a caring human being. I am eager to apply the interpersonal skills I have mastered throughout my experiences to my future in the medical field. I look forward to a lifetime of learning, exciting new challenges, and the ability to positively affect the lives of others.

See page 262 to find out where this student got in.

SAMANTHA VIZZINI

*Samantha did neuroscience research at the Medical Univer-
sity of South Carolina and had the opportunity to be a student
observer at the Center for Pain Management in Atlanta, Georgia.
She was a member of the Alpha Epsilon Delta premedical honor
society, a peer tutor, and involved in Greek life.*

Stats
MCAT: Physical Sciences, 10; Verbal Reasoning, 10; Writing Sample, Q; Biological Sciences, 10
Undergraduate overall GPA: 3.30
Undergraduate science GPA: 3.50
Undergraduate colleges attended: Tulane University
Gender: Female
Race: Caucasian
Applied To
Emory University, School of Medicine
Medical College of Georgia, School of Medicine
Tulane University, School of Medicine

AMCAS Personal Statement

The summer before my senior year at Tulane I thought I knew exactly what I wanted out of life, but that was the summer I realized how little I actually know about life and about myself. I had always dreamed of becoming a doctor but until then I did not understand why. It was always a feeling I had and could never really explain. Becoming a doctor just made sense to me. But that summer, after filling out my Medical School applications for the first time, I learned why I truly want to be a doctor.

I spent the entire summer working in a pain management clinic, following the Doctor around picking up after him while trying to pick up any knowledge possible. I was so excited to be in a real Doctor's office, observing patient examinations and procedures, but I had no idea that the real lesson I would learn would be about myself. Not that I didn't learn a great deal that summer observing Dr. Kabakibou, but I learned much more talking with his patients.

There was one patient in particular that I remember more than anyone I met in those few months. She was an older woman, divorced, and in her late fifties. She was a hair dresser running a school and a business out of her home with her daughter who was also a patient of Dr. KK. Like most of Dr. KK's patients they lived far from the metro area and drove many hours each month to see him. She was suffering from chronic back pain and was receiving a series of epidural steroid injections. Every month when she came in Dr. KK would send me to the pharmacy to get her a valium to calm her nerves for the procedure. As the valium started to take effect I would often sit in the exam room with her and discuss her life and her family.

We talked about her daughters, one who worked with her and suffered from endometriosis as well as chronic pain, and the other who ran off with her boyfriend, leaving an infant behind. We talked about everything from her court struggle to get custody of her granddaughter to her realization that the women she taught had been stealing her medication as well as her money. It was through these talks that I learned how strong this woman is. How amazing and resilient she must have been to be fighting against all of this and to still be so tolerant and compassionate. She taught me to see the good in people and to forgive the bad. She believed the people who stole from her were obviously fighting against something bigger than themselves and they could not help what they did, therefore we have no choice but to forgive them.

However, through discussions with this woman, and many other patients, I learned that there are many more people in this world fighting against things that seem bigger than themselves yet are succeeding in this struggle everyday. These people are the reason I want to be a doctor. To help those who are fighting for every moment they get in life. The people who refuse to let anything get in their way. These remarkable people inspired me all summer long to see each problem for what it is: an obstacle that I can overcome, even if it requires asking for help. They taught me so much yet at the end of my summer each one thanked me for helping them. I politely said goodbye to each of them and wished them well yet to this day I am still shocked. I should have been the one thanking them for teaching me the most important lessons I have ever learned; lessons that I could never have learned in school; lessons about myself and about life. To these people I will be eternally grateful, for showing me how what seemed like such a small effort on my part could make such a big difference to so many people, and for helping me understand the massive impact the medical profession has on people's lives, including my own.

See page 262 to find out where this student got in.

TAMARA JETTE

A University Scholar, Tamara graduated valedictorian from her high school and was given a full scholarship to the UMass institution of her choice. She also was able to apply for a CNA license due to completion of the Allied Health program in her high school, which enabled her to work as a nursing assistant during college. Tamara worked multiple other jobs while she was in college including working as an orientation leader, an information desk assistant, a tutor, and as the Student Activities and Events Council coordinator. She was also the president of the Pre-Medical Society and helped to establish a relationship with UMass Medical School and also set up medical school tours for students interested in visiting local campuses.

Stats
MCAT: Physical Sciences, 10; Verbal Reasoning, 10; Writing Sample, P; Biological Sciences, 11
Undergraduate overall GPA: 3.97
Undergraduate science GPA: 4.0
Undergraduate colleges attended: University of Massachusetts—Boston
Gender: Female
Race: Caucasian

Applied To
Harvard Medical School
Temple University School of Medicine
Tufts University, School of Medicine
SUNY Upstate Medical University
University of Massachusetts Medical School

Scholarship Essay

Tamara used the following essay in her application to University of Massachusetts Medical School.

Why do you want to be a doctor?

My pursuit of a medical career began before I knew I was in pursuit of a medical career. I responded to a pink flyer I saw hanging on the bulletin board at my high school, asking for a caretaker for recently born triplets. All I knew about babies was that they cried a lot. But coming from a family where a drug addiction created chaos, and having received little help from the outside world, I knew that if I could give help, I could not say no. This was what brought me to medicine: the idea that if you have it, you give it. Once I was old enough, having seen the triplets through their first year and a half of life, I became a certified nursing assistant. At the nursing home, I was, ostensibly, there because of my medical knowledge. But in dealing with the patients, I was both a trained caretaker and a person. While I knew how to drain a catheter, or get a bedridden patient showered, equally important was the fact that I knew how to talk to people, how to care for people with love. These two experiences – caring for triplets in the capacity of one human being helping another, and caring for the elderly in the capacity of a trained professional – pushed me towards a career in medicine, towards the belief that medicine is not just cold facts, the seconds between a heartbeat, but the beating heart itself.

The triplets' names were Alexia, Cassandra, and Maxwell. They were born almost two months premature, to an elementary school teacher named Judith and an engineer named Kevin. The babies had been conceived through in vitro fertilization. After a failed first attempt, three fertilized eggs were implanted in her womb, with the hope that one would take. Unexpectedly, they all took. This left Judith and Kevin in an impossible situation – financially unprepared, but unwilling to have any of the babies aborted, they would raise the children on small salaries, asking for any help they could get.

For a year and a half, I was at their house three nights a week, and on weekends. At first, I was only allowed to sit with the babies in my arms, because they were very fragile. After a while, I was responsible for bathing them, feeding them, teaching them to walk. I became a part of the family, and I loved the triplets like they were my own.

When I turned 18, I was one of two students in the rigorous Allied Health Program at my school to become a certified nursing assistant. I applied to an agency called Horizons Healthcare, and they placed me at a nursing home called Sterling Home.

At Sterling Home, I was given eight patients as my charges for every shift. I was responsible for waking them up, getting them showered and dressed, tending to complaints that they had about their health, checking for bedsores, and noting changes in complexion, bodily fluids, and alertness.

The Allied Health Program had prepared me for the analytical and physical parts of the job. It was my own curiosity that prompted me to talk to the patients. Standing in their rooms, I turned their failing bodies over in bed to prevent bedsores, I washed their faces and I did their hair, and I asked them about their lives. Women told me about their husbands, which wars they'd fought in, the honors they had claimed. Their children, where they went to college. The granddaughter that looked just like me. Men told me the jobs they used to have, jokingly flirting with me, calling me 'Sunshine'.

It was in the midst of all these people whose lives were coming to a close, who wanted to give me their last bits of wisdom, that I learned that I could never be just a girl who makes sure they're clean and fed. I had to be a person who connected, who learned the human side of the medicine I practiced as well as the charts and the numbers and the correlations.

I wanted to be a doctor because I want to make every moment count. I want to work in a field that is dynamic and always needs me. I want to work with people who share my love of medicine, and I want to work to make this field as good as it can be in my lifetime. I want to bring to the bedside not only the scientific facts but the human element that makes these facts relevant. This is what a doctor is to me and this is why I came to medical school.

Throughout my first year of school I was forced to be an agent of the facts, learning everything and forgetting nothing to get the grades I wanted to succeed. A few patient encounters were scattered throughout our curriculum including case presentations but to seek out the world that I had known as a CNA I had to make my own time to travel across Broad Street to Temple University Hospital. I shadowed as much as I was able to last year, including taking a surgery elective, shadowing my gastroenterologist preceptor, and completing a medical student service in the neurosurgery department during my first (and last) summer off. I also made sure to get involved beyond the classroom and the bedside by volunteering in the community and working with and eventually gaining leadership positions on a number of the outreach programs at Temple. I work with Prevention Point, a local needle exchange program and street-side health clinic that works to keep the spread of infection down and to provide healthcare to those who would otherwise not be able to receive it. I work with Big Friends, a tutoring and mentoring program at a local elementary school. I work with the Student National Medical Association, or SNMA, developing the Minority Association of Pre-medical Students, or MAPS, a program that helps to put in place mentors for pre-medical students at Temple's main campus. I am also Co-president in both the American Medical Student Association, or AMSA, and the American Medical Association, AMA.

The opportunity that I have been given is one that I cannot even begin to comprehend at times. I am grateful and I am in awe of the responsibilities that wearing a white coat, even a short one, bestow upon me. I plan to continue to work to not only thrive in the classroom but also outside. Because it takes more than medical school to make a physician and I hope that someday my patients will benefit form that philosophy.

Thank you for your time and consideration concerning this scholarship.

See page 262 to find out where this student got in.

VICKI ROBIN MCGOWAN II

While still in college, Vicki was a volunteer in the outpatient surgery recovery room of St. Agnes Hospital in Baltimore, Maryland. During this time she also worked as a resident assistant at her college, and was a science tutor and mentor at a local middle school. In addition, for two years she helped underserved sickle cell patients through a fellowship at the National Institutes of Health. She has received many awards, including Dean's List, Potomac Hall Paraprofessional of the Year, and the RSA Three Year Service Award.

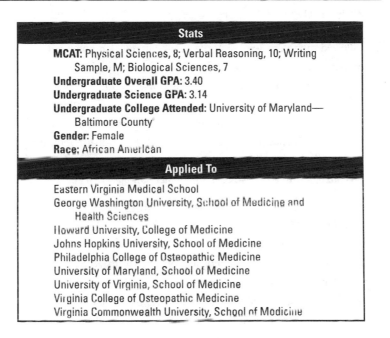

Stats

MCAT: Physical Sciences, 8; Verbal Reasoning, 10; Writing Sample, M; Biological Sciences, 7
Undergraduate Overall GPA: 3.40
Undergraduate Science GPA: 3.14
Undergraduate College Attended: University of Maryland—Baltimore County
Gender: Female
Race: African American

Applied To

Eastern Virginia Medical School
George Washington University, School of Medicine and Health Sciences
Howard University, College of Medicine
Johns Hopkins University, School of Medicine
Philadelphia College of Osteopathic Medicine
University of Maryland, School of Medicine
University of Virginia, School of Medicine
Virginia College of Osteopathic Medicine
Virginia Commonwealth University, School of Medicine

AMCAS Personal Statement

When questioned at the age of seven the proverbial inquiry asked of all school age children, I always responded simply with the word "doctor". Although I do not remember how that goal became my number one answer, I have held fast to that ambition ever since. Beginning in the third grade, I was considered the neighborhood nurse's aid for injured children, administering first aid remedies to their minor cuts and bruises. I became an avid spectator of public television programs involving hospital themes and I could often be found studying detailed photographs of the human body. By the age of fourteen, I had realized my passion for medicine and the human body and I decided to pursue it as a career. I was accepted into a magnet public high school in Baltimore

City with an emphasis on Health Care Delivery. Through my high school's partnership with Johns Hopkins Hospital, I was given the opportunity to witness a neurosurgery procedure. After seeing my first nerve biopsy, I left the room feeling both fascinated and informed. I was in awe of the surgeon for her expertise with the instruments but I also felt assured that with the proper training, I could also complete the procedure. That experience deepened my fascination for the human body and the practice of medicine.

During the first semester of my freshman year at UMBC, I was enrolled in the Basic Concepts of Sociology class. This course challenged my perceptions about life and the role of society. I was intrigued by the many sociological theorists' explanations of cultural differences among civilizations. I developed a new passion, one rooted in understanding the complexities of the American social structure. Although my interest in medicine had not diminished, I began to search for a major that would combine my interests of understanding health care and society. The interdisciplinary studies program allowed me to create an entirely unique major that combined the scientific basis of medicine with the social theories of American society. My major, Health and American Society, has broadened my knowledge base regarding the interaction of society with the administration of healthcare. Through the courses within my curriculum, I have been encouraged to question the present and to examine the past. As a result, I have noticed the influence that social aspects have on the distribution of health care. I have unearthed the reality of health disparities among the underprivileged classes in society and I am determined to overcome such inequalities when I become a physician.

Through my research training fellowship with the NIH, I work directly with the underserved sickle cell community from the Washington, DC metropolitan area. On a daily basis, I witness the difficulties these patients confront, often directly related to poverty. Under the direction of my mentors, I help these patients to cope with other chronic illnesses, homelessness, immigration, medical insurance problems and transportation issues in addition to assisting with the management of their sickle cell disease. This experience has further inspired me to serve disadvantaged urban communities when I become a practicing physician.

It is with this new outlook that I approach the next step of my career. In medical school, I wish to discover not only what I can do as a physician to treat illness and disease but also how I can assist the patient with healing himself thereby contributing to his autonomy as a patient and compensating for the health disparities within his social class. My childhood desire to become a doctor is maturing into a drive to assist with the improvement of the American medical systems from the inside out. I have learned that the reality of life today is malleable for the future and I hope to become an innovator of positive change in the world of medicine.

See page 263 to find out where this student got in.

VIVEK KALIA

Vivek was accepted into the University of Alabama at Birmingham's EMSAP (Early Medical School Acceptance Program) right out of high school. He spent a summer overseas in rural Kolkata, India conducting public health research, and received many academic distinctions and honors while in college including designation as UAB's official Rhodes Scholarship nominee.

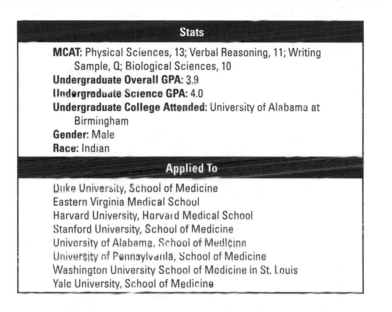

Stats
MCAT: Physical Sciences, 13; Verbal Reasoning, 11; Writing Sample, Q; Biological Sciences, 10
Undergraduate Overall GPA: 3.9
Undergraduate Science GPA: 4.0
Undergraduate College Attended: University of Alabama at Birmingham
Gender: Male
Race: Indian

Applied To
Duke University, School of Medicine
Eastern Virginia Medical School
Harvard University, Harvard Medical School
Stanford University, School of Medicine
University of Alabama, School of Medicine
University of Pennsylvania, School of Medicine
Washington University School of Medicine in St. Louis
Yale University, School of Medicine

AMCAS Personal Statement

As she lay there in her sleep, a trickle of blood coming from her nose went down the side of her face, dripping onto the pristine white cloth next to her. My aunt, who had already been frantic, became even more hysterical and was crying maniacally and praying out loud "Someone wipe the blood! Don't let her bleed now! God please have mercy now!" It was the hardest thing I ever had to witness and the hardest I ever remember crying. My cousin, Sejal Sharma, lay there before her entire family at the young age of 23 in an elegant mahogany casket, claimed by the demonic and relentless monster we've termed cancer. It was only about half an hour before the funeral ceremony was to begin. I was but a mere child and couldn't understand the incredible impact this event would have on my life until I was a teenager.

One thing I will always remember my aunt telling me about my cousin, Sejal, whom I unfortunately never got to spend a significant amount of time with, was that "nobody could ever say anything bad about a person like her. She was an angel." Every time I saw Sejal, she adorned her beautiful face with a most charming smile that would warm my insides. She was the eldest of my uncle's five children on my mom's side and was a sort of mother figure to two of her younger brothers, Sunil and Sanjay, who were 18 and 19 respectively at the time of Sejal's death.

Sejal's exact condition was unclear for a long while before we discovered that she had a brain tumor. My aunt and uncle did not know who to turn to for help in explaining the cause of her constant headaches. She had many eye exams performed and was referred to an ophthalmologist after the optometrists couldn't tell her anything that they thought was abnormal. The ophthalmologist told Sejal that he detected too much pressure on her optic nerves and that she should get an MRI performed on herself to reveal anything hidden inside causing such pressure. After the MRI, my aunt and uncle bore the unforgettable news: "Your daughter has a brain tumor."

Sejal was hospitalized soon afterwards. The neurosurgeons told her parents that the tumor was deep inside the brain, near the center, rendering it inoperable and thereby prescribing her eventual death due to this mass of uncontrollable cells. I remember going to hospital and seeing her lying in her hospital bed, as cheery as ever, as if she, in all her childish giddiness, didn't know of the demon taking over inside her head. My sisters could not hold the tears back and cried uncontrollably whenever we left the hospital, knowing that our beloved cousin's inevitable death had been set.

A shunt had been put into her brain to drain some fluid, but the pressure would surely, the neurosurgeons said, increase over time. Sejal was sent home because the hospital could do nothing else for her. She was feeling a little better after the shunt had been put in, but inside the tumor grew unremittingly. My aunt and uncle never stopped the search for other neurosurgeons who could somehow help their daughter. Unfortunately for our entire family, the tumor wouldn't allow us enough time to find someone who thought they could operate with even a slight chance of success: it determined that Sejal's time on earth was rapidly coming to a close.

As Sejal's condition deteriorated, she was readmitted to the hospital, which would end up being her last time. I'll never forget the beautiful smile she gave me the last time I saw her alive laying there in her hospital bed in Grady Memorial Hospital in Atlanta, her chin tucked against her chest, her dark brown eyes affixed with mine. I'm sure she knew the end was near, but her loving heart wouldn't let us grieve in her presence. I remember her saying, "I wonder how much hair they're going to have to take off by the time I'm out of here. I don't want to end up looking like Sinéad

O' Conner," a comment so unexpected and so funny that only Sejal would say. Thinking back now, that humor and light-heartedness made her so irresistible and makes her a role model of mine.

At nine years of age, death was a perplexity that I didn't know how to deal with. Now that I am applying to medical school, I want only to become part of the field that could have helped my dear cousin. Though she is not here with us now, I know that she knows the real reason I want to do all this: I want to lessen the number of people who have to find themselves in the same position our family found itself in that horrible summer in 1994. I was devastated at the time to see my cousin die, and in such a horrible way – deteriorating day by day, with more and more pain inflicted until her body could no longer take it. I know that, because of the fighter she was, she didn't let go until she absolutely could no longer hold on. Because we didn't have any physicians in our family at the time to help us understand what was happening, we couldn't understand what was going on. After all: aren't doctors and surgeons supposed to be able to fix things like these? During my continued education in medical sciences, I will surely learn to understand how the human body, resilient as it is, is also in many respects fragile and unpredictable. Then I will be able to console myself on the subject of Sejal's death. Until then, it all remains a mystery to me.

Now that I have come to the point in my life where I can choose a profession for myself, there is no other that I have the passion and drive for as I do to become a physician. I have long loved science and have been compelled to study it in depth. Sejal's death made me look into myself over the years and realize that insatiable desire I have to understand and treat the conglomeration of cells we call the human body. Only through being a physician will I be able to satisfy my intellectual curiosities and the irrepressible need I have to help others.

See page 263 to find out where this student got in.

ANONYMOUS 1

The applicant participated in the Vagelos Scholars Program at the University of Pennsylvania, which allowed her to earn a bachelor's degree in biochemistry and a master's degree in chemistry in four years. As part of the program, she did two summers of research, completed a significant amount of laboratory work in her junior and senior years, and took graduate courses. While at Penn, the applicant sang in an a cappella group and earned various leadership positions within the group. A Phi Beta Kappa member, she graduated summa cum laude and received an award of distinction from Penn's biochemistry department.

Stats

MCAT: Physical Sciences, 12; Verbal Reasoning, 10; Writing Sample, Q; Biological Sciences, 12
Graduate school GPA: 3.80
Graduate degree earned: Master of Science (MS) in Chemistry
Graduate school attended: University of Pennsylvania
Undergraduate overall GPA: 3.82
Undergraduate science GPA: 3.75
Undergraduate college attended: University of Pennsylvania
Gender: Female
Race: Caucasian

Applied To

Boston University, School of Medicine
Columbia University, College of Physicians and Surgeons
Cornell University, Joan & Sanford I. Weill Medical Center
Emory University, School of Medicine
Harvard University, Harvard Medical School
New York University, Mount Sinai School of Medicine
New York University, NYU School of Medicine
Stanford University, School of Medicine
Tufts University, School of Medicine
University of Massachusetts, Medical School
University of Pennsylvania, School of Medicine
Washington University in St. Louis, School of Medicine

AMCAS Personal Statement

I had an appointment, a gig, in another world, only ten minutes and a half-dozen blocks away. I left my lab early and walked quickly through the Friday afternoon rain to meet up with my a cappella group, Dischord. The eleven of us met at my house on the edge of Penn's campus, and walked past dilapidated houses to an old church. This was the home of New Beginnings, an after-school program for low-income West Philadelphia families. As strangers, we entered a room overflowing with children and set up on a small makeshift stage at the front. I played an "A" on the pitch pipe, bringing Dischord to the ready and silencing the crowded room. We led off with Jenny, an upbeat tune—one of our best arrangements. After the second verse, the room lit up with smiles and wide-eyed excitement. Some children even danced! We performed three more songs and then divided the children into groups to teach them our different voice parts. A chorus of eight little hands grabbed me, pleading: "Can you please teach me your part?" We crowded into a tight circle and sang the soprano line to Jenny over and over again. In no time they had it mastered. Together we made music. While they learned a new song to hum on the way home, I learned something about myself that lent a new clarity to my future goals. For me, the greatest sense of fulfillment would come from using the passions that drive me, as a vehicle to reach others.

While I truly enjoyed the challenge of my undergraduate research experience, this exchange at New Beginnings made me better understand what was lacking. No matter how many new techniques I mastered or how many problems I solved, there was always a void. How could investigating interesting and challenging scientific problems not bring me the sense of fulfillment I expected? Not understanding the answer, I worked harder and became a better, more independent scientist. Experiments grew easier to plan, and my work involving the crystallization trials of lambda integrase moved closer to completion. Despite my progress, something important was still missing.

The challenge of research needed the same sharing of passion I experienced at New Beginnings. This to me is the essence of the medical profession—a passion for science and problem solving, coupled with the emotional satisfaction derived from caring for and interacting with people. These two important aspects of medicine became more apparent to me when I recently spent some time shadowing a medical geneticist. The doctor I followed explained her thinking processes and dealings in regard to patient risk, benefit, and available therapeutic options. What I appreciated about this doctor was not only her ability to think critically and scientifically, but also her ability to communicate this information to her patients in a compassionate and clear manner. The combination of all of these experiences brought me to the realization that practicing medicine would best synthesize my love of science with my desire to share my passions with others.

Specifically, I am most interested in pursuing pediatrics or oncology. Pediatrics is appealing because I love interacting with children, and appreciate their fresh world perspective. Oncology also interests me, because it is an intellectually stimulating, quickly evolving field, requiring ongoing education to remain current. Learning about cancer has become increasingly important to me in the past few years, as I witnessed firsthand its affects on the lives of so many people for whom I have cared. I watched helplessly as lung cancer took the life of my grandmother, and as many of my mother's friends underwent lumpectomies, chemotherapy, and radiation for breast cancer. I want to become empowered to help make a difference in people's lives, and the medical profession is a challenging and fulfilling way to do so.

See page 263 to find out where this student got in.

ANONYMOUS 2

After college, the applicant served as an investigator on legal defense teams representing death row inmates, volunteered at an inner-city family practice clinic, assisted in research on schizophrenia and bipolar disorder, and started a nonprofit organization providing mental health services to Rwandese genocide survivors.

Stats
MCAT: Physical Sciences, 12; Verbal Reasoning, 12; Writing Sample, O; Biological Sciences, 11 **Undergraduate overall GPA:** 3.44 **Undergraduate science GPA:** 4.00 **Undergraduate college attended:** Harvard College **Gender:** Female **Race:** Caucasian
Applied To
Columbia University, College of Physicians and Surgeons Cornell University, Weill Medical College Emory University, School of Medicine Harvard University, Harvard Medical School New York University, Mount Sinai School of Medicine New York University, NYU School of Medicine Northwestern University, Feinberg School of Medicine Oregon Health and Science University, School of Medicine Stanford University, School of Medicine Tulane University, School of Medicine University of California—Davis, School of Medicine University of California—Irvine, College of Medicine University of California—Los Angeles, David Geffen School of Medicine University of California—San Diego, School of Medicine University of California—San Francisco, School of Medicine University of Chicago, Pritzker School of Medicine University of Miami, School of Medicine University of Southern California, Keck School of Medicine University of Washington, School of Medicine Yeshiva University, Albert Einstein College of Medicine

AMCAS Personal Statement

The attorney-client conference room at North Carolina's Guilford County Jail has three gray plastic chairs. They are old chairs, the kind that have been warped by humidity and wear such that that they never sit evenly on the floor. Miguel and I sat in those chairs together all day every day for three straight weeks. Miguel liked to switch every few hours from his chair to the empty one. He liked to rock the uneven chairs back and forth on the cement floor. When we talked about his involvement with East LA gangs, he rocked harder. When we talked about the execution of his family by guerilla terrorists in El Salvador, he rocked even harder. When we talked about his methamphetamine addiction, he picked up the chair underneath him and began dragging it around the room. Sometimes Miguel made so much noise the guards outside came to make sure everything was all right. One of the first phrases Miguel learned to say in English was, "We're fine, thank you."

Miguel was not fine. He was facing a first-degree murder charge and capital punishment. He was actively psychotic and was diagnosed with bipolar and post-traumatic stress disorders. Moreover, the unclean needles Miguel had used to shoot meth had left him, years later, with an advanced case of Hepatitis C.

As an investigator assigned to Miguel's case, I had spent the last six months traveling between North Carolina, San Francisco and Los Angeles uncovering all this. Because I spoke Spanish, I was the first professional to whom Miguel had been able to communicate his symptoms and experiences since coming to the United States. I worked feverishly with physicians, psychiatrists and defense attorneys to prepare a bio-psycho-social case history for the Guilford County Court, with the hope that the court would come to see the degree to which Miguel required both medical and mental health care. When the Guilford County district attorney's office at last offered a deal for life in prison, with a clause ensuring adequate mental and physical health facilities, I flew once more to North Carolina to meet with Miguel. It took us three weeks of sitting all day in those gray chairs before Miguel was able to take in what he was facing and make a decision to save his life.

When Miguel finally accepted the deal, I rose from my plastic chair for the last time, exhausted by all I had been through, still coming to terms with what I had experienced. My time with Miguel led me to understand the inextricability of physical and mental illness, and the complexity of the skills required in their treatment. I realized I wanted to learn these skills, to appreciate better the origin and consequence of conditions such as Miguel's. Additionally, I realized how critical personal connection is in being able to help people like Miguel. The research and investigation I had been able to do for Miguel's case, the final plea bargain— all of that resulted from the relationship that Miguel and I had built.

Though my work with Miguel crystallized these ideas, they had been growing in me for a number of years. They traced back to my junior year in college, when my mother became critically ill with intestinal scleroderma. I know that the hours I spent sitting by my mother's bed, working with her to manage the physical realities of her illness, steered me towards the hours I later spent sitting in those gray chairs with Miguel. My mother died not long after Miguel's life was spared. Though my mother's situation couldn't have been more different from Miguel's, both relationships left me with a clear vision of the work I wanted to pursue.

Other experiences I have had— traveling solo through rural Bolivia, discussing trauma care with Rwandese genocide survivors, communicating with doctors in Zanzibar who treat malaria-induced epilepsy— have confirmed my understanding of medicine as an emotionally rewarding and socially active career. They have also confirmed my belief that the skills involved in achieving good medical care are numerous, complicated, and critical to master. This past year, working at the Contra Costa Center for Health and the San Francisco VA hospital, I have seen these skills in action. I have been inspired to see patients outside of the terrifying context of criminal defense and third world conditions, patients at ease with their doctors and their treatments. I think about Miguel and try to imagine what might have been different had he received treatment before his crime. I think about someday having the resources and expertise to treat the potential Miguels. Whether I end up a free-clinic internist, a Doctors Without Borders obstetrician, or a jail psychiatrist, I cannot envision a more rewarding or important career.

Secondary Essay #1

The applicant used the following essay in her application to Columbia University, College of Physicians and Surgeons.

What satisfaction do you expect to receive from being a physician?

There are many ways in which I expect to find a career as a physician satisfying. I expect that the science and the daily problem solving will be interesting and exciting. I expect that my relationships with patients will be instructive and affecting. I expect to be challenged, both emotionally and intellectually, by my efforts to improve the medical, social, and psychological well being of the communities in which I work. In fact, what I expect to find rewarding about a career as a physician is precisely that it offers an array of intellectual, emotional, and social-political satisfactions.

I've come to learn that a complex combination of satisfactions is important to me. I spent much of college trying to achieve a balance among them—how to be stimulated intellectually without becoming too self-involved, how to help others without losing sight of my own needs. My senior thesis as an English major became a quest to solve this very dilemma. I wrote my thesis on the poetry of Robert Hass because I was fascinated by Hass's unique ability to explore political and theoretical issues through a personal and phenomenological framework, pulling large and important ideas out of the abstract and into a more intimate and empathic realm. Hass's poems use various literary devices to demonstrate that seemingly disparate political and personal spheres can coexist and inform one another. Hass makes clear how the capacity for self-understanding is what gives rise to the capacity for compassion, and how capacity for compassion is what drives political idealism.

My decision to pursue medicine arose in the context of my study of Hass's poetry. In medicine, I believe I can find what Hass describes: intellectual excitement and interpersonal engagement driving social-political accomplishment. Hass's poetry fit well with my efforts to find my way out of my senior year quandary, and I believe that a career in medicine fits well with what I know I want to do in my life. I'm sure that there will be times of heart-ache—dying patients, long hours, working with inadequate resources—and I expect to falter in some moments just as I expect to soar in others. But even in those times of complete exhaustion I think that I will maintain a deep and personal investment in my work that I already feel fortunate to have found.

Secondary Essay #2

The applicant used the following essay in her application to Northwestern University, Feinberg School of Medicine.

> *Describe the distinguishable characteristics you possess and tell us how you think these characteristics will enhance your success as a FSM medical student and future physician.*

My beliefs in social justice and helping others have always been very important to me, and working diligently and competently to follow these beliefs has always been something I have found myself able to do as well as enjoy. I am able to remain calm in chaotic situations, whether I am talking down a psychotic patient or managing a group of summer interns assisting our legal team during a death penalty trial. I can successfully mediate between parties in conflict, whether I am working with an angry mother and her terrified daughter who has recently received a positive pregnancy test or with an inmate and a prison guard, each of whom insists the other is out to get him. I don't tire easily, and when passionately invested in a project I will work until its completion. I am a fast learner, and I am inspired and eager to learn from people with experience greater than my own in order to more efficiently and effectively achieve my goals. Lastly, I am a competent Spanish speaker, and find it extremely satisfying to communicate successfully with people in need who have been isolated and intimidated by an existing language barrier.

I expect these skills to prove useful in medical school and in my career as a physician. In medical school I anticipate being challenged by long hours, difficult material, and clinical inexperience. I will need to be eager, unassuming, and dedicated in order to meet these challenges successfully. I will need to call upon the skills I already possess and be open to learning from the skills of others, mentors and peers alike. I believe the experience I have had working with various medical, legal, and research teams will help me to strike this balance effectively. I also believe that my unremitting dedication to helping others and achieving social justice will only get stronger as I acquire the skills needed to become a physician. I hope that the combination of my passionate beliefs, enthusiasm, and willingness to learn will make me a devoted and effective health care provider.

Secondary Essay #3

The applicant used the following essay in her application to University of California—Davis, School of Medicine.

Who would you consider to be the most influential person in your life and why?

My mother was, and continues to be, the most influential person in my life. My mother gave me a sense of security and empowerment in the world that is fundamental to the choices I have made and the paths I intend to follow. One of my earliest memories is of the two of us sitting together in our bathroom when I was three. I was in the tub, dressed in my bathing suit, swim cap and goggles. She was just outside the tub, reaching her arm over the side so her hand was flat at the bottom. I remember holding my breath, ducking my face in the water, kissing my mother's fingers, and spluttering back up for air. Years later my father explained this puzzling recollection to me. Apparently, I wanted to learn to swim but was terrified of putting my head under water. Kissing my mother's hand, however, was something I loved to do. So, night after night, my mother helped me practice kissing her hand at the bottom of the bathtub until I was comfortable putting my head underwater and could join my friends in swim class.

My mother's love for me and her belief in all I could accomplish have enabled me to do so much more than learn to swim. My ability to work hard, follow my passions and expect success is directly linked to those early days in the tub and the many variations of those days that followed.

My mother died this past January of intestinal scleroderma, an illness she had been battling for almost twenty years. She got sick when I was a little girl, and lived on powdered food and IV-feeding for much of my childhood. It wasn't until I was in college, however, that I realized how sick she was. I remember being a teenager and describing my mother's condition to people by saying, "Oh, it's not life-threatening; she just can't always eat." I had no idea of the magnitude of her daily struggle with pain and deprivation. I knew the details of her illness — the circumference of her G-tube, the antibiotics she rotated through — yet I never connected these facts with the reality that my mother was slowly dying. Talking to other family members, friends, my mother's colleagues, and even the physicians who treated her, I've come to realize that we were all living with a positive and hopeful view of my mother's condition that she constructed, for us and for herself. My mother taught me the powerful lesson that we can define our own realities. Her optimism and her refusal to live as an invalid defined her world and mine as I was growing up. Today, my life is filled with excitement, a sense of opportunity, and a belief that I can make a difference. I know I would be a very different person had my mother raised me in a climate of fear and suffering.

I learned from my mother that one's approach to a problem defines the problem. I learned from her what truly excellent care-taking can be. I remember the absolute trust I had in my mother, the encouragement I felt when I saw her hand at the bottom of the tub. If I can give my patients one ounce of that encouragement, if I can communicate to them the same courageous optimism that informed my childhood, I know I will become an effective physician.

Secondary Essay #4

The applicant used the following essay in her application to University of California—Davis, School of Medicine.

Each applicant brings with them goals of what they want to accomplish as a physician. They also have their larger dreams with regards to what they hope to accomplish in their lifetime. In a brief paragraph, please describe how you would want to be remembered at the end of your life.

The final line of Shakespeare's "Sonnet 73"— "Love that well, which thou must lose ere long"—captures how I would like to be remembered at the end of my life. I want to be remembered not just as somebody who loved her community, but as somebody who loved it well, somebody who didn't just take but also gave back, somebody who put attention and effort toward following her ideals. Shakespeare deliberately includes the word "well" at the end of his sonnet to avoid a clichéd statement about love and loss, to convey that the idealized notion of love being all that matters is false. He indicates that love alone is not enough; it must be accompanied by dedication and hard work. I think these are crucial words of advice for a future doctor. They help me understand that my strong desire to help my community is not, in itself, enough to make me an effective health care provider. I will need to read article upon article as research progresses. I will need to deliver bad news to patients in a calm and encouraging manner. I will need to work long hours when I'm tired. I look forward to medical school as a place in which I can apply Shakespeare's instructions to my life as a physician and continue to construct a legacy of one who loved well the world in which she lived.

See page 264 to find out where this student got in.

ANONYMOUS 3

The applicant volunteered at Stony Brook University Hospital in the Pediatric, Pediatric Intensive Care, and Pediatric Oncology units. She did research on the evolution of pelvic asymmetry in the threespine stickleback—a type of fish—that was presented at several conferences. A teaching assistant for the Biology and Psychology departments, the allpicant was involved in course planning and held review sessions for students. She was a member of the Sigma Beta Honor Society Steering Committee, Phi Beta Kappa Honor Society, Golden Key International Honor Society, and the National Society of Collegiate Scholars. She also assisted physicians in a medical office for four years.

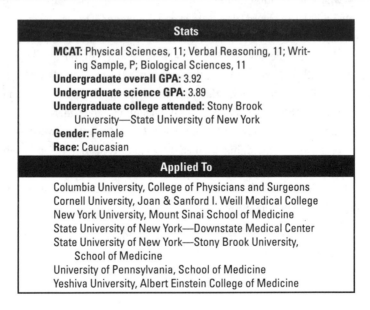

Stats
MCAT: Physical Sciences, 11; Verbal Reasoning, 11; Writing Sample, P; Biological Sciences, 11
Undergraduate overall GPA: 3.92
Undergraduate science GPA: 3.89
Undergraduate college attended: Stony Brook University—State University of New York
Gender: Female
Race: Caucasian

Applied To
Columbia University, College of Physicians and Surgeons
Cornell University, Joan & Sanford I. Weill Medical College
New York University, Mount Sinai School of Medicine
State University of New York—Downstate Medical Center
State University of New York—Stony Brook University, School of Medicine
University of Pennsylvania, School of Medicine
Yeshiva University, Albert Einstein College of Medicine

AMCAS Personal Statement

"What do you want to be when you grow up?" That is the magic question that is most often asked of children. For many youngsters the answer wavers between a lawyer, a teacher, a policeman or an astronaut, and alternates every week. For me, however, the answer has always been a consistent "I want to be a doctor."

The inspiration to become a physician first came when I was eight years old. My two year old brother was ill and no one knew what was wrong with him. He could not explain what was hurting him because he had not learned to speak yet. Sophisticated imaging technology, such as a sonogram, that was necessary to reveal my brother's acute appendicitis was simply not available, and thus neither the pediatrician nor the emergency room doctors were able to come up with a diagnosis. Luckily, a physician family friend correctly suspected appendicitis and encouraged us to take my brother to the hospital before it was too late. Finally, not a moment too soon, my brother was operated on and his ruptured appendix was removed. If any more time had been wasted, he would have died. Watching my little brother go through this painful ordeal, and seeing my family in such distress was extremely difficult for me. I wished I could do something to ease his pain and help him get better. It was frustrating, sitting in the sidelines, witnessing a loved one suffering, and not being able to do anything about it. But the surgeon and the doctor who diagnosed him were able to help him. By telling my parents that their son would be well again, they were able to make a difference. In my young eyes they were real heroes for saving him. After that day I wanted to be just like them, I wanted to be able to at least have the chance to help others deal with their illnesses. I wanted to be some little girl's hero someday too. It was then that I decided that when I grew up I would become a doctor.

At the time, it was probably just a childish dream, but this dream has stayed with me all along, maturing as I matured. As I got older and more knowledgeable, I became even more confident that this was the right path for me. In addition to the healing and interpersonal aspect of being a physician, I am also especially interested in the science of medicine itself. All throughout my scholastic career I was always drawn to the natural sciences. I was very curious about how things work or why certain phenomena take place. The more answers I discovered, the more captivated I became, and that fascination continued to drive my hunger for more scientific knowledge.

In preparation for the future, I attended Brooklyn Technical High School, one of the top three science school in New York City and was part of the Bio-Medical Sciences major. I challenged myself by taking Genetics, Anatomy and Physiology, Organic Chemistry, and Advanced Placement courses in Biology, Physics, and Calculus. Ultimately, I graduated as one of the top ten students with honors in my major and chose to attend Stony Brook University, knowing it was one of the top research universities concentrated on the sciences. I chose the biology major since it closely fit my interests, and again offered sufficient challenges. In addition to focusing on the sciences, I kept my focus on a future in medicine as well. One of the most rewarding experiences was taking a class in Darwinian Medicine. Learning about this newly emerging field was truly enthralling. The core of this course was centered on the evolution of pathogens and the resulting counter human evolution. For a potential physician, the notions presented were eye-opening and provided me with an improved grasp of, and better perspective on, the prominent health issues of today and tomorrow. Taking this course made me want to strive even harder to achieve my goal and be able to apply my knowledge. Currently, I am working on a study concerning the evolution of loss of bony armor in fish. In the near future this research will lead to the discovery and isolation of a growth factor that is responsible for the growth of bone. This finding has a potential use in the medical field in dealing with bone injuries. I also spend time volunteering in the Pediatrics unit of Stony Brook University Hospital. I have learned a great deal about the doctor-patient relationship by observing doctors and interacting with the patients and their families.

For me a medical profession presents the opportunity to learn continuously throughout my career and to employ my knowledge directly in a beneficial manner. It is an exigent, and yet extremely rewarding field, the rigorous path to which is paved with sacrifice and determination. Without the willpower and a real desire to practice medicine in accordance to its doctrines, this goal cannot be achieved. The aspiration to enter the medical field and make a difference in people's lives has motivated me to do everything I have accomplished so far. That eight year old girl who was inspired by a doctor saving her brother's life is now all grown up and is ready to embark on the first step of the journey that will allow her to make a significant impact on the healthcare of other people.

See page 265 to find out where this student got in.

ANONYMOUS 4

The applicant volunteered at Pattengil Middle School, where she helped students in math and social studies, provided after-school homework help, and created activities that encouraged students to be involved in school. She also volunteered at Huron Valley Sinai Hospital in Commerce, Michigan, where she fed, bathed, and took the vitals of patients. Proficient in Indian classical dance, the applicant's performances raised money for the education of underprivileged children in India.

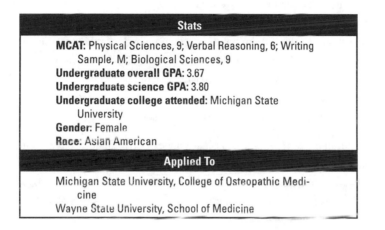

Stats
MCAT: Physical Sciences, 9; Verbal Reasoning, 6; Writing Sample, M; Biological Sciences, 9
Undergraduate overall GPA: 3.67
Undergraduate science GPA: 3.80
Undergraduate college attended: Michigan State University
Gender: Female
Race: Asian American
Applied To
Michigan State University, College of Osteopathic Medicine
Wayne State University, School of Medicine

AMCAS Personal Statement

"That's the last box," my dad said as we just finished loading the truck to be shipped to India. Moving: a word very familiar to me, as I have moved three times during a span of twenty-one years. At the age of five we moved to Curacao, a small island in the Caribbean, at eleven back to India, and again at thirteen to the United States of America. Traveling and living in different communities has taught me how to understand different kinds of people and their unique situations. These experiences have also instilled in me a deep desire to interact with others different from myself and serve my community. As a physician, I want to help, educate and value the needs of people in various situations.

Irrespective of the country, in both developing and developed societies, every individual seeks for help. In India, I watched mothers carrying their kids as they were begging for money when cars halted at stoplights, just to gather a few pennies to feed their children. This made me realize that their role as mothers made them stand in the scorching heat so their kids would not go to sleep on an empty stomach. In America, I have seen homeless people searching for pop cans in the trash bins so they can make a little money to buy dinner. Observing these conditions has made me understand that every person acts according to their situation and they do whatever necessary, within their limits, for survival. My desire to help society awakened in me when I saw these people in these situations and this led me to explore the medical profession. My exploration of the medical field started off in a school setting and progressed further through volunteering at a hospital. These experiences have built my passion towards being a physician.

My determination to educate people is why I decided to volunteer at Pattengil Middle School in East Lansing, Michigan. By volunteering at Pattengil, I hoped to make students aware of the importance of education, the impact it has on one's future, and the role it plays in one's survival. I was paired with a sixth grader who was significantly behind in school, as she did not get the necessary support at home. She did not have anyone to help her with her schoolwork, until I provided her with after school help and made sure she completed her homework for the next day. My role in educating her helped me to understand her situation, as she was just a young child who wanted some love and support when she got home from school.

My Bharatanatyam (Indian classical dance) performances have contributed to raise funds for several organizations to help support the education of the underprivileged. My contribution has helped children to obtain a better education, which ultimately provides them with several options for their future. I feel a doctor's primary role is to educate and promote awareness to patients about various diseases and their treatments. My love of educating and interacting with people enhanced my interest in medicine.

As a volunteer at the Huron Valley Sinai Hospital in Commerce, Michigan, I had an opportunity to observe and value the needs of people in various situations. My experience in the hospital has helped educate me on what being a physician is all about: their driving passion to help people, to be challenged, and to learn throughout their life. It has also given me first hand experience as a care provider. I wanted to assist patients by providing them with a comfortable healing environment so that they could heal faster. I helped Patient Care Assistants in the hospital by taking patient vitals, bathing immobile patients, and feeding those that needed assistance. Even though most of the patients were several generations older than I was, they all looked to me for compassion and comfort. They enjoyed my company, as I would watch television with them, talk to them about their hobbies, and give them a helping hand when needed. I realized that my perfect vision of the hospital environment was distorted, as some patients do die and some act aggressively. I never lost sight of the fact that they are human beings who just want some love and guidance to feel better. These are all experiences that have helped me build a stronger passion for the field of medicine. This passion includes my wish to provide people with the prospect of good health, and my respect for people in various settings and situations. As a doctor I want to work with people and assist them in the healing process.

Observing different societies has made me the person I am today, broadened my horizons, and above all made me realize that my goal is to be a physician. I chose to become a doctor because it is the perfect career in which I will be able to acquire humanistic rewards, which to me are priceless. Living in different countries around the world has shown me the meaning of responsibility, flexibility, cooperation and respect towards different ideas and principles. Most of all it has enhanced my lifelong commitment to better society.

Secondary Essay

The applicant used the following essay in her application to Michigan State University, College of Osteopathic Medicine.

Describe a personal experience or ethical challenge you have faced that has influenced the development of your character. How has this experience helped you to develop specific skills and/or abilities that are essential to becoming an osteopathic physician?

My life in general has been different from the life led by the normal American youth. I was born in India and raised with the customs and traditions of a conservative Indian family. We lived in a joint family where my parents lived with their parents and siblings, and their families. Girls did not have the same privileges as boys in several circumstances. For example, girls were not allowed to go out of the house to watch movies and go shopping with friends. We were also constrained in the clothes we are supposed to wear. We were only supposed to wear clothes that cover our entire body. Our house ran in a timely manner, people are not allowed to do as they pleased. Breakfast, lunch and dinner are only served at a certain time, and the schedule had to be followed. Everyone is very disciplined as they all rise early and sleep early. Through this part of my life I learnt discipline that is necessary to make a good osteopathic physician.

At the age of thirteen, we moved to Detroit, Michigan. Moving to the United States has been a big change and almost the turning point of my life. When we first moved here, I was amazed by the American culture. The fact that children get so much independence was something new to me. After living in a joint family for several years of my life, it took me a while to adjust to a house with only four people living in it. When I moved here in the eighth grade, it was hard for me to make friends too. Everyone had already made his or her friends group and I did not quite know which group I belonged to. Everyone was very different from me; in the way they spoke, behaved and presented themselves. I also had to adapt to the different educational systems. In India, we were evaluated solely on our class exam results, but in America, we are encouraged to be well-rounded individuals. It took sometime to get used to the idea of extracurricular activities, volunteering, lab work and sports, which characterize a well-rounded person. After moving to America I have learnt adaptability and flexibility that are essential to becoming an osteopathic physician.

Staying in different parts of the world has allowed me to experience how life differs in a developed nation and a third world society. It has also enhanced my interest in the medical field. Not being able to afford for a medical checkup, millions of people in India are left clueless, not knowing the symptoms of the disease and what needs to be done to control it. Watching mothers carrying their kids and begging for money as cars halt at a stoplight so they can gather a few pennies to feed their children made me realize how fortunate I am for being able to have three meals a day. Not even having enough money to eat a proper meal, they definitely have never gotten a medical checkup. Experiencing all these situations has motivated me to become a physician and provide an opportunity where underprivileged people can turn to physicians for guidance irrespective of their financial status. Seeing the poverty has made me compassionate and wanting to help the underprivileged and the poor.

Having been raised in either of the two hemispheres, I have learnt to adapt and be open-minded about different cultures, educational systems, and different lifestyles. Visiting the world and meeting people of all different backgrounds has built my desire to interact and learn more about people. Living in India has taught me bonding, respect, and responsibility. In America I have learnt flexibility, good judgment and cooperation, which I feel, are qualities that will make me be a better osteopathic physician.

See page 265 to find out where this student got in.

Chapter 9

WHERE THEY GOT IN

Adam John Defoe

University of North Dakota, School of Medicine and Health Sciences
Applied to:

Creighton University, School of Medicine .... waitlisted, withdrew

University of Minnesota—Duluth, Medical School .... denied

University of Minnesota—Twin Cities, Medical School .... denied

University of North Dakota, School of Medicine
and Health Services .... accepted

University of Wisconsin—Madison, School of Medicine
and Public Health .... denied

Alexandra Paul

Johns Hopkins University, School of Medicine
Applied to:

Dartmouth Medical School .... accepted

Georgetown University, School of Medicine .... accepted

Harvard University, Harvard Medical School .... denied

SUNY Upstate Medical Center .... accepted

Tufts University, School of Medicine .... accepted

University of Pennsylvania, School of Medicine .... accepted

Yale University, School of Medicine .... waitlisted

Bashir Hakim

Undecided
Applied to:

Boston University School of Medicine .... denied

Michigan State University College of Osteopathic Medicine .... accepted

New York University, NYU School of Medicine .... denied

Ohio State University, College of Medicine .... waitlisted

University of Michigan Medical School .... denied

Wayne State University, School of Medicine .... waitlisted

Brandon Devers

Baylor College of Medicine
Applied to:

Baylor College of Medicine .... accepted

Duke University, School of Medicine .... accepted

Johns Hopkins University, School of Medicine .... accepted

Stanford University, School of Medicine .... waitlisted

University of California—Los Angeles,
David Geffen School of Medicine .... accepted

University of California—San Francisco,
School of Medicine .... accepted
University of Kentucky, College of Medicine .... accepted
Washington University in St. Louis, School of Medicine .... accepted

CAELAN JOHNSON

Rush University, Rush Medical College
Applied to:

Case Western Reserve University, School of Medicin........................... accepted
Loyola University Chicago, Stritch School of Medicine............................. denied
Northwestern University, Feinberg School of Medicine............................. denied
Rush University, Rush Medical College .... accepted
Southern Illinois University, School of Medicine .... accepted
University of Chicago, Pritzker School of Medicine .... denied
University of Illinois at Chicago,
UIC College of Medicine.. accepted
University of Iowa,
Roy J. and Lucille A. Carver College of Medicine................................... denied
University of Wisconsin—Madison,
School of Medicine and Public Health   denied
Washington University in St. Louis, School of Medicine .... denied

CAROLYN HAUS

University of North Dakota, School of Medicine and Health Sciences
Applied to:

Creighton University, School of Medicine... withdrew
Mayo Clinic College of Medicine, Mayo Medical School .... denied
University of Minnesota—Duluth, Medical School.............................. withdrew
University of Minnesota—Twin Cities, Medical School .... accepted
University of North Dakota, School of Medicine
and Health Services.. accepted
University of South Dakota, School of Medicine .... accepted

CHRISTINA AHN

Washington University in St. Louis, School of Medicine
Applied to:

Columbia University, College of Physicians and Surgeons .... denied
Duke University, School of Medicine .... accepted
Johns Hopkins University, School of Medicine...................................... accepted
Harvard University, Harvard Medical School .... denied
Stanford University, School of Medicine....................................waitlisted, denied

University of California—Los Angeles,

   David Geffen School of Medicine .... accepted

University of California—San Diego, School of Medicine .... accepted

University of California—San Francisco,

   School of Medicine .... waitlisted, denied

University of Michigan, Medical School .... accepted

Washington University in Saint Louis, School of Medicine................... accepted

COLLEEN KNIFFIN

University of Minnesota—Twin Cities, Medical School

Applied to:

   Baylor College of Medicine .... denied

   Loma Linda University, School of Medicine.. accepted

   University of California—Davis, School of Medicine .... withdrew

   University of California—Los Angeles,

      David Geffen School of Medicine.. denied

   University of California—San Diego, School of Medicine .... denied

   University of Illinois at Chicago,

      UIC College of Medicine... accepted

   University of Minnesota—Duluth, Medical School................................ withdrew

   University of Minnesota—Twin Cities, Medical School .... accepted

   University of Southern California,

      Keck School of Medicine .... withdrew

DAN NAYLOR

University of Southern California, Keck School of Medicine

Applied To:

   Boston University, School of Medicine... denied

   Case Western Reserve University, School of Medicine .... withdrew

   Dartmouth College, Dartmouth Medical School .... denied

   Drexel University, College of Medicine................................. waitlisted, withdrew

   Duke University, School of Medicine .... withdrew

   George Washington University, School of Medicine

      and Health Sciences.. denied

   Georgetown University, School of Medicine .... withdrew

   Harvard University, Harvard Medical School .... denied

   Johns Hopkins University, School of Medicine.. denied

   Loma Linda University, School of Medicine.. withdrew

   New York Medical College.. waitlisted, withdrew

   New York University, NYU School of Medicine .... denied

   Northwestern University, Feinberg School of Medicine............................ denied

Oregon Health & Science University, School of Medicine......................... denied
Pennsylvania State University, College of Medicine.................................... denied
Stanford University, School of Medicine.. denied
Thomas Jefferson University, Jefferson Medical College .... denied
Tulane University, School of Medicine .... denied
University of California—Davis, School of Medicine............................... denied
University of California—Irvine, College of Medicine................................ denied
University of California—Los Angeles,
    David Geffen School of Medicine... denied
University of California—San Diego, School of Medicine .... denied
University of California—San Francisco,
    School of Medicine .... denied
University of Chicago, Pritzker School of Medicine .... denied
University of Michigan, Medical School .... denied
University of Southern California,
    Keck School of Medicine .... accepted
University of Vermont, College of Medicine... denied
Vanderbilt University, School of Medicine.. denied
Yale University, School of Medicine.. denied

DEEPIKA RAO

Washington University in St. Louis, School of Medicine
Applied to:

Case Western Reserve University, School of Medicine .... accepted
Columbia University, College of Physicians and Surgeons................... accepted
Duke University, School of Medicine ....waitlisted, withdrew
Harvard University, Harvard Medical School ....waitlisted, withdrew
Pennsylvania State University, College of Medicine............................. accepted
Stanford University, School of Medicin... denied
Tufts University, School of Medicine.. accepted
UMDNJ, Robert Wood Johnson Medical School .... accepted
University of California—San Francisco,
    School of Medicine .... denied
University of North Carolina at Chapel Hill, School of Medicine........... accepted
University of Pittsburgh, School of Medicine .... accepted
University of Rochester, School of Medicine and Dentistry.................. accepted
University of Southern California, Keck School of Medicine................ accepted
Washington University in St. Louis, School of Medicine .... accepted

Drew Joel Schwartz

Washington University in St. Louis, School of Medicine

Applied to:

Harvard University, Harvard Medical School .... denied

University of Pittsburgh, School of Medicine .... denied

University of Virginia, School of Medicine .... accepted

Vanderbilt University, School of Medicine .... accepted

Washington University in St. Louis, School of Medicine .... accepted

Yale University, School of Medicine .... waitlisted, withdrew

Dustin Y. Yoon

Case Western Reserve University, Cleveland Clinic Lerner College of Medicine

Applied to:

Drexel University, College of Medicine .... accepted

George Washington University, School of Medicine

and Health Sciences .... denied

Georgetown University, School of Medicine .... denied

Johns Hopkins University, School of Medicine .... waitlisted

Thomas Jefferson University, Jefferson Medical College .... denied

University of Maryland, School of Medicine .... accepted

University of Pennsylvania, Perelman School of Medicine .... denied

University of Rochester, School of Medicine and Dentistry.................. accepted

Vanderbilt University, School of Medicine .... waitlisted

Yale University, Yale School of Medicine .... waitlisted

Eddie Silver

Thomas Jefferson University, Jefferson Medical College

Applied To:

Thomas Jefferson University,

Jefferson Medical College... accepted, early decision

Elizabeth Kim

University of South Florida, College of Medicine

Applied to:

Albany Medical College .... denied

Drexel University, College of Medicine.. denied

Eastern Virginia Medical School..waitlisted, withdrew

George Washington University, School of Medicine and Health Sciences

Loma Linda University, School of Medicine .... denied

Loyola University Chicago, Stritch School of Medicine............................. denied

New York Medical College.. denied

New York University, NYU School of Medicine .... denied

Pennsylvania State University, School of Medicine...................... denied

Rosalind Franklin University of Medicine & Science .... denied

Saint Louis University, School of Medicine................................... denied

Tufts University, School of Medicine... denied

Tulane University, School of Medicine .... denied

UMDNJ, New Jersey Medical School.. denied

University of California—Davis, School of Medicine.................... denied

University of California—Irvine, College of Medicine................... denied

University of California—Los Angeles,

   David Geffen School of Medicine .... denied

University of California—San Diego, School of Medicine .... denied

University of California—San Francisco, School of Medicine .... denied

University of Illinois at Chicago, UIC College of Medicine .... denied

University of Maryland, School of Medicine .... denied

University of Pittsburgh, School of Medicine .... denied

University of Toledo, Health Science Campus........................... accepted

University of South Florida, College of Medicine.................... accepted

University of Southern California, Keck School of Medicine..................... denied

University of Washington, School of Medicine .... denied

Yeshiva University, Albert Einstein College of Medicine .... denied

---

ERIC RANDOLPH SCOTT

University of Virginia, School of Medicine
Applied To:

   Boston University, School of Medicine.................................... withdrew

   Dartmouth College, Dartmouth Medical School .... denied

   Duke University, School of Medicine .... denied

   Georgetown University, School of Medicine .... withdrew

   Johns Hopkins University, School of Medicine........................... denied

   University of Chicago, Pritzker School of Medicine .... withdrew

   University of Virginia, School of Medicine............................... accepted

   Virginia Commonwealth University, School of Medicine...................... accepted

   Wake Forest University, School of Medicine........................... accepted

   Yale University, School of Medicine.. denied

GEORGE ISSA

Medical College of Georgia
Applied To:

   East Virginia Medical School..waitlisted

   Morehouse Medical School .... accepted

   University of Alabama, School of Medicine.............................waitlisted

Gwendolyn Riddick

Edward Via Virginia College of Osteopathic Medicine

Applied to:

Edward Via Virginia College of Osteopathic Medicine .... accepted

Hannah Brotzman

Georgetown University, School of Medicine

Applied to:

Albany Medical College .... denied

Boston University, School Of Medicine .... accepted

Brown University School of Medicine .... denied

Dartmouth Medical School... denied

Emory University, School of Medicine .... denied

Georgetown University, School of Medicine.. denied

Tufts University, School of Medicine... denied

Ohio State University, College of Medicine.. withdrew

University of Pennsylvania, School of Medicine .... waitlisted

University of Vermont, College of Medicine.. waitlisted

Wake Forest University, School of Medicine... denied

Jacques Courseault

Tulane University, School of Medicine

Applied to:

Baylor College of Medicine .... withdrew

Duke University, School of Medicine .... denied

Emory University, School of Medicine .... withdrew

Johns Hopkins University, School of Medicine....................................... withdrew

Louisiana State University, School of Medicine...................................... accepted

Medical College of Georgia, School of Medicine .... withdrew

Morehouse School of Medicine .... withdrew

Northwestern University, Feinberg School of Medicine...... waitlisted, withdrew

Saint Louis University, School of Medicine.. accepted

Stanford University, School of Medicine... denied

Tulane University, School of Medicine .... accepted

Wake Forest University, School of Medicine.. withdrew

Washington University in St. Louis, School of Medicine .... withdrew

JILL HUDGENS LEE

University of South Alabama, College of Medicine

Applied To:

University of Alabama—Birmingham,

    School of Medicine .... accepted

University of South Alabama, College of Medicine .... accepted

JIMMY LEE KERRIGAN

Washington University in St. Louis, School of Medicine

Applied to:

Duke University, School of Medicine .... waitlisted, withdrew

Emory University, School of Medicine .... waitlisted, withdrew

Harvard University, Harvard Medical School .... denied

Johns Hopkins University, School of Medicine .... denied

Northwestern University, Feinberg School of Medicine .... denied

University of Alabama—Birmingham,

    School of Medicine .... waitlisted, withdrew

University of Chicago, Pritzker School of Medicine .... accepted

University of Pennsylvania, School of Medicine .... waitlisted, withdrew

University of Tennessee—Memphis, College of Medicine .... accepted

Vanderbilt University, School of Medicine .... accepted

Washington University in St. Louis, School of Medicine .... accepted

MANSOOR KHAN

Washington University in St. Louis, School of Medicine

Applied to:

Boston University, School of Medicine .... withdrew

Brown University, Brown Medical School .... withdrew

Columbia University, College of Physicians and Surgeons ...... waitlisted, denied

Cornell University, Joan & Sanford I. Weill Medical Center .... denied

Duke University, School of Medicine .... accepted

Emory University, School of Medicine .... accepted

Harvard University, Harvard Medical School .... denied

Johns Hopkins University, School of Medicine .... denied

State University of New York—Stony Brook University,

    School of Medicine .... accepted

University of Michigan, Medical School .... accepted

University of Pennsylvania, School of Medicine .... waitlisted, denied

Washington University in St. Louis, School of Medicine .... accepted

Yale University, School of Medicine .... waitlisted, denied

Yeshiva University, Albert Einstein College of Medicine .... withdrew

Meghan Allison Nesmith

University of South Florida, College of Medicine

Applied to:

Emory University, School of Medicine .... denied

Florida State University, College of Medicine .... withdrew

Medical University of South Carolina .... denied

University of Florida, College of Medicine .... withdrew

University of Miami, Miller School of Medicine .... accepted

University of Miami, Miller School of Medicine at Florida Atlantic

    University .... accepted

University of South Florida, College of Medicine .... accepted

MeKeisha Givan

Meharry Medical College, School of Medicine

Applied To:

Meharry Medical College, School of Medicine .... accepted

Michael Curley

University of Wisconsin—Madison, School of Medicine and Public Health

Applied To:

Creighton University, School of Medicine .... accepted

Loyola University Chicago, Stritch School of Medicine .... accepted

Medical College of Wisconsin .... accepted

Saint Louis University, School of Medicine .... accepted

Tulane University, School of Medicine .... withdrew

University of Wisconsin—Madison,

    School of Medicine and Public Health .... accepted

Michael Franco

Temple University, School of Medicine

Applied To:

Cornell University, Joan & Sanford I. Weill

    Medical College .... waitlisted, denied

Harvard University, Harvard Medical School .... denied

Johns Hopkins University, School of Medicine .... denied

Temple University, School of Medicine .... accepted

Thomas Jefferson University,

    Jefferson Medical College .... waitlisted, withdrew

UMDNJ, New Jersey Medical School .... accepted

UMDNJ, Robert Wood Johnson Medical School .... accepted

University of Pennsylvania,

    School of Medicine .... waitlisted, denied

MICHAEL SOULE

Yale University School of Medicine

Applied To:

Harvard University, Harvard Medical School .... accepted

New York University, Mount Sinai School of Medicine .... accepted

New York University, NYU School of Medicine .... accepted

Stanford University, School of Medicine... denied

University of California—San Francisco, School of Medicine .... waitlisted

University of Chicago, Pritzker School of Medicine .... accepted

University of Illinois, College of Medicine.. accepted

University of Miami, School of Medicine .... withdrew

University of Pennsylvania, School of Medicine .... waitlisted

MICHAEL YIP

Washington University in St. Louis, School of Medicine

Applied to:

Baylor College of Medicine .... denied

Loyola University of Chicago, Strich School of Medicine .... withdrew

Northwestern University, Feinberg School of Medicine........................ accepted

Rush Medical College of Rush University .... accepted

University of Chicago, Pritzker School of Medicine .... denied

University of Illinois at Chicago, UIC College of Medicine .... accepted

University of Michigan, Medical School .... accepted

University of Pennsylvania, School of Medicine................................... denied

University of Wisconsin—Madison, School of Medicine and

   Public Health .... withdrew

Washington University in St Louis, School of Medicine .... accepted

NAVID EGHBALIEH

University of South Florida, College of Medicine

Applied to:

University of South Florida, College of Medicine.................................. accepted

NIKUNJ NARENDRA TRIVEDI

Cornell University, Weill Medical College

Applied to:

Brown University, Albert Medical School .... withdrew

Dartmouth College, Dartmouth School of Medicine............................. withdrew

Drexel University, College of Medicine... withdrew

Emory University, School of Medicine .... withdrew

George Washington University,

   School of Medicine and Health Sciences.. withdrew

Georgetown University, School of Medicine .... withdrew
Harvard University, Harvard Medical College .... denied
Mount Sinai School of Medicine .... accepted
New York University, NYU School of Medicine ....waitlisted
Northwestern University, Feinberg School of Medicine............................. denied
Rosalind Franklin University of Medicine and Science .... withdrew
Stanford University, School of Medicine... denied
Temple University, School of Medicine... withdrew
Thomas Jefferson University, Jefferson Medical College .... withdrew
University of California, Davis, School of Medicine .... denied
University of California, Irvine, School of Medicine .... withdrew
University of California, Los Angeles,
     David Geffen School of Medicine..interviewed/denied
University of California, San Diego, School of Medicine....................... accepted
University of California, San Francisco, School of Medicine.................... denied
University of Chicago, Pritzker School of Medicine .... denied
University of Illinois, College of Medicine.. accepted
University of Pennsylvania, Perelman School of Medicine .... denied
University of Southern California, Keck School of Medicine of USC.... withdrew
Yale University, Yale School of Medicine .... withdrew
Yeshiva University, Albert Einstein College of Medicine .... withdrew

REBECCA SHARIM

Temple University, School of Medicine
Applied To:

Temple University, School of Medicine........................... accepted early decision

SAMANTHA VIZZINI

Tulane University, School of Medicine
Applied To:

Emory University, School of Medicine .... denied
Medical College of Georgia, School of Medicine .... denied
Tulane University, School of Medicine .... accepted

TAMARA JETTE

Temple University, School of Medicine
 Applied To:

Harvard Medical School .... denied
Tufts University, School of Medicine.. denied
SUNY Upstate Medical University... denied
University of Massachusetts Medical School.. denied

VICKI ROBIN MCGOWAN II

Virginia College of Osteopathic Medicine
Applied to:

Eastern Virginia Medical School.. denied

George Washington University, School of Medicine and Health
Sciences...waitlisted, withdrew

Howard University, College of Medicine .... accepted

Johns Hopkins University, School of Medicine................................. denied

Philadelphia College of Osteopathic Medicine .... accepted

University of Maryland, School of Medicine .... denied

University of Virginia, School of Medicine .... denied

Virginia College of Osteopathic Medicine.. accepted

Virginia Commonwealth University, School of Medicine........................... denied

VIVEK KALIA

Johns Hopkins University, School of Medicine
Applied to:

Case Western Reserve University, School of Medicine .... accepted

Duke University, School of Medicine ....waitlisted

Harvard University, Harvard Medical School .... denied

Stanford University, School of Medicine.. accepted

University of Alabama, School of Medicine... accepted

University of Miami, School of Medicine .... accepted

University of Pennsylvania, School of Medicine ....waitlisted

Washington University School of Medicine in St. Louis............................. denied

Yale University, School of Medicine... accepted

ANONYMOUS 1

New York University, NYU School of Medicine
Applied to:

Boston University, School of Medicine... accepted

Columbia University, College of Physicians
and Surgeons ....waitlisted, withdrew

Cornell University, Joan & Sanford I. Weill
Medical Center.. denied

Emory University, School of Medicine .... accepted

Harvard University, Harvard Medical School.. denied

New York University,
Mount Sinai School of Medicine ....waitlisted, withdrew

New York University, NYU School of Medicine .... accepted

Stanford University, School of Medicine...............................waitlisted, withdrew

Tufts University, School of Medicine.. accepted

University of Massachusetts, Medical School....................................... accepted

University of Pennsylvania, School of Medicine .... accepted
Washington University in St. Louis,
   School of Medicine .... waitlisted, withdrew

Anonymous 2

University of California—San Francisco

Applied To:

Columbia University,
   College of Physicians and Surgeons .... withdrew
Cornell University, Weill Medical College .... withdrew
Emory University, School of Medicine .... accepted
Harvard University, Harvard Medical School .... withdrew
New York University, Mount Sinai School of Medicine .... withdrew
New York University, NYU School of Medicine .... withdrew
Northwestern University, Feinberg School of Medicine........................ withdrew
Oregon Health & Science University,
   School of Medicine .... withdrew
Stanford University, School of Medicine... withdrew
Tulane University, School of Medicine .... withdrew
University of California—Davis, School of Medicine............................. withdrew
University of California—Irvine, College of Medicine............................ withdrew
University of California—Los Angeles,
   David Geffen School of Medicine... withdrew
University of California—San Diego,
   School of Medicine .... accepted
University of California—San Francisco,
   School of Medicine .... accepted
University of Chicago, Pritzker School of Medicine .... withdrew
University of Miami, School of Medicine .... denied
University of Southern California,
   Keck School of Medicine .... withdrew
University of Washington, School of Medicine .... denied
Yeshiva University,
   Albert Einstein College of Medicine.. withdrew

ANONYMOUS 3

Yeshiva University, Albert Einstein College of Medicine

Applied To:

Columbia University,

College of Physicians and Surgeons..denied

Cornell University,

Joan & Sanford I. Weill Medical College ....denied

New York University,

Mount Sinai School of Medicine ....waitlisted, denied

State University of New York—

Downstate Medical Center..accepted

State University of New York—Stony Brook University,

School of Medicine ....accepted

University of Pennsylvania, School of Medicine..denied

Yeshiva University,

Albert Einstein College of Medicine..accepted

ANONYMOUS 4

Michigan State University, College of Osteopathic Medicine

Applied To:

Michigan State University,

College of Osteopathic Medicine ....accepted

Wayne State University, School of Medicine..denied